Local Government in the Soviet Union

The last two decades have seen an increasing drive toward centralized control of policy in the Soviet Union. Despite this only a very limited success has been achieved in improving local government. This book analyses the reasons for this, examining both the institutional framework and changes in crucial policy areas. It argues that a fragmented vertical power structure involving the three bureaucracies of Party, ministries and the city and regional soviets has been unproductive. It shows how group interests have moulded and adapted policies and how the Party's initiative in centralizing policy has been thwarted. It also outlines the significance of the industrial base in determining local budgets and the provision of amenities, as opposed to overtly political factors. At a time when there are great expectations of reform from the new leadership, this book provides much insight on the institutional and practical barriers to change which are likely to remain for some time.

LOCAL GOVERNMENT IN THE SOVIET UNION

Problems of Implementation and Control

Cameron Ross

ST. MARTIN'S PRESS
New York

© 1987 Cameron Ross
All rights reserved. For information, write:
Scholarly & Reference Division,
St. Martin's Press, Inc., 175 Fifth Avenue, New York, NY 10010
First published in the United States of America in 1987
Printed in Great Britain

Library of Congress Cataloging-in-Publication Data

Ross, Cameron, 1951-
   Local government in the Soviet Union.

   Bibliography p. 222
   Includes index.
   1. Local government — Soviet Union. 2. Soviets.
I. Title.
JS6058.R67   1987   352.047   86-29861
ISBN 0-312-00545-8

Contents

Glossary of Russian Terms
Preface
Introduction   1
1. Party-State Relations   17
2. Local Budgets in the Soviet Union   62
3. Drawing up the Budget   90
4. Local Soviets and Planning in the Soviet Union   110
5. Local Soviets and the Planning of Housing   154
6. Problems of Implementation and Control in Soviet Local Government   181
Conclusion   209
Appendices   217
Selected Bibliography   222
Index   226

Glossary of Russian Terms

All-Union	This refers to the USSR as a whole rather than individual republics
buro	executive body of a Party committee (e.g. obkom buro, gorkom buro)
CPSU	Communist Party of the Soviet Union
gorispolkom	executive committee of a city soviet (plural gorispolkomy)
gorkom	city Party committee (plural gorkomy)
gorplan	city Planning Commission
ispolkom	executive committee (plural ispolkomy)
oblispolkom	oblast executive committee (plural oblispolkomy)
obkom	oblast Party committee (plural obkomy)
oblast	province (administrative level below republic)
otdel	department (plural otdely)
PPO	primary Party organisation
raiispolkom	executive committee of district soviet (plural raiispolkomy)
raikom	district Party committee (plural raikomy)
raion	district level — administrative level below that of oblast or where there is no oblast level, subordinate to the republic. In large cities there are urban raiony which are subordinate to the city level (plural raiony)
RSFSR	Russian Soviet Federative Socialist Republic

Preface

This work arose out of my PhD thesis and would never have been completed without the award of a scholarship from the British Council to Moscow University for 1981–2, and further help from the Council which enabled me to live in Khar'kov in 1982–3. I am most grateful to the Council for giving me the opportunity to live and work in the Soviet Union for this period. My supervisor in Moscow, Professor Georgii Barabashev, was always very kind and helpful to me, and I should like to thank him for making my stay in the Soviet Union so interesting and rewarding. I also wish to thank the members of Ivanovo City Soviet for allowing me the privilege of an interview with them in May 1982.

I should like to take this opportunity to thank my supervisor Dr Caroline Humphrey of King's College, Cambridge, for all her help and encouragement. Thanks also go to Professor Ronald Hill of Trinity College, Dublin, for his detailed comments on the work.

I am indebted to Stuart Rees and his colleagues at Essex University Library for their generous assistance in tracking down Soviet publications. Peter Jackson of Emmanuel College, Cambridge, gave invaluable help with the laborious task of proof-reading. Last but not least a special note of gratitude goes to my wife, Margaret Ross, for her support and encouragement during the course of this research.

Cameron Ross

Introduction

WESTERN STUDIES OF SOVIET POLITICS

In recent years a number of Western scholars have begun to devote more attention to the study of city and regional level politics in the Soviet Union. To a large extent such research has been encouraged by the renewed attention that the Soviet leadership has given to local politics, particularly as during the Brezhnev period (1964–82) a great deal of legislation was adopted which sought to strengthen the role of city and oblast soviets, the status of deputies and the relations of the soviets with enterprises and other state bodies.[1] This legislation was initiated in response to economic and demographic changes within Soviet society. Between 1950 and 1975 there was an eightfold increase in the volume of city budgets, and by 1977 62 per cent of the population of the USSR lived in cities.[2] These developments have led to greater demands being made on the provision of housing and other municipal services. In order to administer these developments city and oblast soviets have been given new rights of 'co-ordination and control' over enterprises situated in their territories, with particular regard to the provision of housing and social and cultural services. There has also been a trend in favour of corporate planning,[3] with the adoption in many cities and oblasts of 'complex economic and social plans' which seek to tackle the problem of harmonising branch and territorial plans.

Western scholars have examined these new developments from various angles. Hill[4] has approached the subject with an interest in political elites, the Soviet electoral system, Party-state relations and the work of Soviet scholars with regard to local government in general. Friedgut[5] has provided us with a study of participation at local level, and the work of the deputies in the sessions of the soviets. Frolic[6] has gone some way towards providing an explanation of the work of the executive committees and departments of the soviets. Jacobs[7] has also examined Soviet elections and more recently, has provided us with information regarding the social background of the deputies of local soviets. Churchward[8] has also examined participation and has documented the general development of the soviets in the 1950s and 1960s. In general it may be said that these writers have all dealt with the *structural–institutional* aspects of local government

Other scholars have concentrated on particular areas of policy or specific aspects of the soviets' work. Lewis[9] has examined local budgets and Sternheimer[10] has written on planning at the local level, while together they have produced a study of urban management in the Soviet Union.[11] Taubman[12] has discussed the problem of enterprise-soviet relations. Morton[13] and DiMaio[14] have looked at management of housing by local soviets. Cattell[15] has provided a case study of Leningrad City Soviet and more recently has examined the provision of services at local level.

Each of these writers has contributed substantially to our knowledge of local politics in the Soviet Union. However, there has still been no study of the work of local soviets which has examined both structural/institutional questions and policy areas. One of the main aims of this study is, therefore, to examine both structural and policy areas and to show how they are related. It is my contention that only by studying the changes that have taken place at the structural level (i.e. in the structure of the departments of local soviets and their executive committees, of local Party bodies and other local level administrations) can we hope to gain a full understanding of policy areas such as finance, planning and housing. In 1983 Jacobs[16] edited a collection of articles on local government which, though wide-ranging, were essentially disparate in nature and did not integrate the two aspects with which I am concerned.

In this study I shall show that problems of a structural nature (i.e. the work of local-level departments, their composition and development, working procedures and operations) have indeed led to serious problems for the central leadership in the implementation and control of policy-making at local level. Bureaucratic problems such as lack of co-ordination between various local level departments, enterprises and Party bodies, as well as shortages of staff and excessive centralisation of decision-making, have led to difficulties in policy implementation.

As the title of this work suggests, I am primarily interested in the implementation and control aspects of policy-making at local level. By contrast, over the last 20 years Western scholars have adopted an approach that concentrates on 'interest groups'. 'Institutional Pluralism', 'Bureaucratic Pluralism', 'Pluralism of Elites' and more recently 'Corporatism', are all interest group based models which are exclusively concerned with the *input* side of policy-making.[17] The question they pose is, 'Who governs?', rather than, 'How is the Soviet Union governed?' While I share many of the views of the interest group/pluralist school, this study will show that there is a need to examine more fully the process of implementation and control—the output side of policy-making. As Cocks has demonstrated, since the early 1970s there has been a concerted movement by the central leadership to reassert its control over policy execution. Systems theory, programme planning and computer technology have been introduced into Soviet administrations. Brezhnev stressed the importance, in the age of the 'Scientific and Technological Revolution', of improving management techniques, and there have been moves to introduce scientific principles of administration, such as the 'Scientific Organisation of Labour', into Soviet bureaucracies.[18] (see Chapter 6).

The pluralist school stresses conflict and bargaining between bureaucratic groups, and views the Party as a mediator of disputes, a political broker, working within an incremental style of decision-making. My study, however, shows that too much emphasis has been placed on group inputs and conflict, and that in the Soviet Union, groups are far more likely to mould and adapt policies in the *implementation* stage. The stress on inputs has tended to obscure the centralising trends which have taken place within Soviet administrations over the last two decades, and the attempts of the central leadership to manipulate and control group behaviour and influence.

My chapter on Party-state relations highlights the work of the central Party leadership and the role of primary Party organisations within the ministries. In recent years we have seen a surge of activity related to strengthening Party control over the ministries and local administrations. While I agree with Hough,[19] that the Party does at times act as a 'political broker', I stress a more activist role for the Party at the local level, particularly in the formulation of policies. However, I also show that the Party's power is far greater at the input stage than at the output stage, i.e. the implementation of policies (see Chapter 1). While at times the Party may mediate in disputes, more often it should be seen as the political boss of its territory, as the chief policy-making body as well as the chief control agent for the centre. The corporatist model[20] better approximates to reality, in that it allows for one dominant actor, the state, to direct and control the work of bureaucratic groups. Both theories, however, stress an incremental style of decision-making. Here, as Cocks states:

> The accent is on achieving consensus, maintaining stability, and limiting the scope and intensity of conflict. There is typically a neglect of outcomes and an avoidance of goal specification and

priority setting that tend to exacerbate conflict . . . Instead of trying to maximize some consistent set of policy objectives and priorities, a 'satisficing' or suboptimal approach is pursued whereby everyone is partially satisfied and no one is wholly alienated.[21]

Further, Smith notes that 'Incrementalism assumes the dispersal or decentralization of decision-making power—in other words, a pluralistic social and political environment. It is the only model of decision making consistent with the group basis of politics.'[22]

While incrementalism may at times be seen in Soviet administrative practice, we should not allow ourselves to be blinded to opposing tendencies at work within Soviet bureaucracies. Marxist-Leninist ideology (as perceived and used by the Soviet leadership) and traditional concepts of Soviet administration such as 'Democratic Centralism' and 'Dual Subordination' give a powerful centralising thrust to decision-making. Thus the interest group/pluralist models, by concentrating too much on inputs, have ignored the importance of the implementation process in Soviet politics and the ability of groups to mould policies in the execution stage, and failed to uncover the control and centralising aspects of Soviet administrative practice over the last two decades.

However, while the central leadership has aimed at improving its control techniques, my study will show that it has been largely unsuccessful in this venture. There are two principal reasons for this which I shall outline in my study.

Structural problems

The Soviet system suffers from having not one bureaucracy, as there is in the West, but three—those of Party, ministries and soviets; a fact which leads inevitably to increased difficulties in co-ordination. Moreover, the economic system is vertically fragmented into tens of ministries and thousands of enterprises at both central and local levels, each ministry possessing a highly autonomous and hierarchical system of decision-making. The problem for the central leadership is to provide for horizontal integration of its policies at the local level. Much of the legislation of the last two decades has thus been addressed to the question of strengthening the local soviets' control over the myriad of enterprises situated at the local level. Harmonising branch and territorial plans has become a major preoccupation of the last decade, as has the introduction of corporate planning into the local administrations; but the vertical and fragmented aspects of Soviet administration have defeated attempts at greater horizontal integration. This is readily seen in the unplanned development of many cities and the selfish attitude of enterprises towards city planning. Often enterprises will create self-sufficient economies within their territories and will turn a blind eye to the overall needs of the cities or regions in which they are situated (see Chapter 4).

Structural problems are also to be found at local level, where the soviets are badly equipped to deal with the many new demands placed upon them and the new rights entrusted to them. The departments are often badly staffed, officials receive low wages, and the departmental struture is not standardised throughout the system. As we shall see in Chapter 6, the executive committees have not yet developed adequate control procedures to deal effectively with the great number of central resolutions and decrees which are sent to them; and my discussion in Chapter 1 of Party-state relations will show that the poorly defined nature of the Party's role in leading and guiding the state also leads to control problems.

Bureaucratic group interests

Policies may, as I have contended, be poorly implemented because of inefficiencies and dysfunctions within and across Soviet bureaucracies caused by structural problems. But policies will also fail or be changed because of the influence of bureaucratic groups, who may drag their feet over the implementation of certain policies or who may adapt policies to suit their personal interests or those of their administrations. Chapter 5 shows clearly the ability of the ministries and their enterprises to thwart central policies with regard to the transfer of housing to the jurisdiction of the soviets.

Thus while I agree that groups can and do influence the policy process, I contend that in the Soviet Union this is much more likely to take place in the implementation process. I stress the failure of the centre to enforce its policies and to create adequate control mechanisms at the output stage, whereas the interest group approach emphasises the success of bureaucratic groups at bargaining and influencing policies at the input stage. Given that inputs and outputs are inter-related I would accept that changes in the implementation stage may affect inputs into the system; but too great a concentration on inputs fails to give a true picture of Soviet administrative practice, with its centralising ethos and political culture as reflected in the concept of 'democratic centralism' and supported by the ideology of Marxism-Leninism.

In addition to the central theme of implementation and control, I will also examine a number of other important questions. Much of the work will seek to provide a better understanding of the relations between city and regional soviets and their respective positions over the period 1964–82. It is only by looking at the work of the soviets across two levels (e.g. oblast and city) that one can really appreciate the role and status of each. Throughout, I shall consider in particular the work of Moscow Oblast Soviet and also make a more general examination of cities and oblasts in the Soviet Union.

My examination of local budgets in Chapter 2 and planning in Chapter 4 has led me to the hypothesis that the industrial structure of a city or region is the most important single factor in determining its budget. Thus I shall argue that such factors as the size, type, jurisdiction and number of enterprises situated in any one area are more important (in the majority of cases) than overtly political features such as patronage and local representative ties with the central leadership. The budget structure is highly variable from city to city, region to region. Turnover tax, and income from profits, the two major sources of local budgets, come directly from enterprises situated in the territory of the soviets.

In order that the work of the city and oblast soviets, and the administrative framework in which implementation problems arise, may be more clearly understood, I shall first give a brief outline of the Soviet administrative and political system, followed by a short account of the basic structure of city and oblast soviets. Then I shall move on to the first of my principal concerns, the work of local Party and soviet leaders and the relations between them.

THE BASIC STRUCTURE OF THE SOVIET POLITICAL AND ADMINISTRATIVE SYSTEM

In *Governing Soviet Cities*,[23] Taubman gives an account of the hierarchical structure of the Soviet political system and the status of the various Party and state bodies. In this brief summary I have followed Taubman's work, while adapting his findings to my particular interest in both oblast and city soviets.

As can be seen from Figure 1 there are six basic administrative

Figure 1: The Soviet administrative and political structure

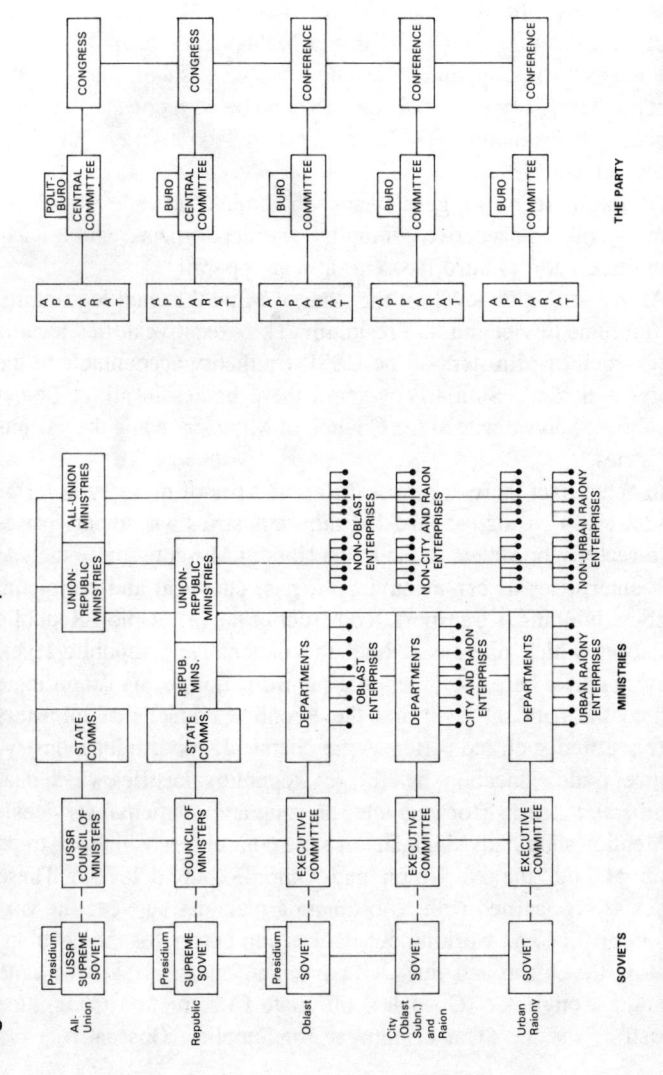

Source: Adapted from Williams Taubman, *Governing Soviet Cities: Bureaucratic Politics and Urban Development in the USSR* (New York, Washington and London, 1973), p.12

levels, each with its own soviet, Party body and ministerial agency. At the highest level we find the All-Union bodies which are responsible for the USSR as a whole. Next come the Republic-level bodies which deal with the work of the 15 different Soviet Republics. Below these are the oblasts and certain cities of Republic subordination such as Leningrad and Moscow. Below the oblasts come cities of oblast subordination and raiony. At the bottom we find rural and settlement soviets. We should note that certain very small cities will be subordinate to the raion level. In larger cities there will also be urban raiony. In the republics of Estonia, Latvia, Lithuania, Georgia, Armenia, Azerbaidzhan and Moldavia, there are no oblasts and thus the raiony and cities here will be subordinate to the Republic level. My principal concern shall be with oblasts and cities of oblast subordination. The term 'local soviets' refers to all levels below republic level.

As can be seen in Figure 1, at each administrative level there is a soviet with its executive committee and departments, and a Party committee with its buro, secretariat and apparat.

At the All-Union level for the state, we find the chief legislature, the Supreme Soviet and its Presidium. The executive at this level is the Council of Ministers of the USSR (in theory accountable to the Supreme Soviet). Similarly we find these bodies in all 15 Soviet Republics. Subordinate to the Council of Ministers come the various ministries.

In actual fact there are three different types of ministry in terms of administrative status: (a) All-Union ministries whose enterprises are directly subordinate to their superiors in Moscow (these include such enterprises as car manufacture, gas, chemical and petroleum machine-building, transport construction); (b) Union-Republic ministries which operate at both the national and republic level. These agencies here are under dual subordination, being subordinate both to the national level and the Republic councils of ministers (here we find such industries as the chemical, food, light industry, finance, trade, education, health); (c) Republic ministries which deal with local concerns (for example, housing and municipal services).

Mention should also be made of state committees which are to be found at both the All-Union and Union-Republic levels. These bodies are concerned with co-ordinating planning between the various ministries and working out indices and norms for the developments of the oblasts and cities. Of particular importance are the State Planning Committee (Gosplan), the State Construction Committee (Gosstroi) and the State Committee for Supplies (Gossnab).

Of special importance is the relation between ministries and enterprises of All-Union, Union-Republic and Republic subordination (e.g. non-city/non-oblast, as outlined in Figure 1) and the soviets. These must be distinguished from enterprises which come under the jurisdiction of the cities and oblasts (these are labelled city/oblast enterprises). This aspect of the soviets' work will be dealt with particularly in Chapters 4 and 5.

Turning to examine the Party structure we can see that the Party bodies shadow the soviets at each level, from the chief policy-making body, the Politburo, to the buros of Republic, oblast, city, down to the bottom level. At each level the executive of the Party is engaged in guiding and controlling the work of the state bodies. As we shall see in Chapter 1, this duplication of Party and state bodies often creates bureaucratic problems of role definition and leads to problems of co-ordination of policy guidance across the Party/state divide.

CITY AND OBLAST SOVIETS

Figure 2 outlines the basic structure of a typical oblast or city soviet. As can be seen, the deputies meet in full session only four times a year, the sessions lasting at most two days. The deputies entrust the day-to-day running of affairs to the executive committees and departments of the soviets. In oblast soviets with a population of one and a half million and over a presidium may be formed, consisting of the chairman, deputy chairmen and secretary of the executive committee. The city and oblast soviets and their executives are elected for a period of two and a half years. Within the executives the chairmen, deputy chairmen and secretaries are full-time salaried officials. Figure 2 also outlines the relationship between these bodies as seen by Soviet legal scholars and my view of the relationship (in italics). Thus whereas in theory the executive committees are elected by deputies, in practice they are selected from above by Party and state personnel, as are the heads of departments and other leading officials (see Chapter 1).

Figure 2 shows that the deputies also form standing commissions. These are groups of deputies which have been set up in theory to control the work of the executive and its subordinate agencies. There are commissions for most branches of industry. An important development in the late 1960s was the creation of commissions for planning and budget work. The commissions function between the

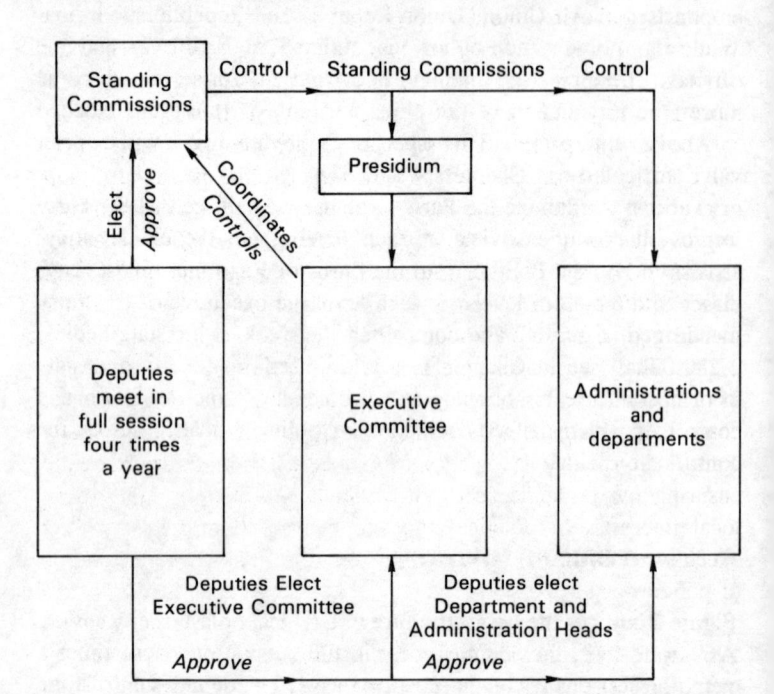

Figure 2: Typical structure of a city or oblast soviet

```
        Standing      Control    Standing Commissions    Control
       Commissions ─────────────────────────────────────────────┐
         │    ↑                        │                        │
       Elect Approve   Coordinates     │                        │
         │    │         Controls       ↓                        │
         │    │                    Presidium                    │
         │    │                        │                        │
         ↓    │                        ↓                        ↓
      ┌──────────┐              ┌──────────┐              ┌──────────────┐
      │ Deputies │              │          │              │Administrations│
      │ meet in  │              │Executive │              │     and      │
      │full session│            │Committee │              │ departments  │
      │four times│              │          │              │              │
      │  a year  │              │          │              │              │
      └──────────┘              └──────────┘              └──────────────┘
              Deputies Elect              Deputies elect
           Executive Committee          Department and
                                       Administration Heads
                Approve                      Approve
```

sessions of the soviets and thus allow constant supervision of the executive by the deputies. In preparing questions for discussion in the sessions of the soviets and executive committees, the commissions can influence to a small degree the formulation of some local decisions. However, the role of the commissions can be seen much more at the implementation stage of the policy process than on the input side. Western studies have shown that the commissions have become more of a control agent for the executive than a controller of it.[24] The commissions have been much more successful in checking the work of enterprises and institutions than in initiating policies.

Throughout our period legislation has been enacted to increase the role and status given to deputies and to encourage greater participation from them in the sessions of the soviets and in the community at large. In 1972 the Supreme Soviet passed a law on the status of deputies[25] which in particular outlined measures to improve the deputies' relations with members of the executive, giving them the right to consult officials and receive replies to requests within specific periods. In 1977 the new Soviet Constitution once more emphasised the important role of the soviets and their deputies. While there are still many infringements of these rights by state officials, it must be said that the sessions of the soviets now meet more regularly and the role of the deputies has indeed increased.

Above all, we should stress that the deputies provide a safety valve for the regime, a means by which citizens can air their grievances. At the lowest level the deputy can (for example) help improve the living conditions of the citizens, arrange for necessary repairs to houses to be carried out, press for surplus funds to be directed to the construction of a kindergarten or club, or see to the mending of a road or bridge. In the election of 20 June 1982, 2,289,023 deputies were elected.[26] The state uses this vast supply of manpower to a large extent to assist it in the implementation and control of policy-making. As we shall show in Chapter 1, Party control over the soviets is very strong and the Party is committed to ensuring the implementation of national policies over and above local interests. In practice, the deputies are dominated by their executives and make only a minimal contribution to the formulation of policies at local level.

My study of deputy participation in Moscow Oblast between 1969 and 1979 shows clearly that the sessions are dominated by members of the oblast executive committee and other state and Party officials, with poor representation of workers and peasants (see Appendix 1). Workers made up only 9.7 per cent of those who spoke at sessions over the period, while comprising 54.6 per cent of the membership of the soviet. Only 11.6 per cent of the deputies spoke at meetings between 1969 and 1971. Thus the sessions should be seen as forums in which the leadership outlines it policies and hears the reports of selected deputies rather than where policies are formulated. Further evidence of this is given in Appendix 2, which shows the occupation of those deputies who gave reports and co-reports over the same period. Here not one single worker was involved and no less than 54.6 per cent of the speeches were made by the top leadership of the oblast executive committee. One of the most important sessions is that held each November/December to ratify the plan and budget of the soviet for the coming year. A study of those who spoke in these sessions of Moscow Oblast Soviet between 1969 and 1970 is given in Appendix 3. The average deputy has little opportunity to contribute to even this most important of debates; a mere 9.2 per cent of the speeches were made by workers.

This is not the only disadvantage from which deputies suffer.

Hill, Friedgut and others have shown that members of the ispolkomy are both better educated and older than deputies, that they serve for longer periods of time, and that a greater proportion of them are Party members.[27] The position in fact is that a great many decisions which in theory are within the exclusive competence of deputies are actually made by executive committees in consultation with higher state and Party bodies; the sessions thus do nothing more than ratify decisions taken elsewhere.

THE EXECUTIVE COMMITTEES

The executive committee is the chief executive of the soviet and it alone has the right 'to make decisions . . . binding on all enterprises, institutions and organisations located within the given soviet's territory, as well as officials and citizens'.[28] The work of executive committees is guided by the principle of 'Democratic Centralism', whereby 'all organs of state power and state administration form a single system and work on the basis of the subordination of lower organs to the leadership and control of higher organs'.[29] Thus city soviets will be subordinate to oblast soviets. An important complement to 'Democratic Centralism' is 'Dual subordination', illustrated by Article 30 of the 1980 Oblast Law: 'The executive committee is directly accountable both to the soviet that elected it, and to higher executive and administrative bodies[30]. Thus the department of finance of a city is subordinate both to the city executive committee and the oblast finance department (see Chapters 3 and 4 for a more detailed discussion of these points). Both of these principles of Soviet administration ensure a high degree of centralisation of decision-making within Soviet bureaucracies.

Table 1 shows the composition of Moscow Oblast Executive Committee. This table is broadly representative of the position throughout the Soviet Union, though the structure of the executive committees and depatments will vary from city to city and between cities and oblasts depending on the size of the territory, the industrial base and the population. The oblasts are traditionally more involved in agriculture and light industry while the cities have greater responsibility over heavy industry and social and cultural matters. In Moscow Oblast Executive Committee there are nine members of the full time apparat (a chairman, two first-deputy chairmen, five deputy chairmen and a secretary) and sixteen members.

As Table 1 shows, Moscow Oblast Executive Committee includes

Table 1: Composition of Moscow Oblast Executive Committees (16th Convocation, 23 June 1977)

Chairman	N.T. Kozlov
First Deputy Chairmen	V.P. Prokhorov, A.A. Kamenov
Deputy Chairmen	V.I. Vinogradov, N.K. Korol'kov, V.G. Krylov, A.S. Sviridov, I.M. Cherepanov (Chairman of Oblast Planning Commission)
Secretary	M.P. Shchetinina
Members	
L.S. Andreeva	Head of Department of Education
O.B. Alekseev	Head of Administration of Material and Technical Supplies
V.M. Borisenkov	Secondary Secretary of Moscow Oblast Party Committee
A.A. Galaktinov	Chairman of Odintsova City Executive Committee
V.P. Grinavtseva	Head of Chief Administration of Health
P.D. Gordeev	Secretary of Moscow Oblast Trade Union Council
V.I. Zharova	Chairman of Executive Committee, Zabolot'ev Rural Soviet, Ramenskoe raion
A.K. Zabaluev	Head of Administration of Agriculture
T.S. Kozlova	First Secretary Istrinsk City Party Committee
I.I. Kukhar	Chairman of 'Vladimir Illyich' Kolkhoz, Lenin Raion
M.N. Petina	Painter, Trust No. 4, Chief Administration of Construction
V.F. Pivkin	Head of Chief Administration of Construction
P.D. Sokolov	Chairman of Oblast Committee of People's Control
E.I. Sukhova	Head of Administration of Statistics
V.K. Tsepkov	Head of Administration of Internal Affairs
I.I. Filippov	Head of Department of Finance
	(25 members)

Source: *Byulleten Ispolnitel'novo Komiteta Moskovskovo Oblastnovo Soveta Narodnykh Deputatov,* no. 14 (1977), p.3.

representatives of the major institutions in the community—Party, trade union and public organisations—as well as of the major industries of the region, heads of key departments of the executive, and members of lower soviets and Party organisations. Subordinate to the executive are Moscow Oblast's 44 departments, which cover a wide range of industries and social and cultural amenities, encompassing many industries that in the West would be under private management.

By studying the structural basis of the Soviet economic and administrative system and structural problems at local level within soviet and Party bodies, we can gain a better understanding of the difficulties encountered by the centre in the implementation process. Chapters 1 and 6 will be primarily concerned with local departments of the Party and state and the bureaucratic nature of policy implementation. Chapters 2–5 will provide a study of the economic and planning systems as seen in central-local relations. As stated earlier, my concern will be to stress the implementation side of policy-making and to show the links that exist between structural problems and policy failure in cities and oblasts throughout the Soviet Union.

NOTES

1. Resolution of the Central Committee of the CPSU, 12 March 1971, 'O Merakh po Dal'neishemu Uluchsheniyu Raboty Raionnykh i Gorodskikh Sovetov Deputatov Trudyashchikhsya', *Pravda*, 14 March 1971, pp. 1–2; abridged in *Kommunisticheskaya Partiya Sovetskovo Soyuza v Rezolyutsiyakh i Resheniyakh S"ezdov, Konferentsii i Plenumov TsK* (hereafter *KPSS v Rezolyutsiyakh*), eighth edition (Moscow, 1970–), X, 1969–71 (1972), 311–6; translated as 'On Measures for the Further Improvement of the Work of the District and City Soviets', *Current Digest of the Soviet Press* (hereafter *CDSP*), 23, no. 11 (13 April 1971), 1–5 (hereafter 1971 City Resolution). Decree of the Presidium of the USSR Supreme Soviet, 19 March 1971, 'Ob Osnovnykh Pravakh i Obyazannostyakh Gorodskikh i Raionnykh v Gorodakh Sovetov Deputatov Trudyashchikhsya', in *Sbornik Zakonov SSSR i Ukazov Prezidiuma Verkhovnovo Soveta SSSR 1938–1975*, 4 vols (Moscow, 1975–76), I, 257–70; translated as 'On the Basic Rights and Duties of the City and Borough Soviets', *CDSP*, 23, no. 13 (27 April 1971), 27–30, 38 (hereafter 1971 City Decree). Resolution of the Council of Ministers of the USSR, 19 March 1971, 'O Merakh po Ukrepleniyu Material'no-Finansovoi Bazy Ispolkomov Raionnykh i Gorodskikh Sovetov Deputatov Trudyashchikhsya', *Pravda*, 20 March 1971, p. 1; translated as 'On Measures for Strengthening the Material and Financial Base of District and City Soviet Executive Committees', *CDSP*, 23, no. 11 (13 April 1971), p. 5 (hereafter 1971 City Resolution (Finance)). Law of the USSR, 20 September 1972, 'O Statuse Deputatov Sovetov Deputatov Trudyashchikhsya v SSSR', in *Sbornik Zakonov SSSR*, I, 334–47; translated as 'On the Status of Deputies to Soviets in the U.S.S.R.', *CDSP*, 24, no. 39 (25 October 1972), 9–13 (hereafter 1972 Legislation (Status)). Law of the USSR, 25 June 1980, 'Ob Osnovnykh Polnomochiyakh Kraevykh, Oblastnykh Sovetov Narodnykh Deputatov, Sovetov Narodnykh Deputatov Avtonomnykh Oblastei i Avtonomnykh Okrugov', *Pravda*, 26 June 1980, pp. 1–3; translated as 'On the Basic Powers of the Territory and Province Soviets of People's Deputies and the Autonomous-Province and Autonomous-Region Soviets of People's Deputies', *CDSP*, 32, no. 27 (6 August 1980), 11–17, 19 (hereafter 1980 Oblast Law). Resolution of the Central Committee of the CPSU, the Presidium of the Supreme Soviet, and the Council of Ministers of the USSR, 19 March 1981, 'O Dal'neishem Povyshenii Roli Sovetov Narodnykh Deputatov v Khozyaistvennom Stroitel'stve', in *KPSS v Rezolyutsiyakh*, XIV, 1980–1 (1982), 346–50; translated as 'On Further Enhancing the Role of the Soviets of People's

Deputies in Economic Construction', *CDSP*, 33, no. 13 (29 April 1981), 11, 24 (hereafter 1981 Resolution (Soviets)).

2. For budget statistics, see G.B. Polyak, *Byudzhet Goroda* (Moscow, 1978), p. 17, and for population statistics, see *SSSR v Tsifrakh v 1978 Godu: Kratkii Statisticheskii Sbornik* (Moscow, 1979), p. 7.

3. These are plans which cover the economic and social development of a particular oblast or city, and which include indices of all enterprises situated in its territory regardless of the enterprise's subordination. (See Chapter 4 for a fuller discussion of these points and of complex economic and social planning.)

4. Ronald J. Hill, *Soviet Political Elites: The Case of Tiraspol* (London, 1977); 'The CPSU in a Soviet Local Election Campaign', *Soviet Studies*, 28 (1976), 590-8; *Soviet Politics, Political Science and Reform* (Oxford, 1980).

5. Theodore H. Friedgut, *Political Participation in the USSR* (Princeton and Guildford, 1979).

6. B. Michael Frolic, 'Decision Making in Soviet Cities', *American Political Science Review*, 66 (1972), 38-52; 'Municipal Administrations, Departments, Commissions and Organizations', *Soviet Studies*, 22 (1970-1), 376-93.

7. Everett M. Jacobs, 'Soviet Local Elections: What They Are, and What They Are Not', *Soviet Studies*, 22 (1970-1), 61-76; 'Norms of Representation and the Composition of Local Soviets', in *Soviet Local Politics*, edited by Jacobs, pp. 78-94 (see n. 16 to this chapter).

8. L.G. Churchward, 'Soviet Local Government Today', *Soviet Studies*, 17 (1965-6), 431-52; *Contemporary Soviet Government*, second edition (London, 1975).

9. Carol Weiss Lewis, 'Politics and the Budget in Soviet Cities' (unpublished PhD dissertation, Princeton University, 1975; abstracted in *Dissertation Abstracts International*, 37 (1976-7), 570-A); 'Comparing City Budgets, the Soviet Case', *Comparative Urban Research*, 1977, 46-57.

10. Stephen Sternheimer, 'Running Russian Cities: Bureaucratic Degeneration, Bureaucratic Politics, or Urban Management?', in *Public Policy and Administration in the Soviet Union*, edited by Gordon B. Smith (New York, 1980), pp. 79-108.

11. Carol W. Lewis and Stephen Sternheimer, *Soviet Urban Management: With Comparisons to the United States* (New York and London, 1979).

12. William Taubman, *Governing Soviet Cities: Bureaucratic Politics and Urban Development in the USSR* (New York, Washington, and London, 1973).

13. Henry W. Morton, 'Housing Problems and the Policies of Eastern Europe and the Soviet Union', *Studies in Comparative Communism*, 12 (1979), 300-21; 'The Soviet Quest for Better Housing—An Impossible Dream?', in US Congress, Joint Economic Committee, *Soviet Economy in a Time of Change* (Washington, 1979), pp. 790-811; 'Local Soviets and the Attempt to Rationalize the Delivery of Urban Services: The Case of Housing', in *Soviet Local Politics*, edited by Jacobs, pp. 186-202.

14. Alfred John DiMaio, Jr., *Soviet Urban Housing: Problems and*

Policies (New York, Washington and London, 1974).

15. David T. Cattell, *Leningrad: A Case Study of Soviet Urban Government* (New York, 1968); 'Local Government and the Provision of Consumer Goods and Services', in *Soviet Local Politics*, edited by Jacobs, pp. 172–85.

16. *Soviet Local Politics and Government*, edited by Everett M. Jacobs (London, 1983).

17. For a discussion of Institutional Pluralism, see Jerry F. Hough, 'The Soviet System: Petrification or Pluralism?', *Problems of Communism*, [21], no. 2 (March–April 1972), 25–45. See also Jerry F. Hough and Merle Fainsod, *How the Soviet Union is Governed* (Cambridge, Mass. and London, 1979). For Hough's most recent remarks, in which he seems to retreat from his pluralist stance, see 'Pluralism, Corporatism and the Soviet Union', in *Pluralism in the Soviet Union: Essays in Honour of H. Gordon Skilling*, edited by Susan Gross Solomon (London and Basingstoke, 1983), pp. 37–60. On Bureaucratic Pluralism, see Darrell P. Hammer, 'Inside the Ministry of Culture: Cultural Policy in the Soviet Union', in *Public Policy*, edited by Smith, pp. 53–78. On 'Pluralism of elites', see H. Gordon Skilling, 'Interest Groups and Communist Politics: An Introduction', in *Interest Groups in Soviet Politics*, edited by H. Gordon Skilling and Franklyn Griffiths (Princeton, 1971), pp. 3–18 (p. 17). On Corporatism, see Valerie Bunce and John M. Echols III, 'Soviet Politics in the Brezhnev Era: "Pluralism" or "Corporatism"?', in *Soviet Politics in the Brezhnev Era*, edited by Donald R. Kelley (New York, 1980), pp. 1–26, and Hough, 'Pluralism'.

18. See in particular Paul Cocks, 'The Policy Process and Bureaucratic Politics', in *The Dynamics of Soviet Politics*, edited by Paul Cocks, Robert V. Daniels and Nancy Whittier Heer (Cambridge, Mass. and London, 1976), pp. 156–79.

19. Hough, 'The Soviet System' and 'Pluralism', and Hough and Fainsod, *How the Soviet Union is Governed*.

20. See Hough, 'Pluralism', and Bunce and Echols, 'Soviet Politics', for a discussion of Corporatism.

21. Cocks, 'Policy Process', p. 160.

22. Gordon B. Smith, 'Bureaucratic Politics and Public Policy in the Soviet Union', in *Public Policy*, edited by Smith, pp. 1–17 (p. 11).

23. Taubman, *Governing Soviet Cities*, pp. 10–14.

24. See Friedgut, *Political Participation*, pp. 188–200.

25. 1972 Legislation (Status).

26. *Itogi Vyborov i Sostav Deputatov Mestnykh Sovetov Narodnykh Deputatov 1982 g. (Satisticheskii Sbornik)* (Moscow, 1982).

27. See especially Friedgut, *Political Participation*, pp. 162–82; Hill, *Soviet Political Elites*, pp. 72–4, and *Soviet Politics*, p. 43.

28. 1980 Oblast Law, Article 29, *CDSP*, p. 17.

29. *Bolshaya Sovetskaya Entsiklopedia*, third edition, 31 vols (Moscow, 1970–81), VIII (1972), p. 79; cited by Jacobs in 'Soviet Local Politics and Government', p. 7.

30. 1980 Oblast Law, Article 30, *CDSP*, p. 17.

1

Party–State Relations

INTRODUCTION

In this chapter we shall examine one of the most complex areas of Soviet politics, Party-state relations. Following the work of scholars such as Stewart,[1] Hough,[2] and Hill,[3] we shall examine the structure and membership of the top Party and state organs, taking Moscow Oblast as our case study. In particular we shall look at such phenomena as 'dual membership' of Party and state executives, 'crossover' of members from Party to state and vice versa, and 'turnover' within the Party leadership.

While in general my conclusions support the views of the writers named above, I shall also draw attention to a new area of research that needs to be considered. In essence, I shall seek to show that we must make a distinction between (1) horizontal Party leadership of the soviets, i.e. obkom-oblispolkom or gorkom-gorispolkom relations; and (2) vertical Party control from the primary party organisations within ministries over the ministries and their subordinate enterprises. I shall maintain that Party control at (1) is very strong, while at (2) recent evidence suggests that it is rather weak and ineffective. A number of important Central Committee resolutions have sought to increase the role of the Party bodies within the ministries.[4] In Chapter 4 we shall see that neither the local soviets nor local Party bodies can 'co-ordinate and control' the actions of the ministries, and that the problem of harmonising branch and territorial planning still looms large.

Hough has put forward the view that the Party is a 'super-co-ordinator' and a 'political broker'[5]. As the only organisation which cuts across all others, the Party is in the best position to co-ordinate policy in the localities. This role is reflected in the Soviet

Constitution, which notes, 'The leading and guiding force of Soviet society and the nucleus of its political system, of all state organisations and public organisations, is the Communist Party of the Soviet Union'[6] But as I have already stressed, the term 'political broker' is too weak as a description of the Party at the local level. As I shall show, the range of the Party's activities will vary from general supervision to 'petty tutelage' of state bodies. Party bodies will be engaged primarily in the implementation and enforcement of *national* policies. However, even the Party cannot co-ordinate planning and is itself defeated by the vertical fragmentation of the economic and administrative system (see Chapter 4). The crux of the matter lies in the fact that a local Party head of a city or oblast is no match for the head of a heavy industry ministry in Moscow. At the same time, as we shall show later, there is a very poor system of control within the ministries and little communication between Party organisations within the central state bodies and local Party committees at oblast and city level. To a large extent, then, the work of the Party bodies is limited to clearing up bureaucratic problems and keeping the wheels of bureaucracy turning. The rapid unplanned development of cities and regions through the illegal expansion of enterprises at the local level is ample proof of the inability of the Party to co-ordinate the activities of the various economic organisations situated in the localities (see Chapter 4).

As Churchward rightly notes, 'the exact relationship of party and state organs is not the same at all levels. Nor has it been the same at all periods.'[7] Thus in some areas the Party will play a much more active role than others. This will depend largely on the industrial structure of the region, the personality and status of state and Party leaders, and the history of such relationships over a period of time. The director of a large and powerful enterprise of All-Union subordination, upon which the soviet relies for a significant part of its revenue, will be more powerful than the director of a small enterprise of oblast subordination. In different oblasts and cities the number and type of enterprises will vary substantially, as will the relations between Party officials and the heads of these enterprises.

Thus, while I shall show that Party control over the work of the soviets is very strong, I shall put foward the hypothesis that a 'control gap' exists between top Party supervision over the ministries, and local Party control of enterprises subordinate to those ministries.

In this chapter we shall first examine the basic structure of Moscow Oblast Party Committee, its composition and turnover of membership, followed by a discussion of (1) the theory of Party-state relations; (2) the promotion of the Party political line; (3) selection and placement of cadres; (4) control over the soviets; and (5) control within the ministries.

Most of the material will come from my own research into Moscow oblast but I shall also draw upon a general reading of scholarly literature for information on the position at city level.

THE LOCAL PARTY ORGANISATION

Figure 1.1 shows the typical structure of the buro and secretariat of an oblast Party committee. Table 1.1 outlines the structure and membership of Moscow Oblast Committee in 1981, and Table 1.2 provides details about the departments of the secretariat over our period.

Moscow Oblast Party Committee (Moscow obkom) comprised 221 members in 1966 and 225 in 1981. In 1981 there were 137 full members, 49 candidate members (without a vote) and 39 members of the revision committee.[8]

The committee, which consists of leading Party and soviet officials, is elected at the Party conference, which according to Party rules must take place once every two or three years. The Party committee in turn elects a buro and secretariat. The buro may be regarded as the chief policy-making body and the secretariat as the chief executive of the oblast. Moscow Obkom Buro consisted in 1966 of 14 members (11 full and 3 candidate), rising to 16 (13 full and 3 candidate) in 1981.[9] An important point to note is that all five members of the secretariat were also members of the buro. The secretariat, which is composed of 5 secretaries and, over our period, 12–17 departments, is the chief control agent of the Party, and with all 5 members in the buro it is the dominant voice in policy-making.

According to Hough, at city level there will normally be three secretaries, one for ideological questions, one for industry and a third for organisational questions. A city of 300,000 will have a full-time Party apparat of 25 to 30.[10]

At oblast level as with Moscow there are normally five secretaries. The first Party secretary deals with general questions and is the leader of the obkom. In Moscow, the second Party secretary dealt with ideological and organisational questions, the others with construction, agriculture and industry.[11]

Figure 1.1: Typical Oblast Party Committee Structure

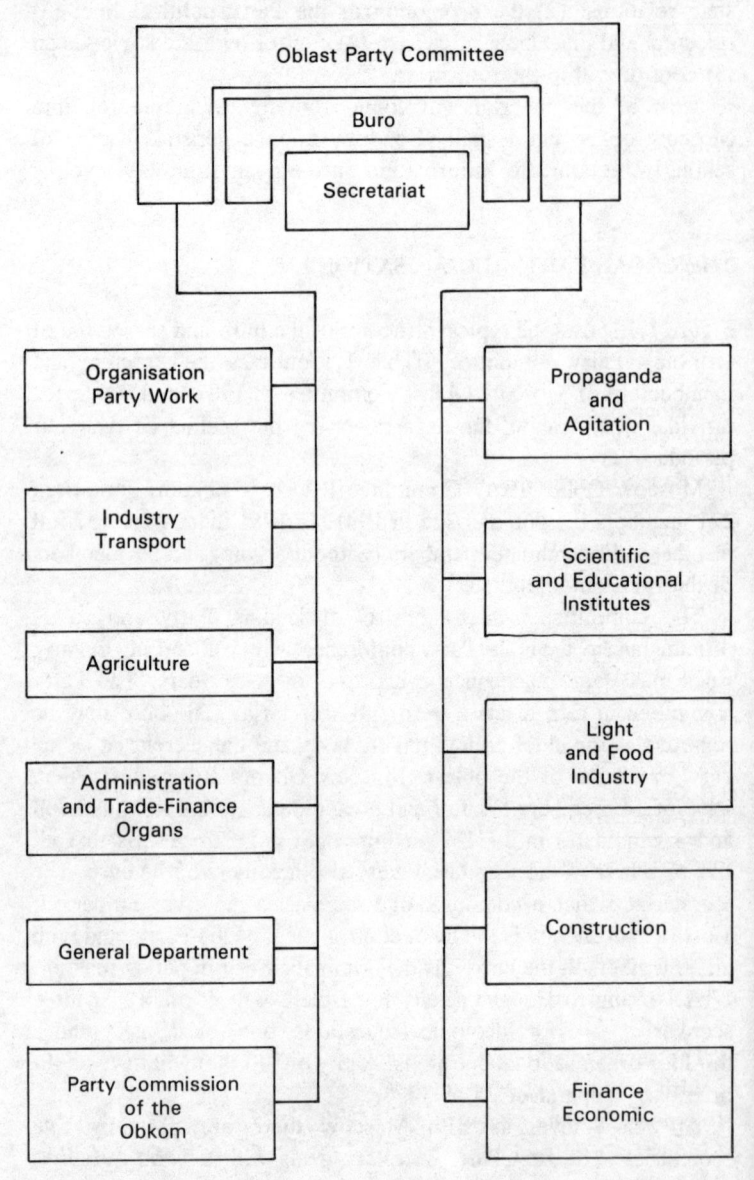

```
                    Oblast Party Committee
                          Buro
                        Secretariat
```

- Organisation Party Work
- Industry Transport
- Agriculture
- Administration and Trade-Finance Organs
- General Department
- Party Commission of the Obkom

- Propaganda and Agitation
- Scientific and Educational Institutes
- Light and Food Industry
- Construction
- Finance Economic

Source: Strukov, V.I., comp., *Kommunisticheskaya Partiya Sovetskovo Soyuza: Naglyadnoe Posobie po Partiinomu Stroitel'stvu* (Moscow, 1980), p. 67.

Table 1.1: Moscow oblast party committee, buro secretariat and departments, 1981

First Secretary and Member of the Buro	V.I. Konotop
Second Secretary and Member of the Buro	V.I. Borisenkov
Secretaries and Members of the Buro	I.E. Klochkov, A.A. Rusanov, A.T. Shamonin
Members of the Buro	A.I. Volgin, K.P. Dvoryaninova, N.I. Ovsyannikov, M.A. Orlov, V.S. Pestov, V.N. Stepnov, M.G. Yazikov, N.T. Kozlov
Candidate Members of the Buro	L.V. Gusev, V.A. Konoplenko, M.I. Semenushkin
Heads of Departments	
(1) Organisation — Party Work	N.I. Ovsyannikov (Member of the Buro)
(2) Propaganda and Agitation	E.N. Bondarenko
(3) Industry	B.I. Balashov
(4) Management	Yu. P. Svyatobogov
(5) Textile and Light Industry	O.V. Semonov
(6) Transport and Communications	L.F. Frolov
(7) Food and Food-processing	V.T. Shul'ginov
(8) Construction and Construction Materials	V.F. Ignumentsev
(9) Agriculture	F.S. Nabarezhnev
(10) Science and Education	N.S. Malofeev
(11) Culture	B.B. Samsonova
(12) City Economy	S.A. Polyakov
(13) Trade and Services	M.E. Makhataeva
(14) Planning and Finance	V.S. Zakharov
(15) Administrative Organs	A.V. Sudakov
(16) Foreign Connections	B.L. Yakubchak
(17) General Department	A.V. Kovylov
(18) Administrative Affairs	B.G. Chubarov

Source: *Leninskoe Znamya,* 17 January 1981, p. 1.

Each secretary deals with a number of departments. As Stewart notes:

> The secretariat through its otdels provides the Party committee with channels of communication to the lower Party committees—the raikoms and gorkoms particularly—to the industrial enterprises, the trade union organizations, the Komsomol organs, the Soviets, and all other organisations in the oblast.[12]

Through the secretariat and its departments the Party buro guides

Table 1.2: The departments of the secretariat of Moscow oblast party committee, 1966–81

	1966	1968	1971	1974	1976	1979	1981
Organisation — Party Work	*	*	*	*	*	*	*
Propaganda and Agitation	*	*	*	*	*	*	*
Science and Education	*	*	*	*	*	*	*
Industry and Transport	*	*	—	—	—	—	—
Textile and Light Industry	*	*	*	*	*	*	*
Food and Food-processing	*	*	*	*	*	*	*
Agriculture	*	*	*	*	*	*	*
Construction and Construction Materials	*	*	*	*	*	*	*
City Economy	*	*	*	*	*	*	*
Trade-Finance	*	*	*	*	*	—	—
Administrative Organs	*	*	*	*	*	*	*
General Department[†]	—	*	*	*	*	*	*
Foreign Connections	—	—	—	*	*	*	*
Culture	—	—	*	*	*	*	*
Industry	—	—	*	*	*	*	*
Transport and Communications	—	—	*	*	*	*	*
Planning and Finance	—	—	—	—	—	*	*
Management	—	—	—	—	—	*	*
Special Sector[†]	*	—	—	—	—	—	—
Trade and Services	—	—	—	—	—	*	*
Number of Departments	12	12	14	15	15	17	17

* = Department is present   — = No department
[†] = Special sector becomes general department in 1968
Source: Compiled from *Leninskoe Znamya*, 1966–81 (see note 13 to this chapter).

and controls all other organisations in the area. The departments, which comprise heads, deputy heads, instructors and staff, process information and statistics which come to them from PPOs (primary Party organs) and other Party and state bodies.

One of the most important departments is that of Organisation-Party Work which engages in the control and organisation of lower Party bodies and plays a leading role in the control of state bodies. The importance of this department is seen by the fact that, in the case of Moscow obkom, its head is the only department head to gain full membership of the Party buro. Thus from 1974–81 Nikitin and Ovsyannikov, successive heads of the department, were full members of the buro.[13]

Over the period a number of new departments were created— General Department (1968), Culture (1971), Foreign Connections (1974), Management (1979)—and a number of departments changed structure. Thus the Department of Industry-Transport split into two, becoming the Departments of Industry and Transport and Communications in 1971. In 1979 an important change took place when the Trade-Finance Department was abolished and the Departments of Finance-Planning and Trade-Services were created.[14] Undoubtedly such changes reflect the growing involvement of local soviets in corporate planning and the economy in general, and the need for the Party to adjust its structures to meet the new conditions.

Turnover of Moscow obkom buro, secretariat and departments

Although the Brezhnev period is epitomised by the phrase 'stability of cadres', over our period there have been quite high turnover rates; see Table 1.3. Thus in 1971, 1976 and 1979 there was a turnover rate of 50 per cent of full members of the buro. If we add candidate members then it was 66 per cent in 1971 and 62.5 per cent in 1979. For the secretariat the rates were lower, the highest being 40 per cent or two of the five secretariats. Turnover in the departments reached a peak of 61.5 per cent in 1971. The turnover rate was higher early on in the period and it was considerably reduced by the end. Thus turnover 1979-81 dropped to 12.5 per cent for full members of the buro and 22.2 per cent for department heads, while there was no change at all to the secretariat.[15]

It is interesting to note that Kozlov, the chairman of Moscow Oblast Executive Committee, and Konotop, the first Party secretary of Moscow Obkom, are the only two members to last the whole period—does this mean that Kozlov could be regarded as the number two in the leadership?[16] Hough puts forward the view that the first Party secretary is number one, the chairman of the executive committee number two, and the second Party secretary number three. He notes the important point that often a second Party secretary will be promoted to chairmanship of the executive committee, and there is a tradition of promoting chairmen to first Party secretary posts. At the same time it is rare for a chairman to be moved to the post of second Party secretary.[17] In Moscow Oblast Konotop was indeed the chairman of the oblast executive committee before being moved to the post of first Party secretary of the obkom. (We shall return to this when we discuss 'crossovers'.)

Now we can move on to discuss the theory of Party-state relations as outlined by Soviet scholars.

Table 1.3: Turnover Moscow obkom buro, secretariat and departments, 1966–81

	1968	1971	1974	1976	1979	1981
Full members buro	33.3%	50.0%	16.6%	50.0%	50.0%	12.5%
Full members + cand. membs.	66.0%	66.0%	33.0%	37.5%	62.5%	9.0%
Secretariat	40.0%	40.0%	20.0%	20.0%	40.0%	0.0%
Departments	30.7%	61.5%	20.0%	53.3%	26.6%	22.2%

Source: Compiled from *Leninskoe Znamya,* 1966–81 (see note 13 to this chapter).

THE THEORY OF PARTY-STATE RELATIONS

The question of Party-state relations has a long history. In 1905 Lenin identified the problem thus: 'The question—and it is a very important one—consists solely in how to differentiate and how to combine the tasks of the soviet and the tasks of the Russian Social-Democratic Labor Party.'[18] At the 8th Party Congress, he stressed that the functions of Party collectives must on no account be confused with the functions of government bodies such as the soviets: 'The Party must implement its decisions through soviet agencies, *within the confines of the Soviet Constitution.* The Party seeks to *guide* the activity of the Soviets, but not to replace them.'[19] This fundamental point has been written into the Party Rules, which declare:

> Party organisations must not act in place of government, trade union, co-operative or other public organisations of the working people; they must not allow either the merging of the functions of Party and other bodies or undue parallelism in work.[20]

However, this is easier said than done, for as Barabashev and Sheremet noted in 1967, the delimitation of Party and state functions 'constitute a very complex problem in both theory and practice'.[21] Hill sums up the work of both bodies in this way:

> While different writers draw up different lists of functions, the overall intention is to allocate policy-making, leadership and general supervision to the party with the functions of legislation and policy application, and to some extent information gathering being assigned to the state . . . .[22]

However, as far as Barabashev and Sheremet are concerned, 'In the final analysis the sphere of Party guidance extends to all measures taken by the soviets'. The basic point they stress is that, no matter what aspect of the work of the soviets the Party concerns itself with, be it cultural, economic or social, 'its relation to them is *political* in character' (my emphasis).[23] And by 'political' is meant not just policy-making but, as Shakhnazarov writes, 'the Party's ability to see beyond current policies and concentrate on general matters of principle, questions of social development of wider scope'.[24] For Shakhnazarov the Party political line is to be found in the Party programmes, which, although in theory are only binding on Party members, are in practice accepted by the general public as a 'kind of ideological constitution'.[25]

Another point which has been stressed in Soviet literature is that the methods of leadership of the Party and the soviets are fundamentally different. Thus Barabashev and Sheremet note:

> The political leadership given by the CPSU is built exclusively on methods of persuasion. But the leadership exercised by the soviets is simply a type of state activity that is clothed in legal forms and combines persuasion and state compulsion.[26]

One danger that would arise if the Party replaced the soviets and took over their administrative functions would be that the political element would become lost, and the long-term assessment of a problem become submerged in solving daily tasks. Shakhnazarov sums up these dangers most forcefully.

> As soon as one admits direct interference by the party organs in everyday administrative activity, they need to adjust their structure in accordance with their new functions, create the necessary departments and expand their staff. The result is that politicians such as party workers should be, tend to be replaced by narrow specialists, which in turn leads to a predominance of pragmatism and a growing unwillingness to deal with the basic tasks of party organisations—the tasks of ideological leadership.[27]

For Shevtsov:

> It is vitally important to note here that the functions of state organs are foreign to Party committees.
> The practical experience of economic management showed

long ago that the direct interference of Party organisations in day to day economic management, the duplication of managerial functions and actual assumption of control do not produce positive results. It removes responsibility from the managers and prevents them from assessing the position objectively and controlling it. What is more, Party organisations that do interfere expend their effort to no avail and so are unable to make full use of the means and opportunities that are available to them as organs of political guidance.[28]

Shakhnazarov notes that Party replacement (podmena) of the soviets leads to a situation of 'confusion', 'turmoil' and 'irresponsibility'—'with negligent officials being able to pass the buck to the Party committees and shelter behind it'. In a remarkable passage he writes:

> A double loss ensues: firstly, the great power embodied in the system of popular representation is not fully tapped; and secondly, the working people develop a rather sceptical attitude to the representative institutions and begin to doubt their effectiveness. This leads to a certain disrespect for socialist legality both on the part of the officials and the general public.[29]

Unfortunately practice does not always square with theory, and there are many cases of podmena reported in the Soviet press. For example, in 1965 the Central Committee of the CPSU in its resolution 'On the Work of the Local Soviets of Working People's Deputies of Poltava Region' warned the Party committees not to 'engage in petty tutelage and unfounded interference in the activities of the soviets and granted them the opportunity to resolve independently all questions within their competence.'[30] Again, in the 1971 resolution of the Central Committee on city and raion soviets, it was noted:

> In the practice of the district and city Party committees, there are still a good many instances of petty tutelage over the Soviets and of usurpation of their functions, as well as the adoptions of Party decisions on questions that fall wholly within the jurisdiction of the Soviets. Some Party committees given instructions to economic executives while bypassing the Soviets and Soviet agencies to which these economic managers are subordinate. Their practice does not correspond to the principles of the Party guidance of the Soviets and fetters the initiative of Soviet officers.[31]

There are many examples of podmena in the contemporary period. Here is just one, as noted by Khakalo:

> We still meet with the situation, whereby instead of daily practical help being given to the deputies by the Party organs, the Party replaces the soviets. They demand that the chairman of the executive committee of the rural soviet report to Party meetings about the work of the soviet, take decisions about the agenda of the sessions, and about how the resources of the executive committee should be distributed. It happens that some Party committees examine the question of soviet construction not as organs of political leadership but like higher bureaucratic agencies. They make decisions of an administrative nature, which is utterly intolerable.[32]

Similarly, the Party often directly engages in the work of the soviets by passing joint decisions with the state bodies. This has been criticised by the Party leadership; the 1965 Central Committee resolution about Poltava Oblast in particular spoke out against the practice. Barabashev and Sheremet also noted the phenomenon:

> As we know the Central Committee of the CPSU has condemned the unsubstantiated wide-spread practice of adoption of joint decisions by Party and local soviet bodies, which in many instances are issued on matters entirely within the competence of the soviets.[33]

In 1971 Chernovtsy City Ispolkom passed a joint decision with the gorkom on 'Fulfilling the Plan of Economic and Social Development of the City over the 9th Five Year Plan'.[34] In one of the raiony of Mogilev Oblast the Party and soviet bodies passed joint decisions in areas which were obviously the exclusive concern of the soviet. Thus these decisions covered such areas as, 'The Preservation of Mineral Fertilisers' and 'The Technical Servicing of Cars and Tractors', while in another raion a joint decision was passed on 'The Preservation of Potato Seeds'.[35] The first Party secretary of Vinnitsa Obkom (Ukraine) notes that officials do not consider a decision obligatory unless it is accompanied by the signature of the relevant Party official.[36]

So far we have noted the importance of the political element in Party leadership and the dangers of Party substitution of the soviets. Now we can turn to examine the basic methods of Party guidance of the state. Fedorinov in a review article of Party-state relations outlines them as follows:

(1) Working out the Party political line, defining the tasks and direction of the activities of all Soviet organizations and institutions on important questions of State economic, social, and cultural construction.
(2) The selection, placement and education of cadres.
(3) Control and verification of the execution of Party and state directives.[37]

The Party exercises such guidance primarily through 'Party groups' in the soviets and 'primary Party organisations' (PPOs) in the ispolkomy, in the departments, and also in ministries and enterprises. After examining the work of these bodies within the soviets and ispolkomy we shall turn to examine each one of Federinov's methods of leadership. Later we shall examine the work of the PPOs in the ministries.

PARTY GROUPS

According to Article 67 of the Rules of the CPSU, Party groups are formed 'at congresses, conferences and meetings and in the elective bodies of Soviets, trade unions, co-operatives and other mass organisations of the working people, having at least three Party members'.[38] Their membership includes all members and candidate members of the CPSU elected to any given representative organ, regardless of what PPO they may belong to. The Party groups are formed and function under the immediate direction of the corresponding Party agencies. The groups are elected for the entire period of office of the state organs in which they function.

Novikov describes the process of election of the Party groups thus: 'Prior to the first meeting of a newly elected soviet, the city committee of the Party assembles the deputies who are Communists, and they, by open ballot choose a Party group organizer from among themselves.'[39] However, there are some qualifications:

> It has become traditional that the deputy working as the first party secretary of the city committee of the CPSU [for city soviets] is placed in this post. Thereafter, meetings of the Party group are scheduled for the same day as the session of the soviet and are

held an hour or two before they open.[40]

In a number of soviets where there are large Party groups, the heads of the groups name deputies and assistants, with the agreement of the other group members. Thus in Vitebsk City Soviet, Byelorussia, 186 members were elected. The first Party secretary was named head of the group, the second secretary was named deputy leader and the secretary of the ispolkom was made responsible for the secretarial work. Other members of the group were a factory director and a worker.[41] Here we see the direct control of the soviet from the Party secretariat with the first and second secretaries leading the work of the Party group. The presence of the secretary of the gorispolkom will allow further co-ordination and control by the Party of the work of the executive committee.

With the re-activation of the local soviets, particularly since 1971, new demands to increase the role of the Party groups have been voiced by the central leadership; and the 1971 resolution on city and raion soviets itself set the goal of ensuring 'the comprehensive intensification of the influence of party groups in the soviets'.[42] All evidence does indeed point to a more active role by the Party groups. Thus Vinogradov notes, 'It must be observed that in recent years meetings of Party groups are conducted considerably more often and with greater regularity.'[43] Meetings are held not only on the eve of the soviet, but also between sessions and after them. Special meetings of the groups are also held to discuss particular economic or social questions, and at times members of particular branches of the economy will meet separately.

The call for increased activity has also led to an increase in the number of topics discussed in the sessions of the Party groups. Thus Vinogradov writes:

> In previous years it was primarily organizational questions that were considered at such meetings, questions that in themselves were quite significant (particularly preliminary discussion and recommendation of candidates for posts of leadership, desirable assignment of members of elective bodies to various commissions, sections and the like). Lately, however, the range of questions discussed has been noticeably enlarged.[44]

The Party rules give very general rights to the Party groups. Article 67 declares:

Party groups are formed for the purpose of strengthening the influence of the Party in every way and carrying out Party policy among non-Party people, strengthening Party and state discipline, combating bureaucracy, and verifying the fulfilment of Party and government directives.[45]

In order to carry out these duties, the Party groups have begun to set out detailed long-term plans for one to two years. These are usually drawn up with the help of the local Party committee and encompass a broad range of questions. Thus Mogilev City Party group in its plan for September 1977–8 included a report from deputies about work in the local automobile enterprise, reports from the director of the city communications department and from the head of a local food enterprise about voters' mandates.[46]

PRIMARY PARTY ORGANISATIONS (PPOs) AND PARTY GROUPS IN THE ISPOLKOM AND DEPARTMENTS

Party groups are also formed in the ispolkomy of the soviets; however, it is much more common for primary Party organisations to function in the apparat of the ispolkom and its departments. PPOs may be formed in each department and in some cases a combined PPO will be formed which includes all the Party members of an ispolkom and its administration.

In the same way as groups, the PPOs will meet before regular meetings of the departments and ispolkomy to discuss organisational and policy proposals. In a similar manner, their function is to promote the Party line within the administrations and control the implementation of Party policy.

As an example of their work we can look at the PPO of Pervokmaisk City Soviet Executive Committee and administration. Here the united PPO of all the departments and ispolkom numbers 34 members. Supported by the city Party committee, it actively carries out work to 'strengthen discipline in the apparat' and takes measures against 'bureaucratism and red-tape'. Over the period 1970–3 at the session of the PPO the following questions were discussed:

(1) The role of communists in fulfilling the tasks set before the ispolkom of the city soviet and its departments 1969–70.
(2) A report on the work of Nikolaev Oblast Party Committee and

the tasks of the Party leadership of the Komsomol.
(3) Progress made in acting upon critical remarks passed by Party members at the election-registration meeting.
(4) The Leninist style of work of the apparat of the ispolkom and the leading role of the communists of the executive committee of the city soviet.
(5) The protocol for examining letters and complaints of workers.[47]

According to Khutin, an analysis of the work of PPOs in ispolkomy shows that the agenda of their meetings is concerned with problems of the functional duties of the apparat, questions of intra-party life, the education of cadres, strengthening discipline and the clear and effective fulfilment by workers of their official duties.[48]

We shall discuss further the work of the Party groups and the PPOs as we cover each of the three areas of Party guidance as outlined by Fedorinov.

WORKING OUT THE PARTY POLITICAL LINE

Party groups and PPOs are not involved to a great extent in policy-making at the oblast and city level, but it is their job to see to it that a strong, unified position is taken up by the Party members on any issue, in order to exert the maximum influence on non-Party deputies. The Party members do not have the right to bind the non-Party deputies to their decisions; they can only recommend policies, and they must in theory rely on persuasion to have their decisions ratified by the soviets. However, this is seldom a difficult task at oblast and city levels, where, as can be seen from Table 1.4, the Party makes up a large majority of the soviets and even more so of the ispolkomy. Thus Party membership of the ispolkomy in 1982 was 93.1 per cent at oblast level USSR and 89.4 per cent for cities. Party membership of soviets, USSR, for oblasts was 54.8 per cent and for cities 46.3 per cent. Members of the Komsomol should, however, be added to these figures, as they will be strong supporters of the Party line, and indeed come under the authority of the Party. Taking Komsomol membership into consideration, the membership for cities in 1982 rises to 71 per cent.[49] In any debate at these levels, then, the Party is assured of support from the majority of the deputies.

The Party groups and PPOs are active in preparing questions and

Table 1.4: Party membership of oblast and city soviets and their isplokomy as elected 1982 USSR

	Oblast Soviet %	City Soviet %
Members + cand.		
membs	54.8	46.3
Komsomol	26.0	24.7
Total	80.8	70.0
	Oblast Ispolkomy	City Ispolkomy
Members + cand.		
membs	93.1	89.4
Komsomol	3.6	6.0
Total	96.7	95.4

Source: *Itogi Vyborov i Sostav Deputatov Mestnykh Sovetov Narodnykh Deputatov 1982g. (Statisticheskii Sbornik)* (Moscow, 1982): for oblast soviets, p. 61, for cities, p. 117, for oblast and for city ispolkomy, p. 197.

setting the agenda of the sessions. Thus I. Klimov, the Deputy Chairman of the Presidium of the Supreme Soviet of Byelorussia, remarks: 'Party groups as a rule set the tone of work in the soviets. They take the initiative in formulating the majority of questions discussed at sessions of the soviets'.[50] The groups normally meet before the session of the soviet or ispolkom and work out a unified Party line on each issue that is to be discussed. Once a decision has been taken, Party members are obliged to take the Party line and are subject to Party discipline if they fail to do so.

One of the most important ways the Party groups enforce the Party line in the soviets is through the standing commissions. Party control of these bodies gives the groups an active influence over the work of the soviets between sessions. The Party groups are involved right from the start in the creation of the standing commissions and the appointment of their members. Thus Novikov writes:

> It is expressed primarily in a more attentive approach to the assignment of Communist deputies to commissions. The group carefully discusses proposals prepared for this purpose and is guided by two objectives: that the Communists be, as far as possible, more evenly distributed among all the standing committees and that each be specifically where his knowledge and abilities can best find application.[51]

In the vast majority of cases, the chairman of a standing commission will be a Party member.

Thus the mere fact that the majority of members of soviets and ispolkomy belong to the Party or the Komsomol, enables the Party to enforce its views on any question without difficulty. In pre-session meetings headed by the powerful figure of the first Party secretary, the Party line is conveyed to the Party groups who are then under Party discipline to comply with it.

Selection, placement and training of cadres

One of the strongest weapons at the disposal of the Party is its power of appointment and dismissal of the leading officials of the oblast or city. The Party groups and PPOs take an active part in this process, discussing in their sessions the composition of the executive committees, heads of departments and other leading posts. Here they will receive instructions from higher Party bodies through the local Party committee. At each election session of Moscow Oblast Soviet the meeting is chaired by the first Party secretary of the Oblast Committee or one of the other secretaries, and it is he who proposes the list of members of the executive committee, heads of departments, and other leading officials who are then voted on at the session. Also present at the election sessions of Moscow Oblast are members of the Central Committee Secretariat.[52]

From the beginning, the Party, as Barabashev and Sheremet note, is busy working out 'guidelines on such cardinal matters as the basic proportions to be maintained with respect to the social origins of deputies, and the problem of continuity and renewal in the ranks of the deputies'.[53]

In general the key positions of chairman, deputy chairman, members of the executive committees and heads of departments will be under the nomenklatura of the Party bodies which are one level up in the administrative hierarchy. Thus the oblast Party committee will have the dominant voice over the selection of the executive committees of the cities under its jurisdiction. In a similar manner the executive committee of the oblast will be under the nomenklatura of the republic central committee of the CPSU.

As the Western scholar Theen notes:

> The term nomenklatura refers to a list of key positions, the appointments to which are directly or indirectly controlled by the

secretariats of the CPSU at the various levels of the political and territorial-administrative structure of the Soviet system. It is the officials in the personnel departments of these secretariats who, together with the relevant political leaders, especially the party secretaries, at a given level serve as the ultimate selectors of the members of the Soviet political elite.[54]

There are three types of nomenklatura: (1) basic nomenklatura, which is the CPSU's exclusive prerogative; (2) the registration and control nomenklatura, which concerns positions which can only be filled with the approval of the CPSU; (3) the reserve nomenklatura, which is a list of potential candidates for future vacancies.[55]

According to Theen, the nomenklatura under the oblast Party committee will include:

such positions as leading party, soviet, trade union and Komsomol officials of the region, its cities, and districts; secretaries of the primary party organizations of large industrial enterprises and construction sites; managers of industrial conglomerates and directors of enterprises, chief engineers, chief economists, as well as other 'responsible workers'; instructors of the regional party committees (gorkomy), secretaries and department chiefs of city and district party committees (raikomy), chairmen of executive committees of the soviets at the city and district level, secretaries of the district Komsomol committee, and so forth.[56]

He estimates that in 1969 there were 88,000 nomenklatura posts at oblast level throughout the USSR, and in 1973, 76,000.[57]

Vinogradov notes that the nomenklatura of Minsk Obkom, with regard to local soviets, numbered 112 in 1978.[58] On 1 January 1978, the reserve nomenklatura ratified by the buro of the obkom included chairmen of the city and raion soviets, 17 secretaries of the city and raion Party committees, 16 deputy chairmen of the ispolkomy, 1 chairman of a raion committee of people's control, 4 secretaries of Party committees of large PPOs and 5 leaders of enterprises and institutions.[59]

The Party nomenklatura of an average city will run into several hundreds. Thus for Tula in 1968 the number was 700, 930 for Kalinin in 1969, and for Novosibirsk 800 in 1971. For Moscow, the figure was 22,000 in 1956, and 17,000 in 1958. In 1965 Leningrad city and oblast together numbered 5,000.[60]

The State Nomenklatura System

In addition to the Party nomenklatura there is a separate state system under the control of the executive committees and ministries. Thus in the early 1970s the Executive Committee of Leningrad City Soviet employed 656,695 people and exercised basic nomenklatura power over 1,600 top positions in the administration of the city.[61] Each department in the city administration in turn maintained its own nomenklatura lists. According to a 1974 work, the Executive Committee of Moscow City Soviet has nomenklatura power (both basic, and registration and control) over 1,851 top positions, and its departmental nomenklatura includes 10,825 positions.[62]

The existence, not only of two parallel bureaucracies, but of parallel nomenklatura systems, has undoubtedly led to problems and confusion over which positions fall under the jurisdiction of Party and state, ministry or obkom. As we shall see in the chapters on finance and planning, there is a great deal of ambiguity and many poorly-defined regulations concerning the selection of the heads of city and oblast planning and finance departments.

One Soviet scholar outlines three different kinds of interaction that may cause difficulties:

(1) When the post is included in the nomenklatura of the raion, city or oblast Party committee and at the same time under the nomenklatura of a state organ situated in the given territory, i.e. a union or Union-Republic ministry.
(2) Where the post is under the nomenklatura of a central Party organ, i.e. Central Committee of the CPSU, and at the same time under that of an oblispolkom or Republic ministry.
(3) When the post comes under the nomenklatura of both Party and state organs at the same level.[63]

'In all such cases', Rozenbaum writes, 'the party and state organs exchange information about their reserve candidates and jointly make a detailed assessment of them, striving to reach a unanimous opinion about such questions'.[64]

The ill-defined nature of the system must lead to a great deal of bureaucratic in-fighting, and in the end many candidates are still promoted to posts for which they are not suited. According to one Soviet study in Byelorussia, turnover is high because of 'mistakes in cadres policy'. Thus in 1978, 193 chairmen of executive committees were replaced, comprising 10.4 per cent of the total, 102 deputy chairmen (4.7 per cent) and 182 secretaries (9.8 per cent).[65]

On 27 March 1973, at a plenum of Moscow Obkom, the secretary of the oblispolkom, M.P. Shchetinina, remarked:

> We are very disturbed by the large turnover of leading workers of the raion and city ispolkomy. Thus, of 54 chairmen, 33 or 62 per cent worked for only 3 years in such posts, and 12 only one year. A similar short tenure is found among deputy chairmen (46 per cent) and secretaries (40 per cent). It is necessary that we stabilise our leading cadres and for this we need more effective work with the reserve. In all the ispolkomy there are such reserve lists but often only on paper. As a result, for nearly six months in the ispolkom of Podolsk City Soviet there was a vacancy for the post of secretary.[66]

While in theory the Party must obtain the approval and support of the soviets for the appointment and dismissal of executive members, there are many cases where the Party merely by-passes the soviets and dismisses the chairman of an ispolkom. Thus the Buro of Kostyukova Raikom sacked the chairman of a subordinate city soviet and entrusted the post to another deputy. As Khakalo points out, 'Perhaps the chairman of the ispolkom got his just deserts. But this ought to have been done in the established manner by a decision of a session of the city soviet'.[67]

Alternatively, Party groups can influence the selection and dismissal process. For example, the members of Chernovtsy Raion Soviet Party group produced evidence of poor work on the part of P. Medvedko, the head of a section in the Department of Communal Housing of the gorispolkom. They turned to the raikom Party and the PPO of which he was a member. Soon afterwards he was dismissed from his post.[68]

In recent years the central leadership has attempted to bring more order into the selection procedure and to improve the whole process. In part they have done this by decentralising the procedure and giving more power to the PPOs over the selection of cadres at local level. Thus a Central Committee resolution in 1979 on 'The Work of Udmurtsk Oblast Party Committee in Selection, Placement and Training of Cadres' criticised the Party committee for shortcomings in the selection of cadres and attributed this in part to the failure of the obkom to consult the PPOs in this work.[69]

Placement of Cadres—Patterns of Membership of Moscow Obkom and Oblispolkom

An examination of the composition of Moscow Obkom Buro, Secretariat and departments, and of Moscow Oblispolkom, shows consistent patterns of cadre policy, with dual membership of some individuals of the Party buro and the oblispolkom, and the crossover of members of the buro and department heads into the oblispolkom, and vice versa.

Dual membership. My study of Moscow Oblispolkom over the period 1969–77 shows clearly that it was dominated by members of Moscow Obkom. Of the 50 members of the oblispolkom, 33 were full members of the obkom, 2 were candidate members, 1 was a member of the revision commission and 14 were non-Party committee members. In total, 72 cent of the pool of 50 were obkom members. Furthermore, we should note that in our pool were six members of the Buro of Moscow Obkom, two of whom were second secretaries of the buro.

In his account of Tiraspol, Hill gives an excellent account of the phenomenon of dual membership, not only of the top bodies, i.e. gorkom and gorispolkom, but also at the Party committee and soviet level. He draws up a hierarchy of officials, moving from group A, who are merely members of the soviet, through to group H, who are members of the soviet, the gorispolkom, the gorkom and the gorkom buro. The elite groups as outlined by Hill had the following percentages:

	A	B	C	D	E	F	G	H
No.	698	290	231	12	7	22	37	13
%	53.3	22.1	17.6	0.9	0.5	1.7	2.8	1.0

The group H percentage of 1.0 refers to the number of individuals who, over the whole period, gained membership of the gorkom and the gorispolkom; the actual percentage for those who maintained dual membership was lower, at 0.8 per cent.[70]

In many oblasts and cities it is common for the first Party secretary to be a member of the ispolkom, and for the chairman of the ispolkom to sit in the party buro. In the case of Moscow Oblast it was the second secretary who performed this function of dual membership; the chairman of the ispolkom was a member of the buro. In the period 1971–4 there was an additional secretary in the oblispolkom. The only other member to possess dual membership

Table 1.5: Dual membership of Moscow Obkom Buro and Oblispolkom, 1969–77

1969	Paputin (Second Secretary)
	Kozlov (Chairman Oblispolkom)
1971	Paputin
	Kozlov
	Isaev (Secretary Obkom)
	Sokolov (Chairman of Peoples' Control Committee)
1973	Kozlov
	Paputin
	Sokolov
1975	Kozlov
	Borisenkov (Second Secretary)
	Sokolov
1977	Kozlov
	Borisenkov
	Sokolov

Source: Compiled from *Leninskoe Znamya*, 1969–77 (see note 13 of this chapter).

was the chairman of the People's Control Committee (see Table 1.5). In the case of Moscow Oblast, the chairman of the oblispolkom may be given greater authority as the only long-standing member of the Party buro and oblispolkom. Konotop, the first Party secretary, has to rely on reports of the second Party secretaries about the work of the ispolkom.[71]

Dual membership gives the Party the ability directly to influence and control the meetings of the ispolkom and to maintain a close check on its work through the Party representation in the executive. At the same time it allows the Party to convey policies quickly to the ispolkom through having the chairman of the executive in the buro. Another important point which Hill notes is that it also provides the Party with an extra source of information from the state bodies, from individuals directly engaged in implementing policies and thus familiar with a number of technical problems not directly available to the Party.

Crossovers. While dual membership is important, it is not the only way in which cadre policy contributes towards Party supervision of the soviets. When one examines the career paths of members of the Party buro, secretariat and its departments, it becomes apparent that there is a deliberate policy of promoting full-time Party workers to the apparat of the oblispolkom. An examination of Moscow Obkom and Oblispolkom shows a number of interesting cases in this respect (see Table 1.6).

Table 1.6: Table of crossovers Moscow Obkom and Oblispolkom

Name	Party Position	State Position
V.I. Konotop	First Party Secretary 1964 (previously 2nd Sec. 1956-9)	Chairman of Oblispolkom 1959-63
N.T. Kozlov	Secretary 1960-3	Chairman of Oblispolkom 1963 until 1981
N.K. Korol'kov	Cm Buro/Head Dept. Org-Party Work 1966 not re-elected 1968	Deputy Chairman Oblispolkom 1971-to close of period
V.G. Krylov	CM Buro/Head Dept. Org-Party Work 1968 not re-elected 1971	Deputy Chairman Oblispolkom 1971-to close of period
A.A. Kamenev	Head of Department Agriculture 1966 and 1968 not re-elected 1971	First Deputy Chairman 1971-to close of period
M.P. Shchetinina	CM Buro/Head Dept. Prop-Agit. 1966 and 1968 not re-elected 1971	Secretary Oblispolkom 1971-to close of period
V.G. Tsepkov	Head Dept. of Admin. Organs 1966 and 1968 not re-elected 1971	Head of Dept. Internal Affairs. 1971 to close of period
V.I. Vinogradov	Head Dept. Const. and Const. Mat. 1971 not re-elected 1974	Deputy Chm. Oblispolkom 1975 to close of period
I.M. Cherepanov	Head of Dept. Science and Educ. 1971 + 1974 not re-elected 1976	Chm. Planning Commission Oblispolkom to close of period + Deputy Chm. Oblispolkom
N.V. Kudryashov	CM Buro 1974, FM Buro 1976 not re-elected 1979	Head Dept. Land. Recl. and Water. Oblispolkom 1977
V.S. Pestov	Head Dept. Industry 1976 not re-elected 1979 FM Member of Buro 1979-81	Chairman of Committee of People's Control 1977 + 1981 Becomes Chm. of Oblispolkom
M.A. Orlov	Head Dept. Industry November 1974 FM Buro 1976-81	Chm. Trade Union Council
L.P. Bogdanov	Head Dept. Prop. Agit. 1971-79	Previously 1969 Head Dept. Labour Resources, Oblispolkom

Source: Compiled from *Leninskoe Znamya*, 1966-81 (see Note 13 of this chapter), and *Prominent Personalities in the USSR*, ed. E.L. Crowley, H.E. Schulz and A.I. Lebed (Metuchen N.J., 1968), pp. 295 (Konotop) and 315 (Kozlov).

One of the most interesting points is that Konotop, the first Party secretary, was previously the chairman of Moscow Oblispolkom. Kozlov, the chairman of the oblispolkom, was also at one time a secretary of the Moscow Obkom. In 1961 the positions were almost the reverse of those at present, with Kozlov a secretary of the obkom and Konotop the chairman of the oblispolkom.[72]

Two heads of the Party Department of Organisation-Party Work (i.e. Korol'kov and Krylov) became deputy chairmen of the oblispolkom. One of the heads of the Party Department of Propaganda and Agitation (Shchetinina) became the secretary of the oblispolkom. A head of the Party Department of Construction and Construction Materials (Vinogradov) became deputy chairman of the oblispolkom. Tsepkov, head of the Department of Administrative Organs, moved over to head the Department of Internal Affairs of the oblispolkom. The head of the Department of Science and Education became chairman of the Planning Commission of the oblispolkom. A candidate member of the buro, Kudryashov, became head of the Department of Land Reclamation of the oblispolkom. One head of the Party Department of Industry (Pestov) moved to chairmanship of the People's Control Committee and then on to chairmanship of the executive committee, while another (Orlov) became the chairman of the Trades Union Council. Moving in the other direction, the head of the oblispolkom Department of Labour Resources (Bogdanov) moved to head the Department of Propaganda and Agitation.[73]

The important point to notice is that these individuals are all following particular career structures, the majority of which, if not all, will be under the nomenklatura of the Party. Thus, even if we note the presence of an individual in the executive committee or as head of a department for a number of years, this should not lead us to assume that he will have a particular loyalty to that department. Indeed the crossing over from one body to another may be designed to stop such loyalties building up.

From an examination of Moscow Oblast it is interesting to note the practice of promoting first Party secretaries of cities and raiony to headships of departments of the secretariat of the obkom and then on to positions in the oblispolkom or to headships of the departments of the oblispolkom. Hough notes that in 1974 34 per cent of oblast first Party secretaries had once been chairmen of the executive committees of oblast soviets, 84 per cent of these immediately before becoming first secretaries.[74] In their study of twelve cities in the RSFSR, Ermolaeva and Khristoforova found that more than 40 per cent of members of the ispolkomy had previously worked in the Party apparat, and more than 33 per cent in the Komsomol and trade union organs.[75]

Vinogradov provides similar information for Yaroslavl' Oblast. Thus he notes that in the late 1970s the obkom transferred more than ten Party workers to leading posts in the oblispolkom. Among these was the first deputy chairman of the oblispolkom, who earlier was the first Party secretary of a raikom; while the head of the Department of Agitation and Propaganda of the obkom became deputy chairman of the oblispolkom. The head of the Department of Light Industry and Trade of the obkom also became a deputy chairman of the oblispolkom. The head of the Department of Agriculture of the oblispolkom was earlier the first secretary of a raikom.[76] Similarly, Dobrik gives us some examples from L'vov Oblast. Here the first Party secretary of a raikom was elected chairman of the oblispolkom. The second secretary of a city Party organisation became chairman of a raispolkom. The deputy head of the Party department of Industry and Transport of L'vov city was made chairman of a raion soviet.[77] Finally, a study carried out by the Academy of Social Science in Minsk and Brest showed that the nomenklatura reserve for the posts of chairmen of city and raion soviets included secretaries, most of them second secretaries of city and raion Party committees.[78]

Vinogradov notes that many members of the ispolkomy also move into the Party apparat. For example, 'In their turn many chairmen of the ispolkomy comprise the basic reserve for the posts of first secretary of city and raion party committees'. In Minsk Obkom their reserve nomenklatura for such posts in 1978 included 16 chairmen of ispolkomy of city and raion soviets, 36.6 per cent of the total.[79]

It is also interesting to see that membership of the buro of Moscow Obkom can be a stepping stone to top Party and state posts. Thus Mesyats, a member of the secretariat and buro, became first Deputy Minister of Agriculture of the RSFSR. Paputin, second secretary and member of the executive committee, was moved to the post of First Deputy Minister of Internal Affairs of the USSR. Isaev, secretary and member of the buro, was promoted to the Central Committee Apparat.

Viewing cadre policy from the above perspective makes the idea of separate Party and state hierarchies extremely dubious and it is difficult to identify individuals as either 'Party' or 'state' people. What we see is a career structure that constantly crosses the

Party/state divide. The most important consideration is, who selects and guides these individuals in this career path, and who has the power to demote or dismiss them in the future—all evidence points to the Party. Similarly this gives us a completely different picture of Party control within the executive committees. Thus if we look at Table 1 (p. 13) on the composition of Moscow Oblispolkom, as elected June 1977, we see not only the second secretary of the obkom, Borisenkov, and members of the buro, Kozlov and Sokolov, but also former members of the obkom apparat, Korol'kov, Kamenev, Vinogradov, Krylov, Cherepanov and Shchetinina, all now serving as key members of the oblispolkom apparat (i.e. first deputy chairman, deputy chairmen and secretary). In addition, among the membership is Tsepkov, former head of the Department of Administrative Organs of the obkom. Viewed in this light the Party's control over the oblispolkom appears overwhelming, giving us a far greater insight into Party-state relations than a static view of the oblispolkom and dual membership.

Thus this study supports the view of Hill and others, that there is a 'unified leadership pool' which cuts across the Party-state divide. Individuals are promoted both upwards from raiony and cities to oblast level and diagonally between Party and state. From the point of view of the central leadership, such a policy has the advantage of stopping the build-up of bureaucratic loyalties, and of giving such personnel a broad range of professional, political and administrative experience.

Training of Cadres. As we have seen, Party and state officials serve under one unified career structure which may promote them across the Party/state divide, and which is firmly under the control of the Party. In a similar manner, Party and soviet officials are trained together in various institutions at central and local level. Until 1976 the leading institutions for such courses were the Higher Party Schols, now renamed Institutions for Raising the Qualifications of Leading Party and Soviet Cadres. At the Central Institute in Moscow top officials from Republic, oblast and city levels will be admitted, while secondary officials from these levels, together with leading personnel from the rainy and below, will attend local institutions in major cities throughout the USSR.[80]

In 1980, leaders of executive committees of local soviets were strongly represented in full-time courses at these local institutes. Some 11,113 chairmen (or 21.8 per cent of the total), 2,171 deputy chairman (3.8 per cent) and 2,409 secretaries of ispolkomy of local soviets (4.7 per cent) undertook such training.[81]

Control

Undoubtedly one of the most important aspects of Party guidance is the verification and control of the implementation of central policies. The Party is able to enforce such control through a number of different channels such as the PPOs, Party groups, the buro, secretariat and departments. In this section we shall first look at the role of the obkoms and gorkoms in controlling the executive committee and state departments. Later we shall move on to a discussion of control within the ministries.

Party groups

As we have already seen, the Party groups in the soviets are active in promoting the Party line in the sessions and ensuring that members of the Party are promoted to the leading posts in the ispolkomy and departments. The groups are also engaged in conducting control work, checking on the work of officials and working with standing commissions and deputy groups in 'raids' on enterprises and departments. Often officials will be called to give reports about their work before the Party groups. With the powerful first Party secretary as their head, the Party groups can wield significant authority over local enterprise heads, and they can give recommendations about their performance to the Party committees. The groups also maintain a firm control over the work of standing commissions. Thus Vinogradov notes, 'the Party group directs the attention of standing committees and groups of deputies toward unflagging monitoring of the implementation of decisions adopted'.[82] Members of the standing commissions also give reports to the Party groups.

As we have seen, the theory of Party control over the soviets is that only those deputies who are Party members are subject to such control, other deputies being free to choose the course of action they think best. However, since the majority of chairmen of standing commissions are Party members, the scope of action left to non-Party members would appear to be minimal. The Soviet writer Novikov spends much time trying to avoid this conclusion:

> Of course, if the Party group were to undertake to hear the reports of the standing committees in the strict meaning of the word, that would be wrong and would evoke just criticism on the grounds of substituting for the soviet. But what we are referring to is something quite different—specifically, checking on how the

43

Communists included in the committees on the recommendations of the group are functioning, something that no way substitutes for the report to the soviet of one of its subsidiary bodies.[83]

Primary Party Organisations

Similarly, the PPOs are active in controlling the work of the departments of the ispolkomy, and they are themselves closely monitored by the Party buro, secretariat and departments. After a greater role had been given to the city and raion soviets in 1971, the 24th Party Congress of the same year outlined new rights to be given to the PPOs:

> In the interests of further enhancing the role of party organizations in the implementation of party policy, the Congress finds it necessary to grant the primary party organizations of scientific-research institutes, educational institutions and cultural and medical institutions the same right as those of primary party organizations in production regarding supervision over the activity of the administration. In view of their specific character, party organizations of central and local soviet and economic institutions and departments must increase their supervision over the activity of the apparatus in fulfilling party and government directives.[84]

This new stress on the role of the PPOs was the result of poor control over the ministries and their subordinate enterprises, which was revealed in a Central Committee resolution with regard to the Meat and Dairy Industry in 1970. Since that time there have been a number of resolutions which show that the problem of control is still a very serious one. In February 1982 a further Central Committee resolution was passed with reference to PPOs in the administrations and a charter was drawn up with the aim of once more strengthening the work of the PPOs.[85] However, there is much evidence to show that the work of both the Party groups and the PPOs is far from satisfactory from the point of view of the Party leadership.

The buro, and the secretariat and its departments

The buro itself also plays a considerable role in controlling the work of the executive committee. In Moscow Oblast the chairman of the Planning Commission and the head of the Department of Finance report each year to the buro about the budget and economic plan, one or two days (on one occasion on the same day) before these plans are ratified by a session of the soviets. They also appear before the obkom to report on progress in the fulfilment of such plans.[86]

In the course of 1968–71 in the sessions of the Buro of Pervomaisk Gorkom twelve questions were examined connected with the work of the gorispolkom and its departments. These covered such topics as crime prevention, the work of trade enterprises and the training of cadres, physical culture and sport.[87]. In Minsk the Obkom Buro heard reports from the heads of the administrations of local industry, cinema and daily services.[88] These reports were drawn up by commissions of the Obkom with the assistance of the PPOs, and of Party and soviet workers.[89] In a similar manner, Mogilev Obkom discussed the activity of the Departments of Social Insurance, Health and Housing and the Communal Economy of the oblispolkom.[90]

According to Frolic, the buro is concerned with making general policy statements and giving political guidance.[91] He quotes a Moscow administration official as reporting, 'direct buro intervention was not a common pattern in large cities . . . [but] in smaller cities, the buro or secretariat is more likely to deal directly with individual administrations and departments.[92] According to this official 'the head of a city administration got his instructions on the telephone directly from the buro and secretariat'.[93] In a fascinating passage Frolic notes a Moscow official's answer to the question— 'What kind of policies are considered by the Party buro and secretariat?':

> It depends on a number of factors. Which individuals are involved? Sometimes Party and government officials know each other in that case regular channels can be bypassed, particularly in smaller cities. Then it can depend on the type of problem involved. If it is an urgent problem of housing construction for example, there is a good chance that the Party will speak directly to the head of the housing administration.[94]

Further, with reference to the distinction between secretariat and buro:

> 'You must separate party buro from secretariat. The latter's interests are more organisational in nature, and through its general direction over party departments the secretariat may become more involved in the work of the municipal administrations'.[95]

With regard to the departments of the secretariat, Frolic points out that their interests will be more technical in nature, involving the collection of plan indices and so on.[96]

THE SECRETARIAT AND ITS DEPARTMENTS

The secretariat is the chief executive body of the Party and to a large extent the chief policy-making force within the buro. Through its departments it implements Party policy and collects and processes information from other Party and state bodies in the region. Each secretary will control a number of different departments. The Department of Organisation-Party Work would appear to be one of the main departments engaged in supervision and control of the state through its guidance of lower Party bodies. The other departments will no doubt control the corresponding municipal departments according to their speciality.

With regard to Moscow Obkom, looking back at Table 1.2, we can see that a number of new departments have been created and that numerous administrative charges have taken place over our period. In a similar manner Party/state relations will have varied according to the different structure of the departments of the secretariat. We have already noted that the new departments of Finance-Planning and Trade-Services reflect the increased role of the soviets in these areas.

A number of general points can be made from an examination of the departments of the secretariat and those of the oblispolkom:

(1) Each Party department will have to supervise a number of state departments, some more than others. This may leave some state departments freer than others.
(2) It is difficult to see in some cases which Party departments will supervise which state departments. In particular it is difficult to place the state departments of Electricity, Gas, Social Insurance and Health. Should these come under the Party's Trade-Services department, or perhaps City Economy? Table 1.7 outlines possible connections between Party and state. Some areas are very simple. Agriculture and Culture, for example, have direct counterparts in the Party and soviet. Where one state department may come under a number of Party departments I have placed a question mark by it.
(3) The creation of the Finance-Planning Department and that of

Table 1.7: Party control in Moscow Oblast Soviet. Possible links between party and Soviet departments

The Party	Soviet
Agriculture	Agriculture
	Land Reclamation and Water
	Timber
	Agro-Chemical Production Association?
Construction and Construction and Building Materials	Construction
	Industrial Building Materials
	Construction and Maintenance of Roads?
	Repair and Construction of City Roads?
	Capital Construction
	Housing?
Culture	Culture
	Physical Culture and Sport
	Cinema?
Food and Food-processing	Food
	Bakeries
	Public Catering
Textile and Light Industry	Crafts and Toys
	Cultural and Household Goods
	Invalid Labour?
Industry	Heat-Energy
	Labour Resources
	Material and Technical Supply
Transport and Communications	Transport
	Canals
	Fuel
Planning and Finance	Planning
	Finance
	Architecture and Planning
Trade-Services	Trade
	Communal Economy
	Pharmacy?
	Supplies and Sales
	Electricity, Gas?
	Health, Social Insurance?
Education and Scientific Institutions	Education
Propaganda and Agitation	Publishing, Printing and Book Trade
	Cinema?
City Economy	Repair and Construction of City Roads?
	Gas? Electricity?
	Health?
	Social Insurance?
Administrative Organs	Judiciary
	Internal Affairs

Source: *Leninskoe Znamya* for Party departments and *Byulleten' Ispolnitel'novo Komiteta Moskovskovo Oblastnovo Soveta* for state departments.

Trade-Services in 1979 must have improved the control of the Party over these areas. It is difficult to see which department would have looked after planning and architecture before the creation of the Finance-Planning Department.

Party-state relations will differ, then, according to the number of state departments that a particular Party department has to control, and the number and kind of departments that are present at any one time. As we have noted, it is difficult to place all the state departments under a particular Party body. Thus it looks as if the Trade-Services Department could have up to eight soviet departments to control, while the Department of Education and Science has only one.

Co-ordination problems

As we have seen, there are a number of different ways in which the party controls the work of the soviets. The Party groups are present in the soviets to promote the Party line, while the PPOs are engaged in similar activities within the executive committees and departments. Control also comes from the buro, secretariat and departments of the Party committees. This is assisted by the policy of giving key members of the obkoms and gorkoms dual membership of the leading bodies, and by promoting officials across the Party-state divide. The buro hears reports from heads of departments of the ispolkomy and other leading state officials, while the secretariat and departments engage in the organisational and technical work of the soviets.

One problem that springs from these different control channels is the possibility of lack of co-ordination between them, and different and even contradictory instructions being passed on to the different levels of the state apparatus, i.e. ispolkomy, departments. The problem becomes exceedingly complex when we consider the process over a number of different administrative levels. Figure 1.2 shows the possible paths that the Party can take to enforce its decisions. Although in theory it should work through the soviets, it will often bypass them and give instructions directly to enterprise managers, PPOs in the departments etc., but in doing this it increases the possibility of co-ordination problems. Thus the Party may be involved in horizontal or diagonal forms of control and leadership. The result may be that state personnel will receive

Figure 1.2: Co-ordination problems

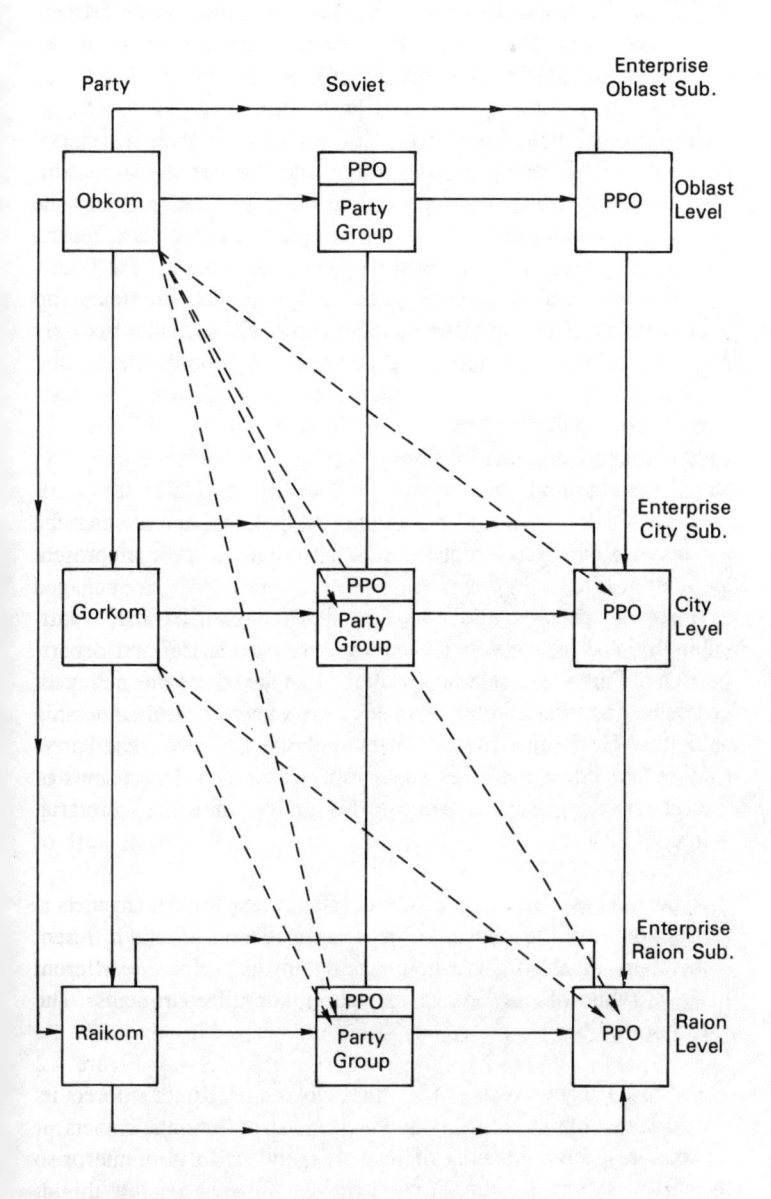

→ Formal channels of communication
--→ Informal channels of communication

contradictory or incompatible commands from different Party bodies. Thus the head of a city housing department may receive instructions from the obkom first Party secretary, or from the department of construction of the obkom secretariat. Similarly, instructions will come from the city Party committee and from PPOs at city level as well as from the leadership within the oblast executive committee, its housing administration and the gorispolkom. The Party at oblast level, wishing to avoid the complications of going through the regular state channels, may instruct officials of PPOs within enterprises without informing the other relevant Party and state bodies. Such an action is liable to produce problems for personnel within the state bureaucracies, who will have to turn to the Party for information about the activities of subordinate bodies which in theory should be under their exclusive control. As we have noted, Party 'podmena' of state bodies is counter-productive and leads to a situation where the soviets come to rely on the Party for even the slightest administrative step. The state gradually draws the Party into its bureaucracy and swamps its political and ideological role under a barrage of requests relating to bureaucratic blockages and administrative problems.

Hoffman observes that Party members may suffer from 'role ambiguity' and 'role conflict', and these are particularly pertinent to the area of Party-state relations, where often the boundaries between leadership and 'substitution' are difficult to gauge precisely. Of 'role ambiguity' Hoffman writes, 'A person may experience [this] when he does not know what his supervisor thinks of his work, what criteria are being used to evaluate his performance . . .', and of 'role conflict':

> A person may experience role conflict when the demands of a superior are unreasonable or incompatible, or when some members of his organization expect him to perform in certain ways, while others believe his job entails different rights and responsibilities . . .[97]

The first Party secretary of Vinnitsa Obkom, P. Kozyr', notes the confusion that often arises among Party and state personnel concerning their respective spheres of responsibility for local administrations. He also stresses that Soviet officials still rely too heavily on the Party to make decisions which by right should be made by the soviets themselves. In the area of agriculture, he points out, the same questions are considered by the secretary of the raikom, the chairman of the raiispolkom and the head of the agriculture department of the soviet. However, when summoned to give their reports to the obkom, all three produce 'identical figures, facts and conclusions'. Yet, as Kozyr' observes, 'each of these has varied functions . . . Why do they always turn to the Party about the majority of economic questions, when by right they should be decided by the raiispolkom?'[98]

PARTY CONTROL OVER THE MINISTRIES

At the beginning of this chapter I suggested there is a 'control gap' between central Party leadership of the ministries and local Party control over the subordinate enterprises of those ministries situated at city and oblast level. It is now time to consider the evidence for such a hypothesis. I base it on the following: First, the large number of Central Committee resolutions relating to control within the ministries and local Party bodies adopted, particularly in the 1970s. These, as we shall show, point to a chronic lack of Party control over the ministries. Secondly, the conclusions which I reach in Chapter 4 with regard to the role of the ministries in the development of the cities and oblasts, and the attempt by local leaders to co-ordinate branch and territorial planning. My research shows the utter failure of local soviets and thus also of local Party bodies to 'co-ordinate and control' the work of the enterprises (particularly those of higher subordination) situated in the territory of these soviets. In this section we shall look at the first part of the evidence (the second part will be discussed in Chapter 4).

In 1971, as we have seen, PPOs were given new rights to control administrations. That there was an urgent need to improve Party control over the ministries was clearly revealed in a 1970 resolution of the Central Committee on the Meat and Dairy Industry,[99] which showed that the work of the Party organisation within the ministry was ineffective, and control over the work of the ministry sporadic and weak. Thus it observed: 'the level of organizational-party and ideological-political work within the apparatus lags considerably behind the requirements placed on ministry party organizations under present conditions.'[100] And further:

> The party committee and party organizations of the administrations do not exert the necessary influence to improve the work of the ministry's apparatus, to strengthen discipline, and to raise the

responsibility of its employees for implementing the directives of the party and government; they do not respond sharply to serious short-comings in their guidance of industry and fail to give the short-comings a principled party evaluation.[101]

Within the ministry 'formalistic and bureaucratic methods of leadership' were tolerated. The Party had not taken the necessary steps to 'eliminate parallelism and duplication in the activity of its different units'.[102] Supervision of the implementation of decisions of the ministry was very poor and 'incidents of bureaucratic delay and a bureaucratic attitude'[103] were not condemned by the Party organisation. Even further, the resolution stated that:

> ... The party committee often displays liberalism and unscrupulousness and fails to provide an incisive political evaluation of incidents where some communists lose their feelings of responsibility for entrusted matters, and of violations of State discipline and incorrect behaviour ... Many decisions of the party committee and party meetings do not pose concrete tasks or define the personal responsbility of Communists for their fulfilment.[104]

The situation reached the point where 'Ministry officials inform the party aktiv and communists *irregularly* of the work of the ministry, the state of affairs in the branch of the economy, and progress in the fulfilment of plans and assignments'[105] (my emphasis). The ministerial officials, it noted, in developing their own autonomy 'do not depend sufficiently on the party organization to improve the work of the administrative apparatus'.[106]

One important point was related to contact between the central Party organisation within the ministry and local Party and state bodies. The resolution noted that often ministry officials fail to visit the localities:

> The weak tie with subordinate organizations, party and soviet organs results in the fact that many questions on industrial work in the ministry are considered without thorough knowledge of the actual state of affairs.[107]

Thus the resolution called for a 'radical reorganisation of the entire work of the party organisation'; it was to 'strengthen party and state discipline in every possible way' and to 'fight for efficient and co-ordinated work of all units of the administrative apparatus'.[108] With regard to control:

> The party committee and party organizations of the administration are to make efforts to achieve a decisive improvement in all subdivisions of the apparatus for organizing supervision over the fulfilment of party and government directives; the personal responsibility of every leader for the state of verification of work is to be raised.[109]

Finally, the communists in the ministry were called upon to guard against 'thriftlessness, squandering, narrow departmentalism and localist tendencies'.[110] Better ties were also called for between the ministry apparatus and local Party and state bodies.

In 1974 the Central Committee passed another resolution relating to control, this time within the Ministry of Communications.[111]

Noting first that the Party still did not use all the methods of control available to it, the resolution observed that 'In the Ministry there was an absence of the necessary system of control over the implementation of adopted decisions'.[112] Again ties with the localities were weak and leading workers seldom visited subordinate organisations; as before, there was a general tolerance of shortcomings by ministerial officials.

In May 1981, the Party was forced to pass yet another resolution, this time with regard to the petrochemical and oil-refining industry. In familiar vein the resolution started with the words, 'In the Ministry there is an absence of a clear system of control . . .'[113] Again it was pointed out that the ministry's directives were too general in nature, often being sent to the localities without being fully worked and 'badly coordinated with the resources and possibilities of the enterprises'.[114] The Party committee and its head were criticised for not using to the full their rights of control over the apparat of the ministry. The Party, it was said, did not consider critical remarks addressed to the ministry and its enterprises from local Party and soviet organisations.[115] In 1982, as we have noted, a new work code for the PPOs was published, outlining the formation of control groups within the PPOs.

That these decisions are taken as general Party policy statements with regard to Party control is seen in an article by the head of the Party organisation of the Ministry of Local Industry in Byelorussia. He cites the resolutions on the Ministry of Communications and on the petrochemical industry as 'codes' and guides for control work within his ministry. Outlining similar control problems to those noted above, he also makes the vital point that 'Of course, the Party organization cannot directly influence the activity of enterprises and associations subordinate to the Ministry'.[116]

Finally, we should note Gorbachev's speech to the 27th Party Congress, where he stressed:

> The CPSU central committee considers that the role of the party committees and departments must be enhanced significantly, that the level of their functions in restructuring the work of the management apparatus and of industry as a whole must be raised.

Party committees in the ministries were 'still using their right of control very timidly and warily' and were not 'the catalysts of the new, of the struggle against departmentalism, paper-work and red tape'.[117]

The above resolutions show that control within the ministries is very weak and that there is a serious problem in controlling the work of subordinate enterprises. The central Party organisations within the leaderships of the ministries have failed to establish adequate ties with local Party and soviet organisations and are unresponsive to the suggestions and complaints of local officials. Co-ordination of control from top to bottom is absent and this allows enterprises to develop their industries in a selfish manner, to the detriment of territorial planning.

But why have the PPOs failed to control the work of the ministries? To answer this question we must look a little closer at the structure of authority within the ministries and the relations between the secretary of a PPO and minister. In theory the authority of a minister is tempered, to some degree, by his ministry collegium (a body which is there specifically to check against too much power being placed in one person's hands). In practice, however, as Jones observes:

> The executive agencies in the Soviet state administrations (i.e. Soviet ministries and their major components) are not collegial organizations at all. They operate on the principle of one-man command (yedinonachaliye) and each yedinonachalnik (one-man commander) has a committee to advise and assist him.[118]

Hammer, in his study of the Ministry of Culture, also points out that, although 'All ministry regulations and instructions are supposed to be reviewed by the collegium before they are promulgated . . . the collegium is, in fact, little more than an advisory board to the minister'.[119] It would appear then that the minister is the senior figure in the PPO secretary/minister relationship. That this is, indeed, the case, is clearly shown in the work of Fortescue, who stresses: 'It is hard to imagine that a ministry party secretary . . . could come close to being the equal of the minister — that would be a truly revolutionary change, not just for the ministries but for the system as a whole.'[120] Indeed, the secretary of a PPO often comes from within the ministry, and is an administrative official formally subordinate to the minister. Often the PPO secretary will depend on the minister for his own career advancement. Thus, as Fortescue notes:

> . . . the pressures on the party secretary to 'collude' with the minister are considerable. Since the end of the 1960s party secretaries have come, as far as we can tell, from within the central ministerial apparatus or from subordinate enterprises and go on to posts in that apparatus after completing their terms. They are making their careers in the apparatus and so rely on the minister for that career.[121]

Another major difficulty is, as Fortescue remarks, that:

> Ministry PPOs often seem to be in fact controlling themselves. The secretary, while perhaps working full-time as a party secretary, nonetheless comes from the ministry bureaucracy, while those working with him on the party committee are senior bureaucrats. Thus in 1984 the head of the party control commission of the Ukrainian Ministry of Food Industry for the implementation of the new economic mechanism was the deputy head of the Planning-Finance Administration of the ministry, that is, one of the key figures responsible for the implementation of the new procedures.[122]

Thus, to conclude, we should stress the dominance of one-man management within the ministries, and the subservience of the PPOs leadership to the ministers.

In Chapter 4 we shall see just how weak the local Party bodies have been in trying to co-ordinate the activities of the myriad of enterprises at the local level. One important point is that, like the soviets, the Party at the oblast and city level has to deal with policies already passed, programmes already set out. Stewart's comments on 1957 are still relevant today. The secretary of Tula Obkom wrote then that 'questions of material-technical supply, planning, finances, and other questions were decided in the ministries, glavks and trusts, and the local Party organs most often had to deal with already prepared decisions'.[123]

The local Party secretary has little authority over the minister of a large heavy industry ministry based in Moscow. Faced with problems he may appeal to higher Party organs, but this can be a long-drawn-out process, and often the damage will have been done by the time higher bodies examine his request. As we have seen, the Party bodies in the ministries are rather dismissive of local Party requests. Similarly, in conflicts between the Party secretary and enterprise directors, the latter usually dominate. Here the economic importance of the enterprise, and its administrative subordination, will be vital. A large enterprise coming under the authority of an All-Union ministry and employing a large workforce, as well as providing much-needed public amenities and services to the territory, will have a powerful hold over the development of the territory. Hough gives us an example of such a struggle as portrayed in a Soviet novel, in which the director of a large enterprise explains to his wife that he has nothing to fear from the first Party secretary of a raikom. 'He is afraid to fight [me], for he would not be able to take me. His raion is a poor one . . . all its economic base is in [my] hands.'[124] In Chapter 4 we shall see just how true to life this remark is, for indeed the city or oblast budget does depend a great deal upon its industrial base for the major part of its revenue.

Thus vertical control from above is poor, and horizontal control from the local Party bodies is limited to dealing with implementation problems and the problems of co-ordinating the activities of the many enterprises in their territories. There is little contact between the central Party leadership of the ministries and local control over the enterprises subordinate to these ministries. The economic importance of the various enterprises to the region, and their ability to provide services and amenities, give them great authority over the development of these territories. Local Party bodies are helpless to change policies and instructions that come from high state officials and ministers in Moscow.

Now that we have examined the basic administrative structures of local Party and state bodies we can turn to the first of my policy areas, that of finance. The next two chapters will be concerned with the structure of city and oblast budgets and the process by which these budgets are drawn up.

NOTES

1. See in particular Philip D. Stewart, *Political Power in the Soviet Union* (Indianapolis and New York, 1979).
2. Jerry F. Hough, *The Soviet Prefects: The Local Party Organs in Industrial Decision-Making* (Cambridge, Mass., 1969); *The Soviet Union and Social Science Theory*, edited by Jerry F. Hough (Cambridge, Mass., 1977); Hough and Fainsod, *How the Soviet Union is Governed*.
3. See in particular Hill, *Soviet Political Elites and Soviet Politics*.
4. See the following resolutions of the Central Committee of the CPSU: 3 February 1970, 'O Rabote Partkoma Ministerstva Myasnoi i Molochnoi Promyshlennosti SSSR', in *KPSS v Rezolyutsiyakh*, X, 1969–71 (1972), 191–7 (excerpts translated as 'On the Work of the Party Committee of the USSR Ministry of Meat and Dairy Industry' in *Resolutions*, V, *The Brezhnev Years 1964–81* (Toronto, Buffalo and London, 1982) edited by Schwartz, 151–8; hereafter 1970 Resolution, Meat and Dairy); 19 November 1974, 'Ob Osushchestvlenii Partkomom Minsterstva Svyazi SSSR Kontrolya za Rabotoi Apparata Po Vypolneniyu Direktiv Partii i Pravitel'stva,' in *KPSS v Rezolyutsiyakh*, XI, 1972–5 (1978), 463–5 (hereafter 1974 Resolution, Communications); 21 May 1980, 'O Sostoyanii Kontrolya i Proverki Ispolneniya v Ministerstve Nefteperabatyvayushchei i Neftekhimicheskoi Promyshlennosti SSSR', in *KPSS v Rezolyutsiyakh*, XIII, 1978–80 (1981), 619–24 (hereafter 1980 Resolution, Oil); 16 February 1982, 'O Komissiyakh Pervichnykh Partiinykh Organizatsii po Osushchestvleniyu Kontrolya Deyatel'nosti Administratsii i za Rabotoi Apparata', *Partiinaya Zhizn'*, 1982, no. 6, 13–16 (hereafter 1982 Resolution, Control).
5. Hough, *Soviet Prefects*, pp. 250–3.
6. *Konstitutsiya (Osnovoi Zakon) Soyuza Sovetskikh Sotsialisticheskikh Respublik* (Moscow, 1977), Article 6 (p. 7), translated as 'The Constitution (Fundamental Law) of the USSR, 1977' in David Lane, *Politics and Society in the USSR*, second edition (London, 1978), pp. 553–84 (p. 555).
7. L.G. Churchward, *Contemporary Soviet Government*, second edition (London, 1975), p. 224.
8. For 1966 see the Moscow oblast newspaper, *Leninskoe Znamya*, 19 February 1966; for 1981 see *Leninskoe Znamya*, 17 January 1981.
9. See n. 8.
10. Hough and Fainsod, *How the Soviet Union is Governed*, p. 495.
11. This is deduced by looking at the topics of the major speeches of the secretaries as reported in *Leninskoe Znamya* between 1966 and 1982.
12. Stewart, *Political Power*, p. 178.
13. Compiled from a study of *Leninskoe Znamya*, 1964–82. Information about elections and the composition of the obkom, buro and secretariat as well as departments are to be found in the following editions: 1966 — *Leninskoe Znamya*, 19 February 1966 (hereafter a); 1968 — *Leninskoe Znamya*,

7 March 1968 (hereafter b); 1971 — *Leninskoe Znamya*, 27 February 1971 (hereafter c); 1974 — *Leninskoe Znamya*, 23 February 1974 (hereafter d); 1976 — *Leninskoe Znamya*, 31 January 1976 (hereafter e); 1979 — *Leninskoe Znamya*, 20 January 1979 (hereafter f); 1981 — *Leninskoe Znamya*, 17 January 1981 (hereafter g).

14. *Leninskoe Znamya*, f.
15. *Leninskoe Znamya*, a–g.
16. *Leninskoe Znamya*, a–g.
17. Hough and Fainsod, *How the Soviet Union is Governed*, p. 504 and footnote no. 52, pp. 654–5.
18. V.I. Lenin, 'Nashi Zadachi i Sovet Rabochikh Deputatov (Pis'mo v Redaktsiyu)', in *Polnoe Sobranie Sochinenii*, 55 vols (Moscow, 1958–65), XII (1960), 61–70 (p. 61); cited in G.V. Barabashev and K.F. Sheremet, 'KPSS i Sovety', *Sovetskoe Gosudarstvo i Pravo*, November 1967, 31–41 (p. 31), translated as 'The CPSU and the Soviets', *Soviet Law and Government*, 7, no. 1 (Summer 1968), 7–16 (p. 7).
19. 18–23 March 1919, 'Vos'moi Sëzd RKP(b).-I. Rezolyutsii Postanovleniya S″ezda', in *KPSS v Rezolyutsiyakh*, II, 1917–24 (1970), 36–86 (p. 77); cited in Barabashev and Sheremet, 'The CPSU', p. 9.
20. *Ustav Kommunisticheskoi Partii Soevtskovo Soyuza* (Moscow, 1980), Article 42c (p. 37); translated as 'Rules of the Communist Party of the Soviet Union', in Lane, *Politics and Society*, pp. 514–31 (p. 532).
21. Barabashev and Sheremet, 'The CPSU', p. 10.
22. Hill, *Soviet Politics*, p. 120.
23. Barabashev and Sheremet, 'The CPSU', p. 10.
24. G.K. Shakhnazarov, *Sotsialisticheskaya Demokratiya: Nekotorye Voprosy Teorii*, first edition (Moscow, 1972), pp. 85–6; translated as *Socialist Democracy: Aspects of Theory* (Moscow, 1974), p. 71.
25. Shakhnazarov, *Socialist Democracy*, p. 68.
26. Barabashev and Sheremet, 'The CPSU', p. 10.
27. Shakhnazarov, *Socialist Democracy*, p. 68.
28. V.S. Shevtsov, *KPSS i Gosudarstvo v Razvitom Sotsialisticheskom Obshchestve* (Moscow, 1974), p. 44, translated as *The CPSU and the Soviet State in Developed Socialist Society* (Moscow, 1978), p. 67.
29. Shakhnazarov, *Socialist Democracy*, pp. 67–8.
30. Resolution of the Central Committee of the CPSU, 16 November 1975, 'O Rabote Mestnykh Sovetov Deputatov Trudyashchikhsya Poltavskoi Oblasti', in *KPSS v Rezolyutsiyakh*, VIII, 1959–65 (Moscow, 1972), 553–8.
31. 1971 City Resolution, p. 2.
32. G. Khakalo, 'Kommunist v Sovete', *Kommunist Byelorussii*, 1978, no. 2, 45–9 (p. 48).
33. Barabashev and Sheremet, 'The CPSU', p. 11.
34. V.S. Kurennoi, 'Kompetentsiya i Formy Deyatel'nosti Ispolnitel'nykh Komitetov Gorodskikh Sovetov Deputatov Trudyashchikhsya' (unpublished Kandidat dissertation, Kiev T.G. Shevchenko University, 1973), p. 40.
35. Khakalo, 'Kommunist v Sov..e', p. 49.
36. P. Kozyr', 'Partiinyi Rabotnik-Chlen Ispolkoma', *Sovety Deputatov Trudyashchikhsya*, August 1969, 11–17 (p. 15).

37. E.I. Fedorinov, 'Rukovodstvo KPSS Soevtami-Obekt Istoriko-Partiinykh Issledovami', *Voprosy Istorii KPSS*, 1974, no. 12, 86–95 (p. 89).
38. *Ustav*, Article 68 (p. 60); translated in Lane (as 67), *Politics and Society*, p. 529.
39. I. Novikov, 'Partiinoe Yadro Soveta', *Sovety Deputatov Trudyashchikhsya*, December 1973, 14–18; translated as 'The Party Nucleus of a Soviet', *Soviet Law and Government*, 13, no. 2 (Fall 1974), 56–64.
40. Novikov, 'The Party Nucleus', p. 57.
41. N.N. Vinogradov, 'Partiinye Gruppy vo Vnepartiinykh Organizatsiyakh', *Voprosy Istorii KPSS*, 1973, no. 5, 39–51; translated as 'Party Groups in Non-Party Organisations', *Soviet Law and Government*, 12, no. 3 (Winter 1973–4), 21-46.
42. 1971 City Resolution, p. 4.
43. Vinogradov, 'Party Groups', p. 39.
44. Ibid., pp. 28–9.
45. *Ustav*, Article 68 (p. 60); translated in Lane (as 67), *Politics and Society*, p. 529.
46. Khakalo, 'Kommunist v Sovete', p. 48.
47. Kurennoi, 'Kompetentsiya', p. 43.
48. A. Khutin, 'Sovershenstvovat' Partiinoe Rukovodstvo Sovetami Deputatov Trudyashchikhsya', *Kommunist Sovetskoi Latvii*, 1975, no. 5, 68–74 (p. 72).
49. See Table 1.4 and source.
50. I. Klimov, 'Organizuyushchaya Rol' partiinykh Grupp v Sovetakh', *Kommunist Byelorussii*, 1974, no. 2, 18–23 (p. 21).
51. Novikov, 'The Party Nucleus', p. 59.
52. *Leninskoe Znamya*, a–g.
53. Barabashev and Sheremet, 'The CPSU', p. 12.
54. Rolf H.W. Theen, 'Party and Bureaucracy', in *Public Policy*, edited by Smith, pp. 18–52 (p. 40).
55. Ibid., p. 40.
56. Ibid., p. 42.
57. Ibid., p. 43.
58. N.N. Vinogradov, *Partiinoe Rukovodstvo Sovetami v Usloviyakh Razvitovo Sotsializma* (Moscow, 1980), p. 169.
59. Ibid., p. 169.
60. Bohdan Harasymiw, '*Nomenklatura*: The Soviet Communist Party's Leadership Recruitment System', *Canadian Journal of Political Science*, 2 (1969), 493–512 (p. 500); cited in Theen, 'Party and Bureaucracy', p. 43.
61. Theen, ibid., p. 44.
62. Bohdan Harasymiw, cited in Theen, ibid., p. 44.
63. Yu. A. Rozenbaum, *Formirovanie Upravlencheskikh Kadrov* (Moscow, 1982), p. 158.
64. Ibid., p. 158.
65. G.V. Khakalo, *Partiinoe Rukovodstvo Sovetami* (Minsk, 1981), p. 29.
66. *Leninskoe Znamya*, 27 March 1973.
67. Khakalo, 'Kommunist v Sovete', p. 49.

68. N.N. Vinogradov, *Kommunisty v Sovetakh* (Moscow, 1979), p. 45.
69. Resolution of the Central Committee of the CPSU, 16 November 1979, 'O Rabote Udmurtskovo Obkoma KPSS po Podboru, Rastanovke i Vospitaniyu Rukovodyashchikh Kadrov', in *KPSS v Rezolyutsiyakh*, XIII, 1978–80 (1981), 501–6.
70. Hill, *Soviet Political Elites*, pp. 114–15.
71. *Leninskoe Znamya*, a–g.
72. *Leninskoe Znamya*, a–g.
73. *Leninskoe Znamya*, a–g.
74. Hough and Fainsod, *How the Soviet Union is Governed*, p. 504.
75. O. Ya. Ermolaeva and T.F. Khristoforova, 'Sotsial'no-Demograficheskie Kharakteristiki Personala Ispolkomov', in *Sistema Organov Gorodskovo Upravleniya (Opyt Sotsiologicheskovo Issledovaniya)*, edited by P.N. Lebedev (Leningrad, 1980), pp. 162–8 (p. 116).
76. Vinogradov, *Partiinoe Rukovodstvo Sovetami*, pp. 176–6.
77. V.F. Dobrik, 'Sovershenstvovanie Partiinovo Rukovodstva Gosudarstvennymi i Obshchestvennymi Organizatsiyami' (unpublished Kandidat dissertation, c. 1979), p. 89.
78. Vinogradov, *Partiinoe Rukovodstvo Sovetami*, p. 168.
79. Vinogradov, *Partiinoe Rukovodstvo Sovetami*, p. 168.
80. Resolution of the Central Committee of the CPSU, 17 August 1976, 'O Dal'neishem Sovershenstvovanii Sistemy Povysheniya Ideino-Teoreticheskovo Urovnya i Delovoi Kyalifikatsii Rukovodyashikh Partiinykh i Sovetskikh Kadrov', in *KPSS v Rezolyutsiyakh*, XII, 1975–7 (1978), 337–41; excerpts translated as 'On Further Improving the System of Raising the Ideological-Theoretical Level and Professional Qualifications of Leading Party and Soviet Cadres' in *Resolutions*, V, edited by Schwartz, 225–6.
81. B.N. Gabrichidze, 'Organizatsiya i Deyatel'nosti Ispolkomov kak Kollegial'nykh Ispolnitel'nykh i Rasporyaditel'nykh Organov Mestnykh Sovetov', in *Ispolnitel'nyi Komitet Mestnovo Soveta Narodnykh Deputatov: Pravovoe Polozhenie Osnovy Organizatsii i Deyatel'nosti*, edited by G.V. Barabashev (Moscow, 1983), pp. 49–76 (p. 55).
82. Vinogradov, 'Party Groups', p. 36.
83. Novikov, 'The Party Nucleus', p. 60.
84. 24th Congress of the CPSU 1971, 9 April 1971, 'Po Otchetnomu Dokladu Tsentral'novo Komiteta KPSS', in *KPSS v Rezolyutsiyakh*, X, 1969–71 (1972), 342–64 (p. 362); translated as 'On the Report of the Central Committee' in *Resolutions*, V, edited by Schwartz, 174–89 (pp. 187–8).
85. See n. 4.
86. See *Leninskoe Znamya*, 25 December 1969 and 1 December 1976.
87. Kurennoi, 'Kompetentsiya', p. 38.
88. V. Mikulich, 'Sila Sovetov v Partiinom Rukovodstve', *Kommunist Byelorussii*, 1980, no. 2, p. 30.
89. Ibid., p. 30.
90. Khakalo, 'Kommunist v Sovete', p. 46.
91. Frolic, 'Municipal Administrations', pp. 391–2.
92. Ibid., p. 390.
93. Ibid., p. 390.

94. Ibid., pp. 390-2.
95. Ibid., p. 392.
96. Ibid., p. 392.
97. Erik Hoffmann, 'Role Conflict and Ambiguity in the Communist Party of the Soviet Union', in *The Behavioral Revolution and Communist Studies*, edited by Roger E. Kanet (New York and London, 1971), pp. 233-58 (p. 234).
98. Kozyr', 'Partiinyi', p. 14.
99. See n. 4.
100. 1970 Resolution, Meat and Dairy, p. 153.
101. 1970 Resolution, Meat and Dairy, p. 153.
102. 1970 Resolution, Meat and Dairy, p. 154.
103. 1970 Resolution, Meat and Dairy, p. 155.
104. 1970 Resolution, Meat and Dairy, p. 155.
105. 1970 Resolution, Meat and Dairy, p. 155.
106. 1970 Resolution, Meat and Dairy, p. 155.
107. 1970 Resolution, Meat and Dairy, p. 154.
108. 1970 Resolution, Meat and Dairy, p. 156.
109. 1970 Resolution, Meat and Dairy, p. 157.
110. 1970 Resolution, Meat and Dairy, p. 157.
111. See n. 4.
112. 1974 Resolution, Communications, p. 464.
113. See n. 4.
114. 1980 Resolution, Oil, p. 619.
115. 1980 Resolution, Oil, p. 621.
116. V. Il'yushenko, 'Partiiny Kontrol' v Ministerstve', *Partiinaya Zhizn'*, 1981, no. 3, 46-50 (p. 46).
117. 'Political Report of the CPSU Central Committee to the 27th Congress of the CPSU' given by Mikhail Gorbachev on the 25 February 1986; translated in *Soviet Weekly*, 8 March 1986, pp. 3-21 (p. 17) (hereafter 'Political Report 27th Congress').
118. Ellen Jones, 'Committee Decision Making in the Soviet Union', *World Politics*, vol. XXXVI, no. 2 (January 1984), pp. 165-88 (p. 169).
119. Darrell P. Hammer, 'Inside the Ministry of Culture: Cultural Policy in the Soviet Union', in *Public Policy*, edited by Smith, pp. 53-78 (pp. 64-5).
120. S. Fortescue, 'The Primary Party Organizations of Branch Ministries', unpublished paper, presented to the Third World Congress for Soviet and East European Studies, Washington, November 1985, p. 21 (hereafter, 'The Primary Party Organizations').
121. Ibid., p. 21.
122. Ibid., p. 22.
123. Stewart, *Political Power in the Soviet Union*, p. 107.
124. V. Dudinstev, *Ne Khlebom Edinym* (Munich, 1957), p. 27; cited in Hough and Fainsod, *How the Soviet Union is Governed*, p. 506.

2
Local Budgets in the Soviet Union

INTRODUCTION

The study of local budgets has largely been neglected by Western scholars. With the notable exception of the work of Lewis, who completed her doctoral dissertation on local finance in 1975, and who has contributed a number of other studies (the most recent in the collection edited by Jacobs, 1983), there has been no other analysis of Soviet local budgets.[1]

While acknowledging the major contribution of Lewis in this field, I shall seek to provide a broader and more detailed analysis of local budgets. I shall cover the budgets of *cities* and *oblasts*, outlining the many changes that have taken place over the period and the relationship of one to the other. Statistics will also be given for raion, rural and settlement soviets, thus providing a complete picture of the budgets of local soviets. Unlike Lewis I shall (through my study of Kandidat dissertations and the *Bulletin* of Moscow Oblast Executive Committee) also provide statistics for individual oblasts and the cities under their subordination. In particular I have examined the six oblasts of Moscow, Leningrad, Yaroslavl', Kalinin, Novgorod and Ryazan'.

By looking at as many different local soviets as possible across different republics over a 10 to 15-year span I will show that:

(1) Wide variations exist in the structure of local budgets—that is, in their income bases and expenditure patterns;
(2) There are also important variations with regard to the degree to which local soviets depend on the resources of the state budget to finance their local economies.

It is part of the overall aim of this book to stress the differences that exist at the local level, with regard not only to social and economic structures, but also to political relationships. To explain the wide variations to be found in income sources and expenditure patterns we must therefore examine both industrial and political factors.

Industrial factors

The importance of the industrial base as a contributor to the structure of local budgets is readily apparent when one examines budget statistics. In each soviet there are many enterprises of different administrative subordination. In any one area there will be wide variations in the number of enterprises subordinate to the local soviet, and those under the jurisdiction of higher administrative levels. For instance, in a large city there will be enterprises of All-Union, Union-Republic, oblast, Republic and city subordination. There will also be differences in their type and size, in resources used (i.e. manpower, land and raw materials) and in the taxes they pay into the local budget.

Soviets with many enterprises under their jurisdiction and a strong industrial base will have good independent sources of income and thus better opportunities to provide their inhabitants with social and cultural facilities; but soviets with a large number of enterprises of higher subordination and a poor local industrial base under their jurisdiction will consequently have a poorer independent income base. Thus many soviets will have to rely on the goodwill of enterprises of higher subordination for funds to provide their citizens with social and cultural amenities.

This study supports the work of Lewis in stressing the importance of 'off-budget' resources. These are funds which are channelled, not through the state budget, but rather through the ministries and enterprises, in the form of social and cultural funds, incentive funds and others, for the construction of housing, polyclinics, kindergartens, clubs, etc. All evidence shows that these 'off-budget' funds have actually increased over our period, with variations being evident from year to year in revenues distributed through the 'ministerial channel' and the state budget. Thus while in 1965 66 per cent of investment flowed through the state budget, this had dropped to only 40.8 per cent in 1976 (see Table 2.1). In the city of Bratsk the budget each year totals approximately 21 million roubles, while enterprises in the city regularly spent five times that amount on capital construction and municipal services.[2] Of the 150 million roubles spent

Table 2.1: Share of Investment Financed from Budget Funds: Selected Years

Year	% of Investment
1935	67.9
1940	67.5
1945	77.8
1950	79.9
1955	71.8
1965	66.0
1971	44.0
1976 (planned)	40.8

Source: D. Bahry, 'Measuring Communist Priorities, Budgets, Investments, and the Problem of Equivalence', *Comparative Political Studies*, 13 (1980), no. 3, pp. 267-92 (p. 272). (These percentages refer to funds which are passed down through the USSR State Budget.)

annually on urban development in Vilnius, only one-third is covered by the city budget.[3]

As we shall discuss in later sections, the development of these 'off-budget' funds is largely the result of changes that took place in 1965 with the advent of the 'New Economic Reforms'. Here the new Brezhnev/Kosygin regime, at the same time as it restored the branch form of ministries, set out measures for decentralising enterprise funds. Enterprises were allowed to retain a greater percentage of the profits they produced each year, and consequently there has been a reduction of funds paid to the budget. Over the years, then, enterprises have been able to build up considerable funds of their own for the construction of social and cultural amenities.

The importance of the industrial base is not only related to 'off-budget' funds but is equally relevant to the structure of local budgets. Turnover tax and payment from profits, which are the main components of local budgets, are directly related to the industrial base of the soviets, and show wide variations from area to area and over a period of time.

Any study of Soviet local budgets must therefore take into account resources which come from the state budget and those 'off-budget' funds which are channelled through the ministries and enterprises. However, at present it is not possible to find statistics on the amount of 'off-budget' resources which flow into individual cities or oblasts, thus making it impossible to know what the totals for non-budget and budget funds are, say, in Novgorod or Yaroslavl' Oblasts. We can only use sporadic pieces of information from different sources and dealing with different periods of time with reference to these funds. The lack of such information invalidates any study which tries to correlate differences in allocations with political factors, when it looks only at budget statistics. We do not know the precise importance of funds from the state budget for any one soviet, particularly in the areas of social and cultural expenditure. Thus until we are able to calculate the total amount of funds which enter a particular administrative locality we cannot undertake such types of analysis.[4]

Political factors

While industrial factors are no doubt of vital importance in explaining the budget structure of any one city or oblast they cannot provide a complete explanation. Indeed it could be argued that the industrial base is itself a product of political factors, for essentially it is political decisions that decide whether an enterprise will be constructed in any particular area. In many respects it is the classic chicken-and-egg situation. We know from previous research[5] that oblasts and cities, when they reach a certain level of industrial development, are automatically represented on the Central Committee of the All-Union Party or, if less developed, at Republic-level central committee. However industrial development itself, as we have noted, must in the first place be related to the status and patronage ties of the leaders of particular soviets. No matter which came first, political factors, such as the representation of city and oblast leaders in higher bodies (e.g. the All-Union Central Committee, Republic central committee, USSR Supreme Soviet, Republic supreme soviets, as well as standing commissions of the supreme soviets and others), must give some soviet and local Party leaders greater access to the decision-making process and thus lead to differences in their ability to attract industry and the allocation of resources to their particular city. It is not surprising, however, that our information about such political patronage and other influences is very limited. Thus we can only contend that such political factors are of crucial importance, but at present they are impossible to gauge with any degree of accuracy.

As we have seen, there are two channels of funds which flow into the city or oblast: the ministerial and the state budget. Over our period the first has increased at the expense of the second. What significance does this have for any particular soviet? I would maintain that it has led to some degree of decentralisation of funds over the areas of social and cultural amenities and the construction of housing. For while funds flowing into the soviets from the state budget are highly centralised, with federal revenues making up two-thirds of the total volume of local budgets,[6] funds from the ministerial channel are concentrated at enterprise level, allowing for a greater degree of bargaining in the localities. Over our period, and particularly since new legislation in 1971,[7] local soviets have been given the right to centralise enterprise funds for the provision of social and cultural facilities and the construction of housing. However, the success rate of individual soviets in this venture has varied greatly, depending on the kind of relations which they have built up with the various enterprises, the status of their leaders and the position of the local Party committees with regard to such activities.

This study will seek to show, therefore, that variations in the structure of local budgets are best explained by: (1) the industrial base of the soviet, the number and kind as well as the jurisdiction of the enterprises situated in its territory; (2) the political status of the Party and soviet leaders of the particular city or oblast and their relationships with the All-Union and Republic leadership as well as with the directors of the enterprises situated in their territory.

In this chapter we shall examine: (1) the basic development of the rights of local soviets with regard to the budget process; (2) the structure of city and oblast soviets, showing the wide variations that exist in terms of their income and expenditure patterns. In Chapter 3 we shall move on to a study of how the budgets are drawn up.

It is not my intention to examine all aspects of the budget structure of local soviets, but rather to isolate those factors which I consider to be of most importance, and which relate primarily to the status of local soviets and their relationships with Party and industrial leaders at the centre and in the localities. The main questions are as follows:

(1) How centralised is the budget process?
(2) How standardised are the income and expenditure patterns of local budgets?
(3) What have been the main developments in legislation over this period and how successful have they worked out in practice?
(4) How crucial is the industrial base and what is the role of enterprises of local and higher subordination in the budget process?
(5) What is the role of the local department of finance in the budget process?

THE DEVELOPMENT OF LEGISLATION WITH REGARD TO THE RIGHTS OF LOCAL SOVIETS OVER THE BUDGET PROCESS

Before dealing with the period 1964–82, we shall first of all examine important developments in legislation which took place in the mid-1950s. In 1956,[8] for the first time, allocations from the USSR State Budget were made for Union Republics without breakdowns for local budgets. From this date, then, with regard to funds from the state budget, local soviets were able to bargain with Republic leaders over allocations to their budgets. This right was further established in what is still today the basic legislation defining the rights and duties of all levels of government over the budget, the 1959 All-Union 'Law on Budget Rights of the USSR and the Union Republics'.[9] On the basis of this law the Republics enacted similar legislation over the period 1959–61.

The 1959–61 legislation began the process of widening the income base of local budgets, which has continued until the present day. Thus from this time they were allowed to keep surplus funds after plan fulfilment, and other incomes produced over expenditure. More importantly the new legislation abolished expenditure limits over a number of areas. Thus national-economic and social-cultural expenditures were to be restricted only in aggregates, without specific area breakdowns. In theory local soviets would receive such funds without specific expenditures being listed. In practice, however, such expenditures have been fixed and indeed the bargaining process would appear to operate on specific expenditures, the overall amounts being the sum of discussions and pleas by the local departments for specific funds.

In 1957 a resolution of the CPSU Central Committee on 'Strengthening the Ties of Local Soviets with the Masses'[10] called for an extension of the powers of local soviets in planning the local economy and in their rights to additional sums from their local industrial bases. This marked the beginning of the transfer of enterprises from higher subordination to the jurisdiction of the local soviets. These were mainly at this time enterprises of local industry.

The period 1957–64 is, however, marked by a great deal of administrative change and confusion. From 1957–64 the creation of the State Economic Councils (sovnarkhozy) robbed the local soviets of many of their industries—a process that was encouraged by the bifurcation of the Party in 1962 (one part for agriculture, the other for industry). Thus we cannot over-estimate the importance of the

September 1965 plenum of the Central Committee in which the new leadership reasserted the branch principle of administration, abolished the economic councils and launched a programme of economic reforms. With a new stress on profits and incentives, enterprises were able to develop social-cultural funds of their own, thus accelerating the division of investments between the state budget and the ministries.

While the 1965 plenum marked the return of the central ministries, it also paved the way for new powers to be decentralised at republic level. The importance of local industry was recognised by the formation of a Republic ministry for this area in 1965, and resolutions of the Central Committee in October 1965 and July 1967[11] gave the Republics new rights to centralise funds of enterprises of All-Union subordination for the construction of housing and social and cultural facilities, kindergartens, etc. They also further extended the rights of the Republics to keep any income in excess of expenditure. This legislation is typical of the general developments over our period. While the power of the central ministries has been retained, attempts have been made to strengthen the local income base of the soviets by stimulating local industry and increasing the amount of profit retained at these levels. In 1966 oblasts and cities of Republic subordination received similar rights with regard to the centralising of funds of enterprises of higher subordination,[12] and legislation in 1971 gave such powers to city soviets.[13]

The 1971 legislation tackled the problem of enterprise-soviet relationships and gave the city soviets new rights over the work of enterprises of higher subordination. Thus city soviets were now called upon to coordinate and control within the bounds of their competence, the work of all enterprises and organisations *regardless* of their departmental subordination' (my emphasis).[14] It also introduced a new stress on the need for complex economic and social planning (see Chapter 4). With regard to finance, the Council of Ministers' resolution of 20 March 1971 on 'Measures for Strenghtening the Material and Financial Base of District and City Soviet Executive Committees'[15] outlined measures to give some economic weight to back up these new political rights, the most important of which were:

(1) The additional transfer of local enterprises of the communal economy, trade and services to the city soviets;
(2) In addition to receiving profits from their subordinate enter-

prises, 'the transfer to the budgets of the districts and the cities of part of the profits of enterprises and economic organisations of republic and oblast subordination';
(3) The right to establish, with the agreement of enterprises (regardless of departmental subordination), questions concerning the joint utilisation of resources earmarked for housing, social and cultural measures, and the municipal economy;
(4) Further rights to keep income over expenditure through overfulfilment of the plan and through economy of expenditure.[16]

In 1972 further legislation strengthened the rights of local soviets over the work of their subordinate economies. From this date they were given the right to keep up to 20 per cent of the profits of enterprises of local industry and 20 per cent from service industries (these rights, however, vary from Republic to Republic).[17] While the 1971 legislation continued the practice of widening the income base of the city soviets, more importantly it also extended the rights of these soviets *vis-à-vis* the enterprises. The soviets were now able to enter into negotiations with all enterprises (regardless of their subordination), over the joint use of 'off-budget' resources for the construction of housing and other amenities. Although there have been problems in implementing this new right (see Chapter 4), there can be no doubt that this has been one of the most significant developments of the period, and that it has given the soviets more opportunities to provide additional housing and other facilities for their citizens.

Looking at the development of the rights of local soviets over our period it soon becomes apparant that the role of enterprises has been of primary importance. Administrative changes have left a confusing situation, with some soviets now better off while others have lost enterprises to higher levels. Thus the introduction of the sovnarkhozy in 1957 meant the loss of many enterprises from the local soviets, while the reintroduction of the branch system of central ministries meant at first the return of more than 2,000[18] enterprises. However:

> with the organisation of new republic ministries and departments, whole branches of the city economy were removed from city jurisdiction; services, electrification, gas and enterprises of construction materials were shifted to republic and oblast jurisdiction.[19]

In 1971, as we have noted, enterprises were once again to be transferred from Republic and oblast subordination to the jurisdiction of the city soviets. However, no sooner had such a process been set in train, than a 1973 resolution of the Central Committee and the Council of Ministers of the USSR (2 March 1973) on 'Several Measures for Further Perfecting the Administration of Industry'[20] once again robbed many of the cities of their local enterprises. This resolution created the 'Industrial Production Associations' (ob″edinenie), which grouped together many enterprises of city and raiony subordination and transferred them to oblast and Republic subordination. One can readily imagine the diversity and complexity of such changes—changes which are still far from complete today.

At present local soviets have the following general rights with regard to budgetary activities:[21]

(1) The right to ratify their budgets (usually each December) in a session of the soviet. The right to raise the sums of income and expenditure over those established by higher levels, so long as the sums do not affect the figures established in the state budget: in other words, the right of local soviets to use above-plan sums and other profits.
(2) The right to receive income in two basic forms: (a) *secured* (zakreplennye)—local taxes and payments of profit of enterprises of local subordination. (b) *regulated* (regulirovannye)—funds which are distributed each year as a percentage of total sums collected in the territory of the soviet each year. These are turnover tax (nalog s oborota), taxes from the population (gosudarstvennye nalogi s naseleniya), and others. To these must be added, in some Republics, profits of enterprises of Republic subordination, and grants.
(3) *Expenditure* — local soviets have a far greater area of competence than local government in Britain and America, and this is well reflected in their areas of expenditure. Thus they have the right, (a) to finance the social-cultural and economic work of enterprises and economic organisations subordinate to them; (b) to finance education, science, culture, health and physical culture, sport, social insurance, trade (i.e. all shops), catering, housing and the municipal economy; and (c) to finance the maintenance of the state administration.
(4) The right to distribute their budget sources in accordance with their own needs and those of their subordinate budgets. Thus

local soviets decide the general volume of income and expenditure for subordinate units as well as the volume (percentage) of turnover tax and other regulated funds to be granted to these lower levels, in accordance with control figures handed down from above.
(5) The right to enter into negotiations with all enterprises regardless of administration with regard to the joint use of funds for the development of the municipal economy, housing and other amenities.

However, while the soviets have been given these rights on paper, it is quite another thing to put them into practice. Local soviets may have impressive legal powers but they have little real authority to implement them. In an interview with members of Ivanovo City Soviet, I found that all members of the ispolkom were in agreement that one of the main difficulties was persuading subordinate soviets fully to utilise their newly-won rights.[22]

My analysis of local budgets will show that, although developments over our period have given the local soviets greater say in the finance of their local economies, administrative changes, such as the formation of the Industrial Production Associations, and increased expenditure, have in fact led to a reduction in their secured income. While there are indeed wide variations in the income base of local soviets, still in general up to two-thirds of all income comes from the federal budget, while only one-third is locally based.

To summarise, it may be said that legislation over the period 1964–80 set out to:

(1) Strengthen the income base of local soviets;
(2) Increase the number of units financed from local budgets;
(3) Widen their connections with non-subordinate enterprises and organisations situated on their territory;
(4) Accelerate the development of local industry, extend the number and use of incentives, and increase the amount of profits retained at the local level.

In order fully to appreciate these developments we will now examine the income and expenditure patterns of local budgets.

THE STRUCTURE OF LOCAL BUDGETS IN THE USSR AND THEIR DEVELOPMENT, 1964–80

Expenditure

Over the period 1960–78 the volume of local budgets grew rapidly from 14 milliard roubles to 40 milliard, comprising 16.5 per cent of the state budget of the USSR in 1978. Table 2.2 shows the enormous speed of growth of city budgets for the USSR, and by Republic, for the period 1950–75. Thus while the growth was 7.9 times for cities throughout the USSR, it was much greater in the newly developed Republics of Kazakhstan (15.4), Turkmenia (11.6), Uzbekistan (11.4), Armenia (11.3) and Moldavia (14.3). The cities of the RSFSR grew 7.1 times. Looking at local budgets by administrative level for the RSFSR 1965–79, Table 2.3 shows that over our period all levels (except raion) more than doubled, while cities maintained their dominant position, comprising in 1979 50.9 per cent of all expenditure by local soviets.

Tables 2.4, 2.5 and 2.6 stress the point that local budgets are predominantly budgets of social and cultural expenditure. Thus expenditure on social and cultural measures exceeded two-thirds of the total expenditure of local soviets in 1973 (see Table 2.4). Table 2.5 shows that for city budgets expenditure in this area made up 56.5 per cent in 1975, a drop from 62.3 per cent in 1965. In Table 2.6, which examines the expenditure of Leningrad Oblast budgets for 1979, it is clear that social and cultural expenditure is dominant. Thus at oblast level it comprises 54.2 per cent, for cities of oblast subordination 78.2 per cent and raiony level 86.7 per cent. The lower down we come in the administrative hierarchy, the greater the soviets' concern with social and cultural expenditure.

A look at the work of local soviets shows that indeed they are engaged largely in administering such areas as trade and public catering, education, health and the provision of services. A Soviet scholar writes:

> Funds are appropriated from the local budgets to finance capital investment in industry, commerce and other locally subordinated enterprises, for the development of agriculture, to expand the repair and service facilities system . . . for housing construction and capital and current repairs, the development of public utilities, transport and amenities . . . education, schools,

Table 2.2: Expenditure of City Budgets in the USSR and Republics, 1950–75 (millions of roubles)

	1950	1955	1960	1965	1970	1975	1975/50[a]
USSR	2258.4	3152.0	6566.2	9697.8	13125.6	17847.6	790.3
RSFSR	1549.5	2138.5	4195.9	5978.9	7978.8	11001.5	710.0
Ukraine	311.1	487.9	1120.8	1566.0	2091.9	2714.9	872.7
Byelorussia	45.6	64.6	151.2	218.1	314.5	577.7	1266.9
Uzbekistan	58.0	80.3	164.9	281.9	520.4	660.9	1139.5
Kazakhstan	40.5	69.7	191.6	426.7	561.9	760.3	1536.0
Georgia	53.5	61.4	138.7	197.3	246.9	334.6	621.9
Azerbaidzhan	45.5	56.7	108.9	211.1	267.3	338.0	742.9
Lithuania	22.2	32.1	74.3	117.4	182.3	252.0	1135.1
Moldavia	13.7	21.0	56.6	89.4	124.8	196.3	1432.8
Latvia	30.7	42.5	93.5	120.0	158.8	202.2	658.6
Kirgizia	13.2	16.2	40.4	74.0	92.0	128.0	969.7
Tadzhikistan	12.5	16.7	51.9	92.7	133.7	130.6	1044.8
Armenia	23.8	29.5	78.2	164.9	218.7	268.9	1129.8
Turkmenia	12.1	14.8	43.1	81.6	131.1	139.9	1156.2
Estonia	17.5	20.0	56.2	77.8	102.3	141.8	810.3

Source: G.B. Polyak, *Byudzhet Goroda* (Moscow, 1978), p. 18.
Note: [a] 1950 equals 100.

Table 2.3: Development of Local Budgets in the USSR, 1965–79 (by Level of Administration) Expenditure

	1965	1970	1975	1979
ASSR, Krai, Oblast				
Millions of roubles	2374.8	3520.7	4557.2	5134.3
Percentage	20.3	22.6	22.1	21.2
Okrug budgets				
Millions of roubles	23.2	36.6	46.3	56.1
Percentage	0.2	0.2	0.2	0.2
City budgets				
Millions of roubles	5873.5	7382.5	10114.0	12316.0
Percentage	50.1	47.3	49.0	50.9
Raion budgets				
Millions of roubles	2516.1	3230.6	3991.2	4492.1
Percentage	21.4	20.7	19.3	18.6
Settlement budgets				
Millions of roubles	313.9	417.1	553.0	632.4
Percentage	2.7	2.7	2.7	2.6
Rural budgets				
Millions of roubles	623.9	1019.2	1381.8	1580.0
Percentage	5.3	6.5	6.7	6.5
Total				
Millions of roubles	11725.3	15606.7	20643.5	24211.8
Percentage	100.0	100.0	100.0	100.0

Source: S. Yu. Kunitsyna, 'Problemy Razvitiya Dokhodnoi Basy Mestnykh Byudzhetov' (unpublished Kandidat dissertation, Leningrad N.A. Voznesensky Finance and Economic Institute, 1980), pp. 25–6.

Table 2.4: Expenditure of Local Soviets in the USSR in Social-Cultural Areas and on the National Economy, 1965–73 (by percentage)

	1960	1964	1965	1970	1971	1972	1973
All expenditure including:	100	100	100	100	100	100	100
National-economic	31.6	32.1	27.0	28.3	29.0	29.7	28.6
Social-cultural	63.9	65.0	69.7	67.2	66.5	66.0	67.1
Admin.	3.2	2.3	2.6	2.5	2.6	2.5	2.5

Source: Ya. B. Khesin, 'Voprosy Ukrepleniya Finansovoi Bazy Mestnykh Sovetov' (unpublished Kandidat dissertation, University of Moscow, 1975), p. 7.

Table 2.5: Expenditure of City Budgets in the USSR in Economic and Social-Cultural Areas, 1950–75 (millions of roubles)

	1950	1955	1960	1965	1970	1975
Expenditure of city budgets on:						
(1) National-economic	550.7	924.8	2913.0	3507.1	5013.1	7256.4
Percentage	24.4	29.3	44.4	36.2	38.2	40.7
(2) Social-cultural	1607.2	2115.6	3532.7	6046.5	7872.6	10083.9
Percentage	71.1	67.2	53.8	62.3	60.0	56.5
Including: education and science	737.1	988.8	1708.0	3183.1	3977.0	5142.5
Percentage	32.6	31.4	26.0	32.8	30.3	28.8
Health and physical culture	846.9	1101.9	1776.5	2783.4	3816.2	4799.8
Percentage	37.5	35.0	27.1	28.7	29.1	26.9
Social insurance	23.2	24.9	48.2	80.0	79.4	141.5
Percentage	1.0	0.8	0.7	0.8	0.6	0.8
(3) Administation	83.1	85.8	83.6	94.5	128.4	160.7
Percentage	3.7	2.7	1.2	1.0	1.0	0.9
Other	17.5	25.8	36.9	49.7	111.5	346.6
Percentage	0.8	0.8	0.6	0.5	0.8	1.9
Total	2258.4	3152.0	6566.2	9697.8	13125.6	17847.6

Source: G.B. Polyak, *Byudzhet Goroda* (1978), p. 21.

Table 2.6: Expenditure of the Budgets of Leningrad Oblast in National-Economic and Social-Cultural Areas, 1979

Budgets	All expd. thousands of roubles	Nat.-economic Sum	Nat.-economic Percent.	Social-cultural Sum	Social-cultural Percent.
Oblast budget	80278	28949	36.1	43509	54.2
Budgets of cities of oblast subordination	91498	17877	19.5	71506	78.2
Raion budgets	18545	1851	10.0	16077	86.7
Budgets of cities of raion subordination	7000	1440	20.6	5415	77.4
Settlement	13175	1358	10.3	11405	86.6
Rural	9616	286	3.0	7929	82.5
Total	220112	51761	23.5	155841	70.8

Source: S.Yu. Kunitsyna, 'Problemy Razvitiya Bazy Mestnykh Byudzhetov' (1980), p. 26.

kindergartens, libraries, clubs, hospitals and the administration of local soviets.[23]

To these we can add the financing of shops and restaurants, cinemas and theatres. Thus local soviets in the Soviet Union encompass a wide range of activities which in capitalist countries would traditionally be under private management.

Table 2.5 shows that although for city soviets social expenditures remain dominant, over our period there has been some increase in financing industry and construction and other national-economic measures. Expenditure in these fields rose from 24.4 per cent in 1950 to 36.2 per cent in 1965, comprising 40.7 per cent in 1975. Variations will exist from soviet to soviet depending on its industrial base, but the main point we must stress is that today soviets are still predominantly engaged in social and cultural activities.

Income

Table 2.7 shows the basic income structure of city soviets in the USSR over the period 1950–75. This consists of two major parts: (1) secured income; and (2) regulated income. The first, as we have noted, is made up of profits of enterprises of local subordination, as well as other local taxes and duties. The soviets have a good deal of local control over these payments and some incentives to increase this income source. The second part consists of federal revenues

Table 2.7: Income of cities in the USSR (millions of roubles)

	1950	1960	1965	1970	1975
Total income of the city budget	2479.6	7482.4	10961.7	15045.7	2038.8
Including:					
(1) Secured income	1169.3	2618.7	2983.9	4529.7	6215.7
Percentage	47.1	35.0	27.2	30.1	30.5
Of this:					
Payments of profits of enterprises and organisations of local subordination	521.9	1761.1	1934.6	3121.0	4390.2
Percentage	21.0	23.5	17.6	22.2	21.5
Local taxes and duties	524.9	524.6	599.7	664.4	778.5
Percentage	21.1	7.0	5.5	4.4	3.8
(2) Regulated income	1190.6	3534.4	5959.8	8312.1	10895.5
Percentage	48.0	47.2	54.4	55.2	53.5
Of this:					
Turnover tax	425.8	2165.3	3879.7	5243.6	6492.5
Percentage	17.2	28.9	35.4	34.8	31.9
Payments of profits of enterprises and organisations of Republic subordination	—	—	334.0	329.1	538.4
Percentage	—	—	3.0	2.2	2.6
Income tax from enterprises and organisations	184.4	308.1	93.8	134.1	170.8
Percentage	7.4	4.1	0.9	0.9	0.8
State taxes from the population	327.2	991.8	1565.9	2343.2	3392.6
Percentage	13.2	13.3	14.3	15.6	16.6
State credits	248.5	14.5	3.5	69.4	102.8
Percentage	10.0	0.2	—	0.5	0.5
State lotteries	—	30.9	55.2	148.3	150.5
Percentage	—	0.4	0.5	0.8	0.8
Income from timber	4.7	23.8	27.7	45.4	47.9
Percentage	0.2	0.3	0.3	0.3	0.3
(3) Grants from higher budgets	7.0	51.4	109.2	57.3	46.4
Percentage	0.3	0.7	1.0	1.4	0.4
(4) Sources from other budgets	112.7	1277.9	1908.9	2146.6	3222.2
Percentage	4.6	17.1	17.4	14.3	15.8
Total regulated income including grants and resources from other budgets	1310.3	4683.3	7977.8	10516.0	14164.1
Percentage	52.9	65.0	72.8	69.9	69.5

Source: G.B. Polyak, *Byudzhet Goroda* (1978), pp. 25-6.

handed down to city and local soviets as a percentage of these taxes collected in their territories. Turnover taxes, and taxes on the population, as well as (in some Republics) profits of enterprises of Republic subordination, make up the basic sources of these centralised sums.

Before examining the basic components of these two income sources, we must first discuss the relative positions of each as part of the overall income of local budgets, and their development over our period.

The first point we must stress is that although from 1971 to 1977 the volume of all local budgets grew by 39.5 per cent (and 45.3 per cent for those to whom the greatest number of enterprises were transferred), the percentage of the cities' secured income in fact declined. From 1960 to 1977 it dropped from 28.4 per cent to 24.8 per cent of the total income. Thus in 1977 the figure for the regulated income of cities was still as high as 75.2 per cent of the total income (including grants and sources from higher budgets). In cities of oblast subordination the figure reached 77.1 per cent, while for raiony it was 88.1 per cent. For local budgets the absolute volume of regulated income increased threefold over the period 1960–77, rising from 57.3 per cent to 63.3 per cent of their incomes.[24]

The all-important factor is the number of enterprises under local subordination, which varies tremendously from area to area. A good illustration of this can be seen in Table 2.8, which lists the secured income of all the oblasts, krais and ASSRs of the RSFSR as well as the two cities of Republic subordination, Moscow and Leningrad. Here variations in secured income range from as low as 7.9 per cent in Yakutsk ASSR to 67.5 per cent in Moscow City Soviet. However, what is astonishing is that in 1975 not one single oblast or krai soviet had a majority secured income. Only the cities of Leningrad and Moscow maintained superior secured incomes—53.8 per cent in the case of Leningrad, and 67.5 per cent in Moscow. Of the total number of RSFSR budgets in 1975, 45.2 per cent had secured incomes of only 20 to 30 per cent. Moscow Oblast had a secured income of 49.6 per cent.

Table 2.9 shows the income structure of local budgets in the RSFSR for 1979 by level of government. Thus, at the end of our period, regulated income for local budgets still represent 67.8 per cent of total income, while for cities of Republic, oblast and okrug subordination the figure is 61.6 per cent, and for raiony as high as 88.0 per cent.

Table 2.8: Secured Income Base of Budgets of ASSR, Krai, Oblast and Cities of Republic Subordination in the RSFSR, 1974 (percentage of total budget)

Bashkirskaya	ASSR	24.9	Kirovskaya	Oblast	25.0
Buryatskaya	ASSR	12.9	Kostromskaya	Oblast	19.4
Checheno-Ingushkaya	ASSR	22.5	Kuibyshevskaya	Oblast	35.1
Chuvashkaya	ASSR	20.9	Kurganskaya	Oblast	21.4
Dagestanskaya	ASSR	12.3	Kurskaya	Oblast	22.6
Kabardino-Balkaskaya	ASSR	29.5	Leningradskaya	Oblast	31.0
Kalmytskaya	ASSR	13.4	Lipetskaya	Oblast	28.5
Karel'skaya	ASSR	12.8	Magadanskaya	Oblast	11.9
Komi	ASSR	11.4	Moskovskaya	Oblast	49.6
Mariiskaya	ASSR	23.6	Murmanskaya	Oblast	9.1
Mordovskaya	ASSR	19.2	Novgorodskaya	Oblast	24.5
Severo-Osetin	ASSR	23.8	Novosibirskaya	Oblast	20.7
Tatarskaya	ASSR	20.0	Omskaya	Oblast	19.9
Tuvinskaya	ASSR	11.3	Orenburgskaya	Oblast	18.9
Udmurskaya	ASSR	23.9	Orlovskaya	Oblast	26.0
Yakutskaya	ASSR	7.9	Penzenskaya	Oblast	24.9
Altaiskii	Krai	18.3	Permskaya	Oblast	23.6
Khabarosvskii	Krai	18.6	Pskovskaya	Oblast	26.4
Krasnodarskii	Krai	38.5	Rostovskay	Oblast	38.3
Krasnoyarskii	Krai	16.8	Ryazanskaya	Oblast	28.4
Primorskii	Krai	18.3	Saratovskaya	Oblast	34.2
Stavropol'skii	Krai	38.9	Sakhalinskaya	Oblast	18.5
Amurskaya	Oblast	15.1	Sverdlovskaya	Oblast	32.6
Arkhangel'skaya	Oblast	12.7	Smolenskaya	Oblast	21.7
Astrakhanskaya	Oblast	17.3	Tambovskaya	Oblast	22.4
Belgorodskaya	Oblast	23.4	Tomskaya	Oblast	12.8
Bryanskaya	Oblast	21.9	Tul'skaya	Oblast	28.3
Chelyabinskaya	Oblast	26.5	Tyumenskaya	Oblast	13.8
Chitinskaya	Oblast	12.7	Ul'yanovskaya	Oblast	24.8
Gor'kovskaya	Oblast	31.9	Vladimirskaya	Oblast	27.7
Ivanovskaya	Oblast	35.8	Volgogradskaya	Oblast	29.0
Irkutskaya	Oblast	14.4	Vologodskaya	Oblast	23.0
Kaliningradskaya	Oblast	20.8	Voronezhskaya	Oblast	33.1
Kalininskaya	Oblast	28.1	Yaroslavskaya	Oblast	36.4
Kaluzhskaya	Oblast	23.6	Leningrad	City	53.8
Kamchatskaya	Oblast	15.2	Moscow	City	67.5
Kemerovskaya	Oblast	29.0	All		29.8

Source: A.F. Bogunova, 'Puti Razvitiya Mestnykh Byudzhetov' (unpublished kandidat dissertation, University of Moscow, 1975), p. 74.

The reasons for this decline in the soviets' secured income are numerous:

(1) The insignificant growth of several local services, and therefore of local taxes. Thus although the income of cities' budgets grew from 1950–75 by a factor of 8.2, the sum from local taxes grew

Table 2.9: Income of Local Budgets in the RSFSR in 1979 (thousands of roubles)

	Local budgets all	Krai, ASSR, oblast, okrug	Cities of repub., oblast, okrug sub.	Raion budgets	Cities of raion subord.
Total income	24220.9	5296.4	11937.2	4412.2	385.7
(1) Secured income					
All	7811.1	2426.8	4579.9	528.4	78.2
Percentage	32.2	45.8	38.4	12.0	20.3
Of this:					
Payment from profits	5688.8	1724.4	3491.3	368.4	30.6
Percentage	23.5	32.6	29.2	8.3	7.9
Local taxes and duties	555.2	0.0	395.9	30.4	39.6
Percentage	2.3	—	3.3	0.4	10.3
(2) Regulated income					
All	16409.8	2869.6	7357.3	3883.8	307.5
Percentage	67.8	54.2	61.6	88.0	79.7
Of this:					
turnover tax	9193.6	2095.4	4616.4	1869.1	60.9
Percentage	38.0	39.6	38.7	42.4	15.8
income tax from Enterprises and co-operatives	499.5	48.6	97.9	204.0	10.5
Percentage	2.1	0.9	0.8	4.6	2.7
Taxes from the population	6055.8	641.6	2441.9	1495.5	226.3
Percentage	25.0	12.1	20.5	33.9	58.7

Source: S. Yu. Kunitsyna, 'Problemy Razvitiya Bazy Mestnykh Byudzhetov' (1980), pp. 83–4.

by only 48.3 per cent.[25]

(2) Many local enterprises under the local soviets' jurisdiction (in particular transport and services) have not been profitable, and demands for higher wages have meant increasing expenditure.[26]

However, by far the most important reason for this decline has been:

(3) The formation of Industrial Production Associations, which has meant the loss by local soviets of a number of enterprises which have been transferred to higher subordination.

Although the absolute growth of incomes from enterprises of *city* subordination rose from 521.9 million roubles in 1950 to 4390.2 million in 1975 — a growth of 8.4 times — the average *yearly* rate of this growth has begun to slow down.

1950–60   12.9 per cent p.a.
1966–70   10.1 per cent p.a.
1971–5   7.1 per cent p.a.

As we noted, there have been many administrative changes with regard to the development of industry over our period. Table 2.10 shows the changes that took place to the secured income base of the budgets of Leningrad Oblast over the period 1971–9. These figures clearly demonstrate the impact of the 1971 legislation on city-level budgets, which showed a dramatic increase in their secured incomes from 10.5 per cent in 1971 to 37.0 per cent in 1973. This was the time when a great many enterprises of Republic and oblast subordination were transferred to the jurisdiction of the city soviets, and this ties in with the corresponding drop in the secured incomes of oblast-level budgets from 60.5 per cent to 50.1 per cent over the same period. However, with the formation of the Industrial Production Associations in 1973 there began a slow return of many enterprises of city subordination to Republic and oblast levels. Thus, after reaching a peak of 37.0 per cent in 1973, the secured income of city soviets fell to 33.7 per cent in 1975 and to 26.2 per cent by 1979. The figures for oblast level show the opposite trend; after falling to 39.0 per cent in 1975 there was a slow but sure upward trend, reaaching 49.9 per cent in 1979. As we have already stressed, there is a wide variation throughout the Soviet Union in the income base of local soviets, and the major determinant of a soviet's secured income is the number of enterprises situated in its territory which are under local jurisdiction. Thus, as Belopukhov points out:

> Local agencies of Soviet power create and develop the infrastructure of complexes with money on hand in the budget, 90% of which comes from the profits and other taxes paid by enterprises under the local soviets jurisdiction. The result is that the size of appropriations for the development of the municipal economy and the volume of services offered in a given city depend not on the population or the level of development of the region's productive forces but *only* on the level of development of the industrial production facilities within the jurisdiction of the city soviet executive committees.[28] (my emphasis)

Table 2.10: Secured Income Base of the Budgets of Leningrad Oblast, 1971–9, in percentage of total volume

Budgets	1971	1973	1975	1977	1979
Oblast	65.0	50.1	39.0	45.0	49.9
Cities of oblast subordination	10.5	37.0	33.7	24.2	26.2
Raiony	3.1	26.5	24.7	14.1	17.3
Cities of raion subordination	12.3	12.3	8.8	7.4	7.5
Settlements	12.6	12.1	13.5	9.9	9.8
Rural	8.1	9.4	8.3	9.5	11.1

Source: S. Yu. Kunitsyna, 'Problemy Razvitiya Bazy Mestnykh Byudzhetov' (1980), p. 76.

Klinetskaya notes the variations in profits entering various city budgets caused by the formation of the Industrial Production Associations. Thus the percentage of profits from enterprises of local subordination in the total budget varied from as little as 10.4 per cent in Orel to 45.5 per cent in Yaroslavl'.[29]

Secured income

Looking at Table 2.11, which shows the secured incomes of Leningrad and Novgorod Oblasts, we can see the major component is *profit* from enterprises of local subordination. In Leningrad this made up 74.4 per cent and in Novgorod 78.4 per cent of the secured incomes of these budgets in 1979. Other local taxes and duties are insignificant at oblast level, making up only 7.0 per cent. Table 2.9 shows that for local soviets in the RSFSR for 1979, local taxes and duties made up only 2.3 per cent of the total budget. Thus the crucial determinant of the secured income of local budgets is without doubt the number of enterprises of local subordination.

Regulated income

As can be seen from Tables 2.7 and 2.9, the main components of regulated income are:

(1) Turnover tax from enterprises of higher subordination (usually in the fields of light and food industry);
(2) State taxes from the population;
(3) Income tax from enterprises and co-operatives;
(4) Profits from enterprises of Republic subordination (new since 1971 and not in all Republics).

Table 2.11: Structure of the Secured Income Base of Leningrad and Novgorod Oblasts in 1979 (thousands of roubles)

	Leningrad	Novgorod
All secured income	70447.0	37046.0
Including:		
Payment from profits of enterprises of local subordination	52423.0	29042.0
Percentage of secured income	74.4	78.4
State duties and other local taxes	4929.0	2779.0
Percentage of secured income	7.0	7.5

Source: S. Yu. Kunitsyna, 'Problemy Razvitiya Bazy Mestnykh Byudzhetov' (1980), p. 74.

Table 2.7 shows that turnover tax rose from 17.2 per cent of regulated income for city budgets in the USSR in 1950 to 31.9 per cent in 1975, while in Table 2.9 we can see that it comprised the largest component of the regulated income of local budgets, being 38.0 per cent in 1979.

Table 2.12 shows the dominance of turnover tax as a percentage of the total income of local budgets in Byelorussia 1950–75. In 1975 we see that it made up 78.4 per cent of the income of oblast level, 54.4 per cent for city and 58.0 per cent for local budgets as a whole. Klinetskaya, in a study of cities in the RSFSR, found that in 10 per cent of the cities, turnover tax made up as much as 80 per cent of the *total* income, while for 42 per cent, it was over 70 per cent.[30] Table 2.13 gives us a more up-to-date picture of turnover tax in the local budgets of the RSFSR and the oblasts of Leningrad and Novgorod in 1979. Here it is interesting to note the wide differences between the budgets of Leningrad and Novgorod, where turnover tax amounts to 12.9 per cent and 58.0 per cent respectively. One of the main drawbacks of turnover tax is its instability as an income source for local budgets. Not only are there wide differences between different oblasts, etc., but also amongst the same soviets from year to year. Table 2.14 illustrates this point clearly with regard to the annual variation in the percentage of payments of turnover tax in three raiony of Novgorod Oblast. Table 2.15 compares the dominant source of the secured income, profits, with the dominant source of the regulated income, turnover tax, as a percentage of local budgets in the RSFSR over the period 1965–78. Here we see that, although the percentage of turnover tax for cities of oblast subordination fell from 42.1 in 1965 to 38.5 in 1978, it was

Table 2.12: Percentage of turnover tax in the income of local budgets in Byelorussia, 1950-75

	1950	1960	1965	1970	1975
Local budgets					
All	54.5	54.4	64.8	57.5	58.0
Including:					
Oblast	86.4	69.2	81.9	76.7	78.4
City	34.1	57.0	56.7	51.6	54.4
Raion	55.3	55.8	65.7	32.6	28.0

Source: P.I. Khodorovich, 'Reservy Ukrepleniya Dokhodnoi Bazy Mestnykh Byudzhetov' (unpublished Kandidat dissertation, University of Minsk, 1976), p. 169.

Table 2.13: Turnover tax as a percentage of the general volume of local budgets in the RSFSR and in Leningrad and Novgorod oblast soviets, 1979

	Oblast, krai, ASSR	Cities of oblast sub.	Raiony	Cities of raion sub.
Local budgets				
RSFSR	39.6	38.7	42.4	15.8
Leningrad Oblast	12.9	26.4	37.7	26.1
Novgorod Oblast	58.0	51.5	30.4	7.7

Source: S. Yu. Kunitsyna, 'Problemy Razvitiya Bazy Mestnykh Byudzhetov' (1980), p. 94.

Table 2.14: Variation in the percentage of payments of turnover tax entering three raiony budgets of Novgorod oblast, 1971-9

Year	Demyanskii Raion	Lyubytinskii Raion	Soletskii Raion
1971	62.2	62.0	46.7
1972	73.0	70.3	64.3
1973	100.0	99.6	78.5
1974	94.2	60.6	93.6
1975	82.5	90.7	98.3
1976	72.6	46.7	97.2
1977	60.4	62.1	60.9
1978	71.7	97.8	59.3
1979	93.3	55.5	76.8

Source: S. Yu. Kunitsyna, 'Problemy Razvitiya Bazy Mestnykh Byudzhetov' (1980), p. 92.

Table 2.15: Turnover Tax and Payment of Profits as a Percentage of Local Budgets in the RSFSR, 1965-78

		1965	1970	1975	1978
Budgets of Republic, ASSR, krai and oblast soviets:					
	– Turnover tax	48.4	44.6	45.6	38.6
	– Profits	29.6	32.1	29.9	34.6
Budgets of cities of Republic, krai, oblast and okrug subordination					
	– Turnover tax	42.1	42.7	39.9	38.5
	– Profits	26.4	26.3	29.1	29.2
Raion budgets:					
	– Turnover tax	53.6	45.9	45.2	41.1
	– Profits	7.3	7.4	7.9	8.3
Cities of raion subordination:					
	– Turnover tax	23.7	18.5	18.3	17.0
	– Profits	6.7	6.1	7.1	8.3
Settlement					
	– Turnover tax	7.8	12.3	14.3	14.1
	– Profits	1.7	1.9	2.2	2.1
Rural budgets					
	– Turnover tax	0.04	17.4	28.3	28.8
	– Profits	11.9	5.1	4.3	4.1

Source: S. Yu. Kunitsyna, 'Problemy Razvitiya Bazy Mestnykh Byudzhetov' (1980), p. 146.

still well above the percentage of profits, which increased from 26.4 to 29.2 over this period.

Thus local soviets must rely predominantly on only one income source to finance their local economies: this source is largely beyond their control, and moreover is very unstable from year to year, depending as it does on the production activities of enterprises of higher subordination. This makes attempts at long-term financial planning by local soviets a largely redundant exercise, and it gives the local soviets little incentive to participate in the production of this tax.

Tables 2.7 and 2.9 show that state taxes from the population made up 16.6 per cent of the regulated income of city soviets in the USSR in 1975, and 25 per cent of the regulated income of local soviets in the RSFSR in 1979.

Tables 2.7 and 2.9 also show that income tax from enterprises and co-operatives makes up only a very small part of the regulated income of cities in the USSR (8.0 per cent in 1975), and local soviets in the RSFSR (2.1 per cent in 1979).

Profits of enterprises of republic subordination

The 1971 legislation added a new form of income, profits from enterprises of Republic subordination. In 1975, 538.4 million roubles from such enterprises were transferred to city budgets. This comprised 2.6 per cent of the regulated income of cities in the USSR, while for city budgets in the Ukraine and Azerbaidzhan it reached 9.8 per cent and 13.6 per cent respectively.[31]

However, in the RSFSR this source has been little used. It is interesting to note, indeed, that there has been opposition from ispolkomy to its introduction. Thus in 1977 when the Ministry of Finance in the RSFSR turned to the executive committees of oblast and krai soviets to ask for their opinion on this subject, almost half of them answered in the negative.[32] The reason for such refusals is that in many ways these sums are even more difficult to plan than turnover tax, and enterprises of Republic subordination are felt to be too remote and uninterested in the work of the local soviets. Changes in their plans would mean further complications for local budgets. Thus Kim notes that with regard to Kazakhstan large sums from profits of enterprises of Republic subordination are paid each year; however, these are planned at Republic level and for the oblasts as a whole, leaving local soviets unable to enter these in their draft budgets. Thus in 1972 these sums were not included in the draft budgets.[33]

As we have seen, over our period there has been a decline in the secured income base of local soviets, with regulated funds making up over two-thirds of total income. This regulated component of the budget is dominated by one unstable income source, turnover tax, over which local soviets have little influence. Turning to the secured income, we have seen that it is mainly composed of profits from enterprises of local subordination, which have varied widely from area to area, depending on the number of such enterprises and the administrative changes which have taken place in the particular soviet. The most recent change with the formation of the Industrial Production Associations in 1973 has tended to favour oblast-level budgets at the expense of city soviets. In both cases it is the industrial base that ultimately is crucial for the particular structure of the local budget.

Although there have been attempts to revitalise the local economy through increasing incentives, and allowing local profits to be ploughed back into the localities, the system of planning local finance has thwarted such aims. The regulated income of local budgets is planned as the difference between expenditure demands and the income produced from the local economy. Thus if a local soviet should increase the sums produced at the local level through mobilising new sources, the sum of regulated income for the following year would be correspondingly reduced by the same amount. This gives the local soviets little incentive to seek to uncover new local sources of income, but rather encourages them to rely on funds from the federal budget. It also leads to a hiding and hoarding of resources. In composing their draft budgets, local soviets will seek to maximise sums from the regulated budget and under-estimate payments from profits of subordinate enterprises. This produces a tendency to accept more from regulated sources and not to try to increase funds from the local economy. For example, the draft budget of Kalinin Oblast in 1975 over-estimated the required funds from turnover tax by 32.3 per cent, while payments from profits were under-estimated by 15.4 per cent. For Ryazan' the corresponding figures were 32.8 per cent and 17.6 per cent, while for Yaroslavl' turnover tax was over-estimated by 27.6 per cent and profits under-estimated by 16.4 per cent.[34] This is one example of excessive centralisation of planning leading in the end to poor control by the centre over the localities. Throughout the Soviet Union the amount of extra resources demanded from the regulated income must be colossal, and the amount of false information that is passed up the hierarchy considerable. In the end such central financial planning is counter-productive and attempts at tighter control are inevitably thwarted by local fiddling.

NOTES

1. See Lewis, 'Politics and the Budget' and 'The Economic Functions'.

2. A. Myasnikov, 'Khozyain Dolzhen Byt' Odin', *Ekonomiki i Organizatsiya Promyshlennovo Proizvodstva*, 1977, no. 4, 124–31 (p. 126); abstracted as 'There Should be One Master', *CDSP*, 29, no. 35 (28 September 1977), 8–9 (p. 8).

3. Lewis and Sternheimer, *Soviet Urban Management*, p. 87.

4. This makes any correlation between political factors such as change of leadership etc., and allocations through the state budget, of limited value.

5. See Robert V. Daniels, 'Office Holding and Elite Status: The Central Committee of the CPSU', in *Dynamics*, edited by Cocks, Daniels, and Heer, pp. 77–95.

6. Polyak, *Byudzhet Goroda*, p. 25.

7. 1971 City Decree and 1971 City Resolution (Finance).

8. Noted in P.I. Khodorovich, 'Reservy Ukrepleniya Dokhodnoi Bazy Mestnykh Byudzhetov' (unpublished Kandidat dissertation, Byelorussian

V.I. Lenin State University, Minsk, 1976), p. 52.

9. Decree of the Presidium of the USSR Supreme Soviet, 30 October 1959, 'O Byudzhetnykh Pravakh Soyuza SSR i Soyuznykh Respublik', in *Sbornik Zakonov SSSR,* I, 517-28; translated as 'Law on Budget Rights of the USSR and the Union Republics', *CDSP,* vol. II, no. 46 (16 December 1959), 6-9.

10. Resolution of the Central Committee of the CPSU, 22 January 1957, 'Ob Uluchshenii Deyatel'nosti Sovetov Deputatov Trudyashchikhsya i Usilenii ikh Svyazei s Massami', in *KPSS v Rezolyutsiyakh,* VII, 1955-9 (1971), 237-48; excerpts translated as 'On Improving the Work of the Soviets of Workers' Deputies and Strengthening their Ties with the Masses', *Resolutions,* IV, *The Khrushchev years, 1953-64,* edited by Grey Hodnett (1974), 73-81.

11. Resolution of the Central Committee of the CPSU and the Council of Ministers of the USSR, 4 October 1965, 'O Peredache Depolnitel'no na Reshenie Sovetov Ministrov Soyuznykh Respublik Voprosov Khozyaistvennovo i Kul'turnovo Stroitel'stva', *Sobranie Postanovlenii Pravitel'stva Soyuza Sovetskikh Sotsialisticheskikh Respublik, Otdel Pervyi,* 1965, no. 19-20, statute 154; Resolution of the Council of Ministers of the USSR, 10 July 1967, 'O Peredache Dopolnitel'no na Reshenie Sovetov Ministrov Soyuznykh Respublik Voprosov Khozyaistvennovo i Kul'turnovo Stroitel'stva', *Sobranie Postanovlenii Pravitel'stva SSSR, Otdel Pervyi,* 1967, no. 17, statute 118.

12. Resolution of the Council of Ministers of the RSFSR, 12 February 1966, 'O Peredache Dopolnitel'no na Reshenie Ministerstv i Vedomstv RSFSR, Sovetov Ministrov Avtonomnykh Respublik Kraiispolkomov, Oblispolkomov, Moskovskovo i Leningradskovo Gorispolkomov Voprosov Khozyaistvennovo i Kul'turnovo Stroitel'stva', *Sobranie Postanovlenii Pravitel'stva RSFSR, Otdel Pervyi,* 1967, no. 17, statute 118.

13. 1971 City Resolution (Finance).
14. 1971 City Resolution, p. 2.
15. 1971 City Resolution (Finance).
16. 1971 City Resolution (Finance), pp. 2-3.
17. Noted in Khodorovich, 'Reservy Ukrepleniya', p. 57.
18. Lewis, 'Politics and the Budget', p. 249.
19. Ibid., p. 249.
20. Resolution of the Central Committee of the CPSU, 2 March 1973, 'O Nekotorykh Meropriyatiyakh po Dal'neishemu Sovershenstvovaniyu Upravleniya Promyshlennost'yu', in *KPSS v Rezolyutsiyakh,* XI, 1972-5 (1978), 242-54.

21. N.I. Khimicheva, *Subekty Sovetskovo Byudzhetnovo Prava* (Saratov, 1979), pp. 196-9.

22. Personal interview with members of the Executive Committee of Ivanovo City Soviet, 18 May 1982.

23. Vasily Lavrov and Lidiya Pavlova, 'Local Budget[s] in the USSR', *Studies in Comparative Local Government,* 4, no. 2 (Winter 1970), 5-14 (pp. 7-8).

24. G.B. Polyak, 'O Pravovom Regulirovanii Finansovoi Deyatel'nosti Mestnykh Sovetov', *Sovetskoe Gosudarstvo i Pravo,* 1979, no. 2, 55-9 (p. 55); translated as 'Regulation by Law of Financial Operations of Local

Soviets', *Soviet Law and Government*, 18, no. 2 (Falls 1979), 42–52 (pp. 43, 45).
25. Polyak, *Byudzhet Goroda*, p. 27.
26. Ibid., p. 27.
27. Ibid., p. 27.
28. Yu. Belopukhov, 'Ustanovlenie Khozrashchetnykh Vzaimootnoshenii Mezhdu Ostraslevymi i Territorial'nymi Organami', *Planovoe Khozyaistvo*, April 1974, 96–9 (p. 97), abstracted as 'Establishing Economic-Accountability between Branch and Territorial Agencies', *CDSP*, 26, no. 30 (21 August 1974), 16–17 (p. 17).
29. N.V. Klinetskaya, 'Funktsiya Finansirovaniya v Mekhanizme Upravleniya Gorodov', in *Sistema Organov*, ed. Lebedev, pp. 112–31 (p. 122).
30. Klinetskaya, 'Funktsiya Finansirovaniya', p. 123.
31. Polyak, *Byudzhet Goroda*, p. 29.
32. S. Yu. Kunitsyna, 'Problemy Razvitiya Bazy Mestnykh Byudzhetov' (unpublished Kandidat dissertation, Leningrad N.A. Voznesenky Finance and Economic Institute, 1980), pp. 147–8.
33. I.L. Kim, *Sovershenstvovanie Poryadka Sostavleniya Byudzheta* (Moscow, 1975), p. 19.
34. A.F. Bogunova, 'Puti Razvitiya Mestnykh Byudzhetov' (unpublished Kandidat dissertation, Moscow M.V. Lomonosov State University, 1975), p. 90.

3

Drawing up the Budget

INTRODUCTION

One of the most difficult areas of research in the field covered by this study is the role played by local executive committees and their finance departments in drawing up their budgets. As yet we have only a very sketchy outline of the work of the oblast and city soviets in this area. There are no minutes or agendas of meetings on which to base our study; similarly, press reports give few such details, and Soviet scholars themselves pay little attention to this process. Thus we have no information at all about the bargaining that goes on in such meetings at oblast level or in the finance ministries of the republics. The role of local and central Party bodies in the drafting of the budget is equally obscure.

However, a change in the method of drawing up the budget which began in 1972–3 has initiated discussion among Soviet scholars, producing new information comparing the old and new systems, and allowing us to put forward some new hypotheses.[1]

The basic principles of Soviet budgetary theory are 'democratic centralism' and 'dual subordination'; a consideration of these is a good starting point for understanding the Soviet budgetary process.

Democratic centralism

According to Article 3 of the Law on Budget Rights of the USSR and Union Republics ratified in 1959:

> The drafting, approval and fulfillment of the USSR State Budget and the allocations of its revenue and expenditures between the union budget and the state budgets of the union republics shall be

carried out according to the principles of *democratic centralism*, which ensures observance of the sovereign rights of the union republics and the local soviets, and the uniting of the budget system and financial policy in the soviet socialist state.[2] (My emphasis.)

Through the unified state budget of the USSR, which comprises all other budgets within it, and which is drafted from the *bottom up* but ratified from the *top down*, democratic centralism is meant to ensure a unified political line based on inputs and initiative from the localities. However, there would appear to be more centralism than democracy. As Lewis points out:

> All evidence suggests that in the great majority of cities, almost all budget outputs of consequence are generated outside the urban area. Most adjustments and accommodations that show up as changes in the soviet city's budget can be traced to decisions taken at higher administrative levels.[3]

Under the 'top down' system of ratification, lower levels must seek to get their draft budgets incorporated in the next level up, and only after the promulgation of the higher level's budget can they themselves bargain for additional income. As the Soviet scholar Piskotin notes, this leads to 'excessive centralisation' in budget planning. Agreeing that socialism requires centralisation, he adds, however, that: 'the forms, methods, and degree of financial centralisation may differ'.[4] Before the adoption of the 1959 law which implemented the 'top down' system, the 'procedure for approving various types of budgets [was] marked by considerably less centralisation, approval of budgets went 'from the bottom up''.[5] As we have already seen, the bulk of income comes down to local soviets from federal taxes, which are granted in amounts established when the next level is promulgated. Although the law states that such incomes should be made as a whole for local soviets without listing specific expenditures, Piskotin notes:

> since these appropriations are assigned anew each year to the republics and local agencies, and in amounts differentiated for each republic and territorial administrative unit, in practice they are established with consideration of concrete demands for funds. Thus the solution of questions that under law, fall within the jurisdiction of the appropriate republic and local agencies is actually *transferred to higher bodies* . . .[6] [My emphasis.]

He goes on to suggest that improvement in the budget process may be effected by decentralisation and the introduction of 'economic accountability'.[7] This idea has also been taken up by the Soviet sociologist A. Myasnikov, who stresses that what is needed is to replace 'psychological dependency' by 'economic accountability'. The city budget should be closely tied to the result of its economic activity. The budget of the city could then be formed 'in exactly the same way that enterprises' incentive funds are formed—by deductions from profits'.[8]

Dual Subordination

Dual subordination provides the administrative back-up to the principle of democratic centralism and calls for the extremely difficult task of co-ordinating vertical and horizontal control (see Chapter 4). In essence it means that any finance department is subordinate, not only to its local soviet, but also to the finance department of the next highest level. Thus a city finance department finds itself subordinate to the city soviet and also to the oblast finance department. The pertinent question thus is whether the finance department of a city is primarily the representative of that city in the budget process, or more correctly a 'field officer' of the Ministry of Finance? All Soviet observers agree that dual subordination, as far as the budget process is concerned, has a *greater* degree of central leadership than horizontal, and that because of the traditionally strong position of the Ministry of Finance, these central directives are stronger here than in other areas. Thus Aivazyan writes: 'Dual subordination with regard to local financial organs has a greater degree of vertical subordination compared to other departments and administrations of the executive committees'.[9]

A study of the work of the departments of finance of local soviets, their duties and rights, shows clearly their role as administrative agents of the centre rather than as representatives of the localities. Most of their work revolves around checking the financial activities of other departments and enterprises, and controlling the implementation of the budget. These functions are clearly seen in the 'Standing Order' ('Reglament') on the work of the finance departments of city soviets, ratified by the Council of Ministers of the USSR on 24 May 1972.[10] While there is great stress on 'control' and 'revision' work, there is no mention of the role of the finance departments in bargaining for greater resources for their areas.

Of crucial importance is the question of who controls the appointment of the heads of finance departments of the local soviets. While in theory the local soviets themselves have the right to participate in such work and to decide questions about the size and structure of their departments, all evidence points to these decisions being taken at higher levels. Thus Chalyi notes, 'It is well known that the most important decisions on the structure and staff of organs depends on whether or not the Ministry of Finance agrees.'[11] With regard to dual subordination, he notes that it is natural that the central bodies will take an active interest in staffing their subordinate departments. The 'Standing Order' mentioned above does not refer to the exact relations between local and central bodies over staff.

Given the traditionally strong position of the USSR Ministry of Finance, and of the Republic finance ministries, there will probably be some bargaining procedure over such appointments between local Party leaders and the ministries. The main point is that the executive committees of oblast and city soviets have little say in these decisions.

Barabashev and Sheremet, in a standard work on Soviet administration, note that for the everyday work of departments, horizontal controls from the executive committees are stronger than vertical ones.[12] Thus we may surmise that after the leading staff have been appointed and the general guidelines set, the work of the finance departments will be under daily control from the executive committees.

In order to understand better these principles and the degree to which the system is centralised, we now discuss the process of budget planning and composition.

In 1981 there were over 51,000 local soviets, including 6 krai, 122 oblasts, 8 autonomous oblasts, 10 autonomous okrugs, 3,100 raiony and nearly 2,100 city, more than 600 raiony-in-city, more than 3,700 settlement and 41,000 rural soviets, each of which has its own budget.[13] Thus the problems of finding the most efficient way of composing these large numbers of budgets are enormous. In desperation the centre has opted for rigid controls and strong centralisation, but, as we have noted, such a path is counter-productive, leading often to less control and to misinformation about the localities being passed to the centre. In 1973 a new system of drawing up the budget was introduced to try to cope with these problems, and by 1974 it was operative in all the Republics except Estonia and Lithuania, which still work under the old system. A comparison of the old and new systems will bring to light the salient points about the budget process and the relation of theory to practice.

THE OLD SYSTEM

The old system (still operative in Estonia and Lithuania) was divided into two clearly-defined stages. The first stage, running from the bottom up, began with the composition by the finance departments of draft budgets, which after gaining approval of their executive committees were then passed up to the next level for incorporation into its budget. The general figures were meant to have been compiled with an eye on the basic indices of the National Economic Plan.

The second stage goes from the top down, with each level being approved and ratified from above. Thus, members of the city soviet, usually the head of the finance department and the chairman of the ispolkom, will visit the oblast department of finance and the oblast executive committee to bargain and amend their figures in line with the oblast budget. It is important to note that under the old system, the oblasts as a rule made many changes to the draft budgets of the cities. After approval from the oblast the budget is sent to the standing committees for planning and budget work; these, after recommending minor changes, normally support its adoption by the soviet in the December session.

Soviet scholars have stressed the complexity and tedium of the process by which the budget was composed under the old system. At each level it was necessary to draw up a draft budget (these often ran into 33 different forms with 87 pages of statistics).[14] Then, major changes often had to be made in the second stage. Moreover, although in theory the budgets were meant to be co-ordinated with the National Economic Plan, this in fact did not take place under the old system, as the budget was drawn up for the half year only. Figures were then often calculated without vital statistics regarding the production plans of enterprises of higher subordination, and without the approval of Gosplans of the Republics.[15]

It is not surprising then that the draft budgets were often worked out with large over-estimations of expenditure. This left the higher authorities to make extensive changes, raising the income sources and reducing expenditure. Thus Filimonov observes, 'There were often cases of *localism* whereby several workers in the finance departments tried to underestimate plans for income and overstate the need for revenues'[16] (my emphasis). In 1973, changes were

Table 3.1: Changes made to the budgets of the oblasts of Kazakhstan and of the city of Alma-Ata by the Ministry of Finance of Kazakhstan, 1972

Income	Draft budgets of oblast and city	Accepted by the Min. of Finance of Kazak. Rep.	Degree of change Sum	Per cent
Turnover tax	1103.3	844.0	− 259.3	21.7
Profits from local enterprises	89.5	104.2	+ 14.7	16.9
Profits from enterprises of republic subordination	—	73.3	+ 73.3	—
Income tax from enterprises	49.2	61.3	+ 12.1	24.6
Taxes from the population	377.7	397.1	+ 19.4	5.1
Income from timber	3.7	4.0	+ 0.3	8.1
Other	95.3	85.5	− 9.8	10.3
Total	1718.7	1569.4	− 149.3	8.7
Expenditure				
National economy	350.0	305.6	− 44.4	12.7
Social and cultural	1296.4	1207.0	− 89.4	7.0
Administrative	52.4	45.5	− 6.9	13.2
Other	19.9	11.3	− 8.6	43.2
Total	1718.7	1569.4	− 149.3	8.7
Including:				
Centralised capital investment	221.4	230.1	+ 8.6	3.9
Wages	771.5	746.5	− 25.0	3.2

Source: I.L. Kim, *Sovershenstvovanie Poryadka Sostavleniya Byudzheta* (Moscow, 1975), p. 18.

made to the draft budget of Kostroma Oblast, which was ratified by the Supreme Soviet of the RSFSR with a 30 per cent cut in the volume of its demands, payments from profit being cut by 27.2 per cent. Figures for Sakhalin Oblast were correspondingly 24.3 per cent and 26.9 per cent. Cuts were also made to profts of the draft budgets of Dagestan ASSR, and of Tula and Kuibyshev Oblasts.[17]

Kim, in his work on the oblasts of Kazakhstan, makes similar points about the impossibility of co-ordinating the draft budgets with the national economic plan and the failure of turnover tax to be calculated because of an absence of figures from enterprises. Table 3.1 shows the changes made in 1972 by the Ministry of Finance of the Republic to the draft budgets of the oblasts of Kazakhstan and of the city of Alma-Ata. Here we see large changes, with turnover tax lowered by 21.7 per cent, and payment from the profits of the local economy raised by 16.9 per cent. Expenditure on national-economic meausres was lowered by 12.7 per cent, and on social-cultural by 7.0 per cent. Overall the changes represented a drop of 8.7 per cent. It was not possible to enter profits from enterprises of Republic subordination in the draft budgets because of lack of information.[18]

Kim also points out that in 1972 the planned amounts of centralised capital investments in one half of the oblasts of Kazakhstan were raised by 26.8 million roubles, while they were lowered in the other oblasts by 17.8 million. In some cases these sums made up as much as 50 per cent of the draft figures.[19] Another problem was that grants for social and cultural measures were calculated on production figures only compiled after 1 August—significantly later than the composition of the first stage of the draft budgets.

Thus the old system was lengthy, complex and unco-ordinated with the National Economic Plan and the production figures of enterprises: there were many cases of 'localism' and attempts by local soviets to overstate demands for revenue, and understate their own revenue base.

THE NEW SYSTEM

Here the drawing up of the budget is not so tightly demarcated into two stages but is carried out in something approaching one long stage. The process does not start at city level at all, as in the old system, with drafts being sent to oblast level, but rather, on the basis of 'control figures' the oblast makes up the general indices of the budgets of its lower soviets, in line with the National Economic Plan. These control figures comprise:

> General sums of income with apportions for the basic income sources, the general sums of expenditure with their apportions, the volume (%) granted to these budgets from state taxes and incomes, and volume of maximum limits on expenditure.[20]

These are worked out for the cities and raiony after the oblast budget has been considered by the ministry of finance of the Republic, and by the departments and administrations of the oblast. The oblasts arrange dates by which time materials and figures must be sent to them. The whole process of drawing up the budget is reduced considerably. While the old system took 35 to 40 days, the new ones takes only 20 to 30 days. According to Rovinkskii and Gorbunova, in Kazakhstan it saves 10,000 man days and up to 30,000 roubles a year.[21]

Disagreements over the control figures are considered by the oblispolkom with the participation of representatives of city and raion soviets. In Kursk Oblast, for instance, the chairman of the city and raion soviets and the head of their finance departments, as in the old system, are given representation in the oblispolkom.[22] Thus, according to Filimonov, the new system allows for more interaction between the city and oblast levels and for officials of the city and raiony to spend ample time discussing various aspects of their budgets.[23] This is difficult to understand when the overall time period of the budget process, and presumably the amount of contact between these two levels, have been reduced. At the same time it would appear that the role of the oblasts in the budget process has significantly increased. They now have responsibility for producing more realistic indices for the cities and raiony under their jurisdiction. This leads Filimonov to formulate the vital question, 'But does not this process strangle the initiative of the ispolkomy and infringe on their democratic rights?'[24] He thinks not, for the following reasons:

(1) The 'Control Figures' are in line with the National Economic Plan and involve the active participation of the city and raiony soviets;
(2) The raiony and cities have time to study the control figures and put their demands before the oblast;
(3) After studying the control figures the raiony and city soviets in session independently ratify their budgets, taking into account changes made by their standing commissions.[25]

Kim also stresses that budgetary rights are fully preserved under the new system (see Table 3.2). Thus the oblast budgets of Kazakhstan composed in 1973 under the new system, (1) were worked out in line with indices from the national economic plan; (2) on the suggestions of the oblasts were raised by the Council of Ministers of Kazakhstan by 7.3 million roubles; (3) on the suggestions of the planning and budget commission of the Supreme Soviet of Kazakhstan they were increased by a further 9.5 million roubles; (4) in their turn the oblasts themselves added a further 4.8 million roubles to the figures approved by the Supreme Soviet.[26]

Filmonov stresses that the soviets can make changes to the control figures as long as these do not interfere with the basic volume of

Table 3.2: Changes made to the budgets of the oblasts of Kazakhstan under the new system of drawing up the budget on the basis of control figures in millions of roubles, (1972–3)

	Control fig. worked out by Min. Fin. Kazak. and placed before oblasts (Oct. 1972)	Control fig. with changes from Min. Fin. USSR (Nov. 1972)	Accepted by C of M Kazak. noting demands of oblasts (18 Dec. 1972)	Accepted by S.S. Kazak. with changes made by Plan-Budget Comm. (27 Dec. 1972)	Accepted by oblast soviets (Dec. 1972–Jan. 1973)
Income					
All	1606.8	1676.9	1684.2	1693.7	1698.5
Including:					
Profits	194.0	201.3	201.1	201.1	205.1
Turnover tax	831.8	744.1	750.9	759.9	759.9
Income tax from pop. and other local taxes	416.8	569.3	569.3	569.3	570.1
Expenditure					
All	1606.8	1676.9	1684.2	1693.7	1696.0
Including:					
National Economy	310.5	304.9	306.5	309.6	312.7
Social and cultural	1235.1	1307.1	1312.9	1318.1	1317.0

Source: I.L. Kim, *Sovershenstvovanie Poryadka Sostavleniya Byudzheta* (1975), p. 28.

grants from the federal government and do not exceed expenditure limits. But in reality such changes are limited, encompassing only an average of 0.14 per cent for income and 0.84 per cent for expenditure by local soviets in the USSR each year.[27]

Further, Kim admits that there have been problems under the new system, with oblasts misusing their rights and only passing on 'control figures' to the cities after they had ratified their budgets, thus allowing no room for bargaining by the cities;[28] and a serious challenge to the idea that the new control figures are more democratic comes from Klinetskaya's study of cities in the RSFSR, which notes: 'It is impossible not to stress that many oblast finance departments instead of actually supervising the composition of city budgets, actually take over the process of composition themselves'.[29] In a questionnaire on this topic 30 per cent of the leaders of the finance departments stated that they had more opportunity to enter changes to their draft budgets under the old system.[30]

As we saw, under the old system there was a lack of co-ordination between the budgetary and planning processes, which often led to major changes having to be made to the draft budgets of cities and oblasts by higher bodies. One of the benefits of the new system is that it is meant to improve such co-ordination. Table 3.3 outlines the budget process in Kazakhstan during the composition of the 1974 oblast budgets. Here we may note that the draft budgets of the oblasts and local budgets were not finally compiled until after the Council of Ministers of Kazakhstan itself had agreed the figures for the Republic budget in line with the indices of the National Economic Plan. Thus we can see that on the 20 November 1973 the Ministry of Finance, in line with the wishes of the Council of Ministers and the requests of the oblasts, increased the income of the oblast budgets by 11.5 million roubles. At this point the budgets were not yet in line with the National Economic Plan, which required that they be raised a further 33.8 million roubles. Undoubtedly such co-ordination will make the budget process more efficient. However, there is evidence to suggest that not all parts of the Soviet Union have achieved the co-ordination present in Kazakhstan.

Klinetskaya questions the greater co-ordination now thought to be present between the finance and planning organs at oblast and city levels. She stresses that often in fact such co-operation is weak and that indices from the planning department are only taken into consideration after the budget work has been completed. Thus in

Table 3.3: Changes made to the budgets of the oblasts of Kazakhstan in 1974 under the new system of drawing up the budget on the basis of control figures (millions of roubles)

	Control fig. placed before the oblasts (2 Oct. 1973)	Control fig. with connection from Min. Fin. USSR and observations of C. of M. Kazak (20 Nov. 1973)	Draft of local budgets composed in line with the National Economic Plan (Dec. 1973)
Income			
All	1722.5	1734.0	1778.6
Including:			
Turnover tax	752.3	785.0	795.2
Profits	218.5	213.0	213.1
Expenditure			
All	1722.5	1734.0	1778.6
Including:			
National economy	326.3	310.3	339.4
Social and cultural	1337.6	1359.2	1369.3

Source: I.L. Kim, *Sovershenstvovanie Poryadka Sostavleniya Byudzheta* (1975), p. 31.

Kaluga, the City Planning Commission receives planning figures from the oblast significantly later than the City Finance Department receives its indices from the Finance Department of the oblast.[31] In the 'Standing Order' of 1972 with regard to the work of the finance departments there is no mention of the need for such co-ordination. For Klinetskaya, these facts help to explain the absence in many cities of long-term complex economic and social planning.

The new system of planning the budget with control figures has strengthened the role of the oblasts, at the expense of city soviets, with some of the cities losing control altogether of budget composition. Although in some areas the process is now better co-ordinated with the national economic plans, this is not true of the whole country. And while the time period for drafting the budget has been significantly reduced, saving thousands of roubles each year, such a reduction must lower the contact between city and oblast leaders and the bargaining possibilities of the city soviets. Indeed under the new system it would appear that efficiency has been bought at the cost of greater centralisation. The whole process now comes from above, with control figures being composed in line with the central national plans. As leaders of city finance departments have remarked, it provides fewer opportunities for them to achieve changes in the indices handed down from above. Although the old system required many changes, it would appear to have been more democratic for city-level soviets. The very fact that changes were made suggests that the cities and oblasts were able to produce draft budgets with some freedom. Under the new system, where there are fewer changes, I would submit that there are also fewer inputs from the localities into the budget process. To show just how centralised the system is, we can look at the drafting process in the Kazakhstan Republic, which became operative after a law of the Presidium of the Supreme Soviet of Kazakhstan in October 1974 formally introduced the new system of budget planning.[32]

The budget process in Kazakhstan has the following sequence:

(1) Administrations and departments of the Ministry of Finance of Kazakhstan, with the participation of ministries and departments, work out control figures for the oblasts based on agreements already made at All-Union level for the Republic budget and on calculations from the Gosplan of Kazakhstan. After the approval of the Council of Ministers of Kazakhstan such control figures are sent to oblast finance departments not later than 1 September.
(2) The oblast finance departments, together with the departments of the ispolkomy, study the control figures and compose a draft budget with suggestions and requests to be presented to the Ministry of Finance and the Council of Ministers of Kazakhstan.
(3) The Ministry of Finance and the Council of Ministers make corrections to the control figures of the oblasts in accordance with changes made to the state budget of Kazakhstan by the USSR Ministry of Finance, and in response to the requests of the oblasts. Then these general figures of income and expenditure are presented to the Council of Ministers of Kazakhstan for their approval not later than 20 September.
(4) Before this approval by the Council of Ministers, the oblast finance departments have, on the basis of new figures, sent on control figures to the cities and raiony, not later than 1 November. The cities and raiony study these, and not later than 10 November present their figures and suggestions to the oblasts.
(5) After approval by the Council of Ministers of Kazakhstan of the oblast budgets, the oblast finance departments, on the basis of the suggestions of the cities and raiony and the departments of

the oblast executive committees, incorporate these into the draft budgets of the oblasts which are then placed before their executive committees not later than 15 November.
(6) Before approval by the oblasts of the budgets of the raiony and cities, the city and raiony finance departments, on the basis of control figures work out, not later than 20 November, the draft budgets of rural and settlement soviets, who after five days give their requests to the city and raiony executive committees.
(7) After approval by the oblispolkomy of the budgets of the cities and raiony, the city and raiony finance departments, on the basis of final control figures and the suggestions of the rural and settlement soviets, present their draft budgets to their executive committees not later than 20 December.
(8) After approval by the city and raion ispolkomy of the rural and settlement draft budgets, these soviets on the basis of final control figures ratify their budgets not later than 1 December.[33]

The above sequence of events involved in drawing up the budgets of Kazakhstan shows the dominance of central bodies over the process. Looking at city level for example, we can see that they have only ten days to prepare draft budgets on the basis of the control figures handed down from the oblasts, and that the oblasts approve the city budgets after only a further five days. This would hardly seem to allow the cities much time for bargaining, remembering that over the same period they are also engaged in drawing up the budgets of their subordinate soviets. The degree to which oblasts take into consideration the demands of the cities is impossible to tell, as we have no information on which to base such a judgement. We must remember that the oblast may have many cities under its jurisdiction and in such a short space of time it would not appear that it would be able adequately to consider all their wishes. The cities would seem to have little initiative in the process and merely respond to the different control figures which are handed down from above.

The above process also reveals the minimal role played by the sessions of the soviets in ratifying the budgets. A local deputy may participate in discussions over finding additional resources from the local economy through greater productivity, and thus additional profits for the budget. As a member of the standing commission for planning and budget questions he may be able to put forward proposals about the expenditure of these additional funds, but all of these refer to moneys which do not affect the basic indices handed down from above, over which the local deputy appears to have no influence. The work of the deputy is much more firmly based on control activities—checking the fulfilment of policies already agreed upon rather than initiating new ones.

The local finance departments and the budget process

As we have already seen, there is much evidence to suggest that the local finance departments are agencies of the centre rather than representatives of the localities. The nomination process of the heads of these departments is dominated by the Republic state and Party bodies. For city level we would suggest that the oblast Party, together with the Republic Ministry of finance and possibly the central committee of the Republic, will together be involved in selecting the leader of the finance departments. Such leaders, knowing that their careers depend on how successfully they carry out the policies of the ministries, are thus more likely to be loyal to such demands rather than to the local interests of their executive committees. However, we have noted instances of 'localism' in which local finance departments have overstated their needs for federal revenue and understated the income coming from their own local economies. Over-centralisation of the budget system can often lead then to instances of 'localism' and to misinformation being sent from the localities to the centre. In a system were fulfilment of the production plans is the key determinant of success, overworked finance departments may use such methods in order to ensure the successful completion of production targets.

The departments of finance

In the majority of large cities the organisational structure of the finance departments is as follows: (1) department of state income; (2) budget department; (3) department of finance for the local economy; (4) staff department; (5) book-keeping; (6) department of control and revision work. However, there are wide variations from city to city, and often shortages of staff and even of departments. Thus in the city of Arkhangel, which has a budget of 80 million roubles, there is no budget department within the Finance Department.[34] Indeed the centrally-approved norms for the staff of such departments are often out of date, taking little account of the size of the budgets, the population or the industrial structure of the cities and oblasts. Thus in Kaluga there are 28 members of the City Finance Department, and the city has a population of 265,000 and a budget of 35 million roubles, while in Orenburg City Finance Department there are 26 members for a population of 459,000, and a budget of 51 million roubles.[35] In the city of Pskov, 1965–77, the department of state income within the Finance Department grew from two to only three people while the enterprises which contributed payments from profits grew by 50 per cent. Three workers had to deal with nearly 500 enterprises and organisations.[36] Thus the over-centralised and outdated systems of norms for staffing the finance departments must in the end lead to inefficiencies and to poor implementation of central policies. The centre's own norms for staffing these departments are thwarting the implementation of its policies.

WHAT IS TO BE DONE?

The dominant view of Soviet scholars is that new incentives, stability of funding and a broader income base need to be given to local soviets. Thus Polyak notes that there are cases when local soviets cannot spend incomes in excess of expenditure because of spending limits. He thus calls for the formation of a 'development fund' which can be:

> accumulated out of: incomes above plan received by local soviets during the current year; utilised residues of budget funds for previous years; and contributions by enterprises and organisations within the territory for the purpose of strengthening the infrastructure. Enterprise and organisation funds for sociocultural measures and housing construction and parts of profits received in excess of plan.[37]

These funds, Polyak notes, may be used for the following expenditures: 'those not scheduled for the current year's budget, chiefly to build the infrastructure, and those associated with reinforcing current budget expenditure (except for those on which there are spending limitations).[38] The development fund may also be used, he suggests, to help cities with weak industrial bases, by transferring such sums from the oblast level.[39]

For Klinetskaya, the budget can be perfected with the achievement of greater stability and equality in the kind of funds that enter each local soviet,[40] while Khesin advocates increasing profits from the service industry, which is under the jurisdiction of local soviets and has developed rapidly over our period. For instance, over the period 1960–73, it increased from 135,800 organisations and 505 million roubles to 259,400 organisations and 1,014 million roubles.[41]

As we noted earlier, Myasnikov and Piskotin have called for the injection of 'economic accountability' into the budget, tying their income bases directly to the economic performance of enterprises under their subordination.[42]

By far the most radical proposals, however, come from Piskotin, who advocates the following sweeping changes to the budgetary process:

(1) conversion of republic and local budgets to a system that covers their expenditures out of their own income sources, permanent or secured to them for a period of years, e.g. for the period of a long-range economic plan, (2) change in the budgeting process introducing a procedure providing: (a) that republic and local budgets be drafted and approved independently in the republics and territorial administrative units, within the limits of the income ensured to them and the indices of the national economic plan; (b) approval of various types of budgets from the bottom up; and (c) that district, urban (cities with internal districts), regional, territorial, republic, and USSR budgets be combined with lower-level budgets only for the purpose of making statistical summaries and introducing, in the required cases corrections in lower-level budgets, approved independently by the corresponding soviets.[43]

Piskotin notes that in order for the above proposals to be implemented there would need to be an equal distribution of Republic and local industry, as well as other income sources, throughout the Soviet Union, and a similar equality over the range of expenditures met by local soviets.[44]

While there is every possibility that the central authorities may try out new ways of increasing the local economy, as suggested by Polyak, Klinetskaya and Khesin, there would appear to be little chance of the radical policies of Myasnikov and Piskotin being implemented in the near future.

CONCLUSION

Chapters 2 and 3 have brought to light the following main conclusions, which fully confirm our original hypotheses regarding the role of local soviets in the budgetary process:

(1) There are wide variations in the income structure of local budgets, in the percentage of secured and regulated income, and in patterns of expenditure. Variations also exist in the importance of profits from the local economy, and turnover tax and profits from enterprises of Republic subordination.
(2) Over our period the secured income of local soviets has dropped and thus their reliance on federal revenues has increased. The dominant regulated tax is turnover tax, which comes mainly from enterprises of higher subordination outside the control of the local soviets. This tax is highly unstable, often being changed from above in accordance with industrial plans which are made with little thought for their impact on local budgets. This makes long-term planning of finance impossible.
(3) Industrial reorganisations have been the main determinants of the changes which have taken place in the structure of local budgets. New legislation in 1971 and since has failed to offset the loss of enterprises and the revenue they bring. This has worked to the detriment of city soviets, while benefiting oblast soviets. The situation from one area to another is highly variable, depending on the industrial structure, the number and type of enterprises and their subordination.
(4) The system of budget planning whereby federal revenues are calculated as the difference between planned expenditure and secured income gives the local soviets few incentives to increase their own local economies, as they know such an expansion would merely lead to reduced federal revenues in the following year. Indeed, local soviets will often attempt to hide the existence of local income sources from the central financial authorities, overstating the need for revenues from federal taxes and understating the amounts coming from their local economies. Excessive centralisation thus leads to *less* control by the Republic ministries of finance, and to misinformation being passed up the bureaucracies.
(5) The new system of control figures has strengthened this centralisation and vastly increased the role of the oblast soviets at the expense of the cities over the drafting of the budgets. The local

finance departments, with weak staffs and little time to prepare their draft budgets, have less opportunity to put their case for increased revenues and other requests. Again, because the central norms regarding staff sizes are out of date and do not consider the development of the particular soviets, it follows that there must be many inefficiencies and a generally poor implementation of central policies. Here centralisation is counter-productive.

(6) Undoubtedly the control exercised by the Party at every stage of the budget process, from the nomination and placement of finance leaders to the daily control over their work, firmly places it in command of the decision-making process. Similarly, the executive committees of the soviets would appear to play a secondary role in their relations with the finance departments, who are first and foremost 'agents' of the Republic ministries of finance.

(7) The state budget is only one channel of the funds that flow into a city or oblast, with 'off-budget' sources now comprising a major share of total investments, particularly in social and cultural fields, which are the main concerns of local soviets. Since 1965, with the introduction of the economic reforms, these funds have increased enormously, giving the local soviets the opportunity to bargain directly at enterprise level for additional funds. Legislation in 1966 and 1971 gave the oblasts and cities respectively the right to pool these 'off-budget' resources for the development of housing, polyclinics, clubs, kindergartens and other social measures which would benefit the overall development of these areas.

(8) While we have stressed the importance of the industrial base as a determinant of the structure of local budgets, we have also suggested that the status of local leaders (their membership of Republic and All-Union central committees of the Party and Supreme Soviets, etc.) will also play an important role in the total amounts of 'off-budget' and state budget funds that an area receives.

(9) The study has revealed the importance of the enterprise/Party/soviet triangle of relationships which will, because of the above reasons, vary from area to area and from one year to another.

To a large extent the budget process itself takes second place to the planning process, which we shall now examine.

NOTES

1. The new system which uses 'control figures' was first experimented with in 1973 in Kursk and Smolensk Oblasts in the RSFSR.
2. 'Law on Budget Rights of the USSR and the Union Republics', Article 3, *CDSP*, p. 7.
3. See Lewis and Sternheimer, *Soviet Urban Management*, p. 83.
4. M.I. Piskotin, 'Ekonomicheskaya Reforma i Sovetskoe Byudzhetnoe Pravo', *Sovetskoe Gosudarstvo i Pravo*, January 1969, 93–102 (p. 98) translated as 'The Economic Reform and Soviet Budgetary Law', *Soviet Law and Government*, 7, no. 4 (Spring 1969), 27–35 (p. 31).
5. Piskotin, 'The Economic Reform', p. 31.
6. Ibid., p. 31.
7. Ibid., p. 31.
8. Myasnikov, 'There Should be One Master', p. 8.
9. G.A. Aivazyan, *Pravovye Osnovy Organizatsii i Deyatel'nosti Finansovykh Organov v SSSR* (Erevan, 1978), p. 26.
10. 'Reglament' of the departments of finance of the RSFSR ratified by the Council of Ministers of the RSFSR, 24 May 1972, *Sobranie Postanovlenii Pravitel'stva RSFSR*, 1972, p. 92.
11. P.F. Chalyi, 'Voprosy Sovershenstvovaniya Raboty Otraslevykh i Funksional'nykh Otdelov i Upravlenii Ispolkomov Raionnykh Sovetov', in *Ispolnitel'nyi Komitet Mestnovo Soveta Narodynkh Deputatov (Problemy Sovershenstvovaniya Organizatsii i Deyatel'nosti)*, edited by I.F. Butko (Kiev, 1980), pp. 133–142 (p. 139).
12. G.V. Barabashev and K.F. Sheremet, *Sovetskoe Stroitel'stvo* (Moscow, 1981), p. 357.
13. N.G. Salishcheva and Yu. V. Evodokimov, *Deputatu Mestnovo Soveta* (Moscow, 1981), pp. 30–1.
14. V.I. Filimonov, *Sovershenstvovanie Sostavleniya Mestnykh Byudzhetov* (Moscow, 1976), p. 55.
15. Kim, *Sovershentsvovanie Poryadka*, p. 19.
16. Filimonov, *Sovershenstvovanie*, p. 58.
17. Ibid., p. 101.
18. Kim, *Sovershentsvovanie Poryadka*, p. 19.
19. Ibid., p. 20.
20. E.A. Rovinskii and O.N. Gorbunova, *Byudzhet Prava Mestnykh Sovetov Narodnykh Deputatov* (Moscow, 1978), p. 40.
21. Ibid., p. 41.
22. N.I. Khimicheva, *Byudzhetnye Prava Raionnovo Gorodskovo Soveta* (Moscow, 1973), p. 74.
23. Filimonov, *Sovershenstvovanie*, p. 146.
24. Ibid., p. 59.
25. Ibid., p. 50.
26. Kim, *Sovershenstvovanie Poryadka*, p. 29.
27. Filimonov, *Sovershenstvovanie*, p. 82.
28. Kim, *Sovershenstvovanie Poryadka*, p. 31.
29. Klinetskaya, 'Problemy Razvitiya', p. 124.
30. Ibid., p. 124.
31. Ibid., p. 117.

32. Kim, *Sovershenstvovanie Poryadka,* pp. 38–40.
33. Ibid., pp. 38–40.
34. Klinetskaya, 'Problemy Razvitiya', p. 118 (n. 14).
35. Ibid., p. 119.
36. Ibid., p. 119.
37. Polyak, 'Regulation by Law', pp. 47–8.
38. Ibid., p. 49.
39. Ibid., p. 49.
40. Klinetskaya, 'Problemy Razvitiya', p. 124.
41. Ya. B. Khesin, 'Voprosy Ukrepleniya Finansovoi Bazy Mestnykh Sovetov' (unpublished Kandidat dissertation, Moscow M.V. Lomonosov State University, 1975), p. 95.
42. See Piskotin, 'The Economic Reform' and Myasnikov, 'There Should be One Master'.
43. Piskotin, 'The Economic Reform', p. 31.
44. Piskotin, 'The Economic Reform', p. 34.

4

Local Soviets and Planning in the Soviet Union

INTRODUCTION

Western literature

The role of local soviets in planning has been examined by a number of Western scholars. Taubman, Cattell and Frolic[1] have provided material related to the decades of the 1950s and 1960s. Sternheimer[2] has given us a more up-to-date picture, taking into consideration the many important changes that took place in the 1970s.

In general, all these authors have pointed to the weak position of the local soviets in the planning process and the dominant role of the enterprises situated in their territories. Taubman, in his seminal work *Governing Soviet Cities,* outlined the struggle between the enterprises and the soviets over the period 1957–73. He showed that enterprises, building up 'self-sufficient economies', often expand into city territory without providing the city soviets with the necessary plans for such development. Once set up, the enterprises are only concerned with the welfare of their own workforces and pay little heed to the overall provision of such services in the cites.

Cattell[3] provided a similar analysis with regard to a case study of Leningrad City Soviet. He noted, however, that from a very early stage, Leningrad City Soviet was able to take a strong line in its relations with the enterprises. With regard to housing construction, it was soon acting as client (zakazchik) for the majority of such building in its territory. Similarly, the policy of transferring housing to the jurisdiction of the soviets was quicker off the mark here than in other cities. Cattell's study shows that if a city has a good industrial base and its leaders are determined enough, the soviets can win out to some extent against the enterprises. However, as we shall show, even Leningrad's plans for the development of the city were inadequate, because of the illegal expansion of enterprises in its territory.

Of the above writers, only Frolic[4] has devoted serious attention to the structure of local planning commissions. He has also provided, in a very general manner, some analysis of how plans are drawn up. Seeking to provide a more integrated study of local politics, I shall look in much more detail at the role of the planning commissions, their structure and composition, and the process of plan formulation. As we noted earlier, many of the structural problems, such as a shortage of staff or the absence of a particular department at a particular level, have had an important bearing on the failure of the local soviets to carry out the new responsibilities given to them. Our study of plan formulation will emphasise the centralised nature of the system.

Sternhemier[5] has provided us with a broad overview of planning at the local level in the 1970s. In particular, he has shown the failure of corporate planning in the Soviet Union. My research on the whole supports his conclusions (see below) and also provides some new information with regard to the role of the Party in working out such plans.

While many of the conclusions of Taubman, Cattell and Frolic (with regard to the 1950s–1960s) remain true today, new developments in the 1970s and 1980s (i.e. legislation in 1971, 1980 and 1981 specifically aimed at the soviets, and in 1979 on planning) must be taken into account. Following Sternheimer, but making a much broader and more detailed analysis, I shall bring the subject up to date.

Although I accept many of the details of Taubman's study, particularly with regard to enterprise-soviet relations, my research points to a much more centralised process of planning (as of finance; see Chapter 3). For Taubman, conflict between enterprises and city soviets was seen as evidence for some kind of 'bureaucratic pluralism' in the Soviet Union. My work shows that conflict certainly still exists, but (going back to our chapter on finance), it is conflict over relatively minor issues and resources. For as we have seen, *all* major allocations come from above.

In this section I shall again stress the importance of the industrial base, and show the very varied situation that exists in the various cities and oblasts throughout the USSR.

The industrial base

In the last chapter we showed that local soviets depend to a large degree on enterprises of higher subordination for the greater part of their revenue, and that across the country there are many variations in budget revenues and income patterns. These result primarily from the industrial base of the soviets but also in some measure (much more difficult to detect) from the political status of Party and state leaders in the various localities.

An examination of the planning process brings out even more clearly the importance of the industrial base as the chief determinant of the cities' and oblasts' economic development. The reinstatement of the branch principle of administration and the 1965 economic reforms strengthened enormously the power of the ministries and accelerated the development of two channels of revenue and resource distribution. Moreover, as we have seen, in recent years there has been a tendency to increase the investments which are passed through the ministerial channel at the expense of the state budget. Thus in the years of the 9th Five-year Plan the share of the Union and Union-Republic ministries' revenues, as a percentage of the total sums invested in construction in the RSFSR, was 60 per cent; for kindergartens the figure was 70 per cent; and for hospitals and polyclinics, 40–50 per cent.[6]

Thus in any one city or oblast a great deal of investment in housing and other communal facilities resides not in the revenue base of the local soviets but rather in the social funds of the enterprises. These enterprises will vary from area to area in number, type, size and political subordination. At city level there may be a predominance of All-Union or Union-Republic enterprises for one soviet, while Republic and oblast enterprises may be in the majority for another. Table 4.1 shows the different industrial patterns which exist in six oblasts of the Ukraine. Thus while in Khar'kov 60 per cent of industry is under All-Union subordination, the figure for Ternopol' Oblast is only 9 per cent. For enterprises of Union-Republic subordination, the corresponding figures were 36.5 per cent and 80.6 per cent, for Republic-subordinate enterprises 3.5 per cent and 10.4 per cent. The table also shows the percentage of Union-, Union-Republic- and Republic-subordinate enterprises is a dynamic one, and over the period 1970–5 for all six oblasts there was some degree of centralisation as a result of the increase in the number of enterprises of Union subordination.

Table 4.1: Percentage of enterprises subordinate to Union, Union-Republic and Republic Ministries in six oblasts of the Ukrainian Republic, 1970–5

Region	Union 1970	Union 1975	Union-Republic 1970	Union-Republic 1975	Republic 1970	Republic 1975
Ukraine Republic	30.3	36.0	65.1	59.2	4.6	4.8
Dnepropetrovsk	16.0	18.3	80.4	77.7	3.6	4.0
Kiev	20.6	22.3	63.4	63.7	16.0	14.0
Odessa	27.8	32.0	65.4	60.1	6.8	7.9
Poltava	39.8	41.5	55.9	54.2	4.3	4.3
Khar'kov	55.3	60.0	41.1	36.5	3.6	3.5
Ternopol'	6.6	9.0	82.6	80.6	10.8	10.4

Source: L.M. Mushketik, *Kompleksnyi Territorial'nyi Plan v Usloviyakh Ostraslevoro Upravleniya* (Kiev, 1974), p. 10.

The percentage of enterprises of different subordination is important because local soviets will have less influence over the work of All-Union and Union-Republic enterprises than Republic ones. In each city or oblast there will also be variations in the number of enterprises which come directly under the soviets' control. In the city of Ufa, for instance, there are 400 enterprises, of which only two are directly subordinate to the city soviet. Here the political relations between the soviet and the enterprises will be very different from those in another city in which the majority of enterprises are of local subordination. While the overall economic status of cities with a predominance of All-Union enterprises will be greater than those with a majority of city-subordinate enterprises, the degree of *control* by the soviet in the former case will be far less.

As we have seen, the basic task of the soviets is to try to 'co-ordinate and control' the activities of these various enterprises and to plan for the integrated development of their territories as a whole. In general, however, the enterprises are concerned only with fulfilling their production plans and keeping their own workforce happy, and not with the well-being of other workers outside their factory gates. Labour shortages in some parts of the country have led enterprise directors to pursue selfish policies in the area of housing construction in order to attract workers. This has led to the unbalanced distribution of these resources throughout the country and within the territories of the oblasts and cities. Thus workers of similar professions may have unequal provisions of housing, etc., depending on the status of the enterprise at which they work and the size of its social fund.

Legislation

The history of legislation over our period has thus largely addressed itself to the question of harmonising branch and territorial plans and giving the soviets greater opportunities to 'co-ordinate' the development of their territories as a whole. As far back as 1957 legislation gave new rights to local soviets in the areas of housing and local services. Thus they were granted the right to transfer to their own jurisdiction housing and communal facilities as well as a number of enterprises in the service sphere. In addition, city soviets were empowered to assume the responsibility of 'client' (zakazchik) for the construction of all housing. This enabled them to concentrate all capital investment in the departments of capital construction of the soviets.[7] Yet the 1957 legislation had little success, and from the outset met strong resistance from the ministries and their enterprises, who jealously guarded their rights of control over housing as a means to attract and keep their labour force.

The 1971 legislation marks a turning point in the development of local soviets in their relationship with enterprises of higher subordination. The Central Committee resolution which introduced the legislation gave the city soviets the right 'to co-ordinate and control within the bounds of their competence, the work of all enterprises and organizations *regardless* of their departmental subordination'[8] (my emphasis), in the areas of housing, social and cultural facilities, health, education, public amenities and other services to the population. Once again the pressing need to transfer housing to the authority of the soviets and their right to act as 'client' for all housing construction was emphasised. The legislation marked the realisation by the leadership of the need to introduce horizontal planning into the system in order to provide a more rational and balanced distribution of funds across the country and to reduce the amount of funds being misused by the branch administrations.

But, as I shall show, the 1971 legislation has also failed to live up to its expectations, and many of the rights given to city soviets in 1971 have not been implemented. The main reason for this is that the soviets are often unwilling to employ sanctions against enterprises and organisations on whom they rely for a significant part of their revenues; and as we shall discuss below, they have few economic sanctions at their disposal.

The 1971 legislation also paved the way for further reforms in the planning process with the moves to 'corporate planning' in the oblasts and cities. The 1970s saw the development of complex economic and social plans which were given official aproval in the new Soviet Constitution of 1977.[9] These plans, which cover the development of all enterprises regardless of subordination, include a wide range of social and economic indices designed to enable the soviets to plan for the integrated and balanced development of their territories. More recently legislation in 1979[10] and 1981[11] has been concerned with the question of soviet-enterprise relations. One of the major difficulties encountered by the soviets has been gaining access to enterprise plans and other statistics. According to this legislation, ministries will have to consider the suggestions of local soviets with regard to the enterprises' plans for housing and social amenities, before such plans are incorporated in the ministries' general plans and ratified by the Council of Ministers. This will allow the soviets greater input into the planning process and give them more information about the development of the enterprises in their territory.

In this chapter we shall discuss the following areas of planning with particular regard to city and oblast soviets: (1) the problems of co-ordinating branch and territorial planning; (2) the structure and composition of the local planning commissions and the process of drawing up the plans; and (3) the centralisation of the planning process.

BRANCH AND TERRITORIAL PLANNING

As we have seen, the basic question to which recent legislation has addressed itself has been the problem of co-ordinating branch and territorial plans, and of increasing the power of local soviets over non-subordinate enterprises. Starting at republic level in 1965[12] and 1967,[13] and moving down to oblast level in 1966[14] and 1980,[15] and to city level in 1971[16] (with additions in 1978[17] and 1981[18]), the soviets have been given new opportunities to develop horizontal plans which cut across the centrally-planned development of the branch administrations.

Indeed the question of horizontal planning was noted in the Report of the 24th Party Congress, which stressed the 'necessity to develop horizontal economic planning'[19] and both the 25th and 26th Party Congresses have continued to call for greater harmonising of branch and territorial plans. Thus the 25th Party Congress stressed that it was necessary to 'ensure the more full harmonization of branch and territorial principles of planning . . . to improve the complex planning of the economic and social development of enterprises, associations, raiony and cities'.[20] The 26th Congress called for 'a complex approach to planning the development of the interdependent branches of the national economy and the economic regions of the country . . . to raise the activity of territorial planning and its role in the development of the regions'.[21] The 27th Congress has more recently urged 'consolidation of the territorial approach to planning and management'.[22]

However, while such powers may be conferred on soviets formally by legislation and may be backed up morally by Party congresses and resolutions, it is quite another matter to implement these new rights. Indeed many Soviet scholars have noted that 'local soviets do not always fully use the rights given to them by law'.[23] As we shall discuss later, there is often a psychological barrier on the part of local soviets, a lack of conviction or belief in themselves, and a tendency to baulk at the might of the ministries and enterprises on whom they depend for the majority of their revenues. It must also be stressed that often the soviets cannot cope with the extra responsibilities entrusted to them by the new legislation. Because of outdated norms for staff size and the low wages paid to personnel in the various departments, there is often a shortage of qualified workers. Indeed, there would appear to be a lack of concerted activity on behalf of the central leadership to carry out the changes in department structure and size that would enable the soviets effectively to carry out their rights. Whether this is related to conflict within the leadership and uncertainty over decentralising decision-making or to bureaucratic blockages is hard to tell, but it reflects the inability of the leadership to co-ordinate decision-making over the various branches of the economy.

In the majority of cases the soviets will not be able to use their rights because of ministerial bullying and 'departmentalism' — the attempt of ministries and their enterprises to build up 'self-contained' economies within the territories of the soviets, ignoring the wider developments of their environment. Indeed, so far do they often go in this direction that they sometimes lose sight of their essential priorties. Thus the director of Gosplan's Economic Research Institute in the Ukraine notes:

> Because the republic, territory and province planning agencies have limited rights, a number of interbranch questions are not resolved. This leads to a situation in which the departments are forced to develop as multibranch economic entities. For example,

the following instance can be cited: During the Eighth Five-year Plan, the Ukraine Republic Ministry of the Food Industry increased the volume of its basic production by 18.1%, while the volume of auxilliary production went up by 57.5%. Is that good? Ministries and departments develop the production of output that is not their speciality while often disregarding the obvious inefficiency of this path. The tendency towards self-sufficiency has brought about a situation in which in some places the production of basic output is growing at a slower rate than the production of articles made by subsidiary production lines. The production of building material is a charcteristic example in this respect. In the Ukraine Republic, building materials are produced by enterprises belonging to more than 50 different departments. Slightly more than one third of the total volume is accounted for by the Ukraine Republic Ministry of the Building Materials Industry.[24]

Legislation, then, may on paper give rights of co-ordination and control, but in practice the local soviets are faced with a bewildering array of departmental development, of which they have little or no knowledge. The soviets may have been reinvigorated by recent legislation, but the difficulty of obtaining information about the work of enterprises has been a serious hindrance to local planning organs in their attempts to compose all-round plans, and enterprises have often changed their plans without informing local soviets, even when such changes involve payment of taxes or the siting and reconstruction of enterprises.

Lebedev and Malyshev note that a problem, particularly for city level, is the obtaining of information and statistics. The city level often has no department of statistics, and the service from the oblasts is frequently poor and unreliable. The city planning organs must then receive statistics from all the various enterprises situated on their territory, and these statistics often do not conform with each other in format, time of collating, etc. They also report that 35 per cent of the workers in planning commissions noted the problem of lack of information or of not receiving information on time.[25] The chairman of Saratov City Soviet Planning Commission stressed that 'if the planning commission is to make the right decisions on social and cultural questions it needs to have reliable information for enterprises of higher subordination, but the statute does not stipulate the necessary guarantees'.[26] In Irkutsk Oblast Soviet great difficulties were found in composing the 1971–5 plan because of the lack of essential statistics. Of 450 enterprises and organisations of higher subordination only 185 answered the soviet's enquiries.[27] In Kiev, in 1972, of 2,000 plans from enterprises, the city received information from only 30 per cent.

The reasons for such discrepancies are in part explained by the very timing of the planning process itself. Thus as Sheremet *et al.* note:

> But what do we see in practice? The plans of development of the district (city) economy usually adopted by the soviets in December are in fact not all inclusive, because they do contain the indices for the development of housing and utilities, the building of roads, social and cultural and service industry facilities, the production of consumer goods and local building materials, by enterprises not belonging to these soviets. The soviets usually do not even have such data at their disposal. Why? Because the final adoption of the amended plans of enterprises occurs in ministries and departments in January or February and sometimes even in March of the following year, i.e., after the holding of the session of the local soviet at which the economic plans are considered and issued.[29]

Thus we find the absurd situation in the city of Salvat in the Bashkir ASSR, where only one of the enterprises, of over 70 different ministries of various subordination, sent plan indices to the executive committee by the required date: all because at this time the enterprises did not have the required data.[30]

Unable to collate the necessary data from enterprises of higher subordination, the Soviet scholar Sukhomlin stresses: 'the city planning commissions in these conditions are reduced to the simple registering of facts. Its role in planning is restricted to the working out of plans for the development of local industry, and summarising materials received from other enterprises'.[31]

Another fundamental problem for the soviets is that plans agreed with enterprises for the construction of housing and other public amenities are often liable to be changed from above, often without the soviets being informed. For example, in Ivanovo Oblast, after the adoption of one such plan, a number of new projects representing 18 million roubles were added to the list to be built. These were primarily industrial projects, while plans for the construction of social amenities totalling eight million roubles were cut.[32] In the city of Bratsk the chairman of the executive committee, frustrated by so much chopping and changing of the plans for the city's first sector, pleaded: 'Give us 300 million rather than 542 million roubles . . . but let it be a firm, planned sum that doesn't change eighteen times'.[33]

Thus the major weakness of the planning system, as Mezhevich observes is basically two-fold:

> One, the city exists as a territorial entity, but its development is often guided by the programs of branches of the economy; two, although there are many elements of economic plans that involve cities, there is *no single plan* that embraces all aspects of urban development and thus makes for unified management.[34] (my emphasis)

For although all cities have five-year plans for social and economic construction, these plans only cover those enterprises which are subordinate to the city soviets. As for enterprises of non-city subordination, Mezhevich writes:

> the city at best consults with them on basic broad guidelines for the development of housing . . . and the construction of social cultural and service facilities. At worst, it must reckon with the plan goals of these enterprises often after they have been adopted by the respective Union or republic agencies.[35]

The local soviets cannot hope to co-ordinate those enterprises because: (1) they are not powerful enough and rely on them for revenues; (2) the city as an integrated whole is not considered at a high enough level. All the soviets can do is try to make sense out of the havoc already imposed upon them from above by the various ministries. Mezhevich concludes: 'Many urban problems can be solved only by including the city in the system of national-economic planning as an independent entity'.[36] The chairman of Saratov City Soviet Planning Commission echoed these words when she noted, 'As a rule, comprehensive plans for the economic development of regions are passsive documents that can scarcely by called constituent elements of a single national-economic plan'.[37] Thus she advocated:

> One thing that should be done to change this procedure is to set uniform deadlines for the development of territorial plans in advance of the drafting of branch plans, so that the provisions of comprehensive territorial plans can be taken into account when

branch plans are drafted . . . Furthermore, if branch plans are to be co-ordinated with territorial plans, enterprises of higher subordination should be required to submit to the city planning commission first their draft plans and later their confirmed plans, in accordance with strict deadlines.[38]

As we have noted, the 1979 and 1981 legislation has (at least on paper) given the city and oblast soviets the right to submit suggestions and remarks about the plans of enterprises to the ministries before such plans are ratified by the Council of Ministers. If enforced this will go some way to solving the above problems. However, the problem of ministries changing the plans of their enterprises without informing the soviets is still unaffected.

The pooling of resources by the Soviets and enterprises for the construction of housing and other social facilities

Undoubtedly one of the most postive developments for local soviets over our period has been their new right to pool the resources of all enterprises on their territory for the provision of housing and amenities. The oblasts received this right in 1966,[39] while it was granted to the cities in 1971. Thus the soviets have an approved access to the second channel of funds. Again, however, we must stress the wide variations from area to area in the implementation of such rights, depending on the role of the enterprises and party bodies and on the persistence of the soviets in asserting their rights. Thus while Klinetskaya found that out of 18 cities studied, only one Pskov, had plans for the pooling of funds for housing construction, reports from other areas suggest that such agreements are becoming more common.[40]

Thus over the years of the 9th Five-year Plan in the city of Kramatorsk the city soviet pooled the sum of 32 million roubles for the construction of 154,000m^2 of housing as well as for children's clinics and other amenities.[41] In the city of Rostov, over four years of the 10th Five-year Plan, the city executive committee mobilised funds totalling 74 million roubles.[42]

However, in 1976 a report of the standing commissions of the USSR Supreme Soviet noted that while there had been an increase in such participation, 'it is still not rare . . . for some managers to attempt to escape this important responsibility'.[43] At present the legislation with regard to shared participation suffers (as far as the soviets are concerned) from two basic weaknesses: (1) the enterprises are not obliged to participate — their entry into such schemes is totally voluntary; (2) even if they do agree to joint utilisation of funds, this agreement does not have the status of a legal document and is not binding on them. The ability of the soviets to be successful will therefore depend on such factors as the support of the local and central Party bodies, and the force with which they are prepared to assert their rights. A great amount of time and energy is needed to fight against 'departmentalism'.

Sheremet *et al.* found that contracts for the pooling of resources were 'unilaterally violated by ministries, departments, and enterprises'.[44] Thus in the city of Riga, about 60 per cent of such 'protocols' are not fulfilled.[45] And in the city of Kurgan in 1974 industrial enterprises paid over only 3 million roubles of a 20 million rouble agreement.[46] Similarly the city of Daugavpils (Latvia) suffered the loss of 2 million roubles through broken contracts.[47] The city executive committee chariman pleaded, 'There is nothing we can do'. The local soviet should not appear before the ministries and departments in the 'role of petitioner', he protested. 'They must have economic sanctions.'[48] In theory the soviets do have the right to penalise enterprise leaders who fail to comply with their decisions.

> The city or district soviet and its executive committee, in case of the nonfulfilment of their decisions by executives of enterprises, institutions and organisations of higher subordination, submit representatives to the appropriate higher agencies for the imposition of disciplinary penalties on these executives, up to and including dismissal from the positions they hold. The results of the examination of these representatives must be reported to the city or district soviet or its executive committee within a month's time.[49]

However, as the above examples show, the soviets have been unable to enforce such penalties. It is difficult to imagine their succeeding in having a top official from an enterprise of higher subordination dismissed from his post.

The chairman of Minsk City Soviet noted that the enterprises often promise pro rata participation as a bargaining ploy with the soviet for permission to expand their enterprises in city territory. Thus he remarks:

In starting the reconstruction or expansion of an enterprise, ministries and departments usually do not stint on promises in an effort to receive permission for this work from the city soviet executive committee. This is not simply given verbally. These assurances are reinforced with authoritative signatures and seals. In general, unconditional consent is given to pro rata participation in the construction of city wide networks and utility lines. But here's the hitch. When it comes to the realization of these promises, we often run into great difficulties: The capital investments for the development of communal economy facilities and cultural and service enterprises that are envisaged by the designs for the reconstruction of plants are not allocated, citing various pretexts, or are made in insignificant amounts.[50]

In all, for the city of Minsk, these debts amounted to 15 million roubles. Thus the chairman advocates:

It seems to us that it is time to bring order into these questions, which are vitally important to every city. It is necessarsy firmly to establish that the confirmed financial-estimate calculations of the amounts of pro rata participation in the construction of facilities of citywide importance are to be strictly implemented. Funds must be transferred to the local soviets' executive committees in full or in proportion to the amount of funds allocated for industrial construction.[51]

That the ministries can openly flout such agreements suggests that the position of the central authorities concerning such questions is ambivalent to say the least, perhaps allowing for some degree of arbitration by the local party bodies.

The problems of co-ordinating branch and territorial plans and the selfish attitude of the ministries towards such pro rata schemes has led many Soviet scholars to suggest that all such funds should be passed directly to the soviets, bypassing the ministries and their enterprises altogether. For example, Bocharov and Lyubonov stress: 'Well, what about the local Soviets? Let's be candid — they are still not the masters of many cities . . . their power to compel ministries and departments to take account of the interests of comprehensive urban development is rather small',[52] and they go on to propose the widely-held view that:

all funds for housing and municipal services should be concentrated in the hands of the local Soviets, no matter to whom these monies have been allocated. Let the ministries be freed from questions of the development of the non production sphere to concern themselves with the real business — increasing production efficiency and output quality at their enterprises. Everyone — both the population and the state — will benefit from such an arrangment.[53]

However, up to now such suggestions have met been met with silence. The view of a senior Gosplan worker is interesting here, showing as it does the support that ministries have for holding on to their social funds and housing construction investments, etc.:

On numerous occassions the press has published proposals to allocate capital investments for nonproduction construction on a territorial rather than a branch basis . . . The existing procedure for planning centralised capital investments in this area is based on the fact that the relative scarcity of resources makes it impossible to accomplish at once all the social and economic tasks facing the ministries, departments and local Soviets . . . To deprive ministries and departments of the right to distribute capital investments for housing construction among their enterprises would place them in a difficult position, deprive them of the ability to maneuver funds in the interests of the branch's development . . . and ultimately contradict the goal of increasing production efficiency.[54]

Other scholars hold completely the opposite view, that ministries will achieve better productivity if they are free from worries about the construction of housing and the like, and can concentrate on fulfilling their production plans, leaving social and cultural areas to the soviets.

While we should not under-estimate the success that many local soviets have achieved in pooling the funds of enterprises, this new power of the soviets will not really be effective until: (1) all enterprises are compelled to enter such finanacial participation; (2) agreements, once made, are binding on the enterprises; (3) the city and oblast soviets are given the right to impose heavy economic sanctions against violators of such agreements.

The consequences of the poor co-ordination of branch and territorial planning are extremely serious, leading to the following state of affairs: (1) the unplanned development of the cities and oblasts because of the uncontrolled expansion of enterprises; (2) a lag in the development of the infrastructure behind that of industrial production; (3) wide differences in the provision of housing and social-cultural funds throughout the Soviet Union and within oblasts and cities themselves.

Unplanned development

One of the most serious problems faced by planning officials is the gap between the planning of the production sphere and that of the infrastructure. This problem has been brought about largely by the difficulties local soviets have in planning the development of the industrial base of their territories. The problem is also related to the overall demographic features of the USSR, to the growth of cities and the migration of labour. In recent years there has been an attempt to distribute large enterprises more evenly throughout the country, and to encourage their development in small and medium-sized cities. Since 1969 the building of enterprises has been prohibited in 31 cities of the RSFSR.[55] However, the ministries and enterprises have often ignored this prohibition, while the soviets, in need of the revenues provided by such industries, have turned a blind eye to their development. This has led to the accelerated growth of larger cities which have outstripped all plans for their development.

As Mezhevich notes, 'The poorly controlled growth of large cities exaggerates the labour shortages, aggravates commuting problems, and creates acute ecological problems and difficulties in urban build-up.'[56] As Polyak observes, from 1959 to 1976, the number of towns with a population of over 500,000 grew from 13 to 42. While the population of the USSR as a whole grew by 15.8 per cent the increase for small towns was 17.5 per cent and for large cities 58.4 per cent. By 1970 one-third of the population lived in large cities (i.e. those with a population of over 100,000).[57]

The 1971 leglislation gives the city soviets fairly explicit rights over the utilisation of land. Article 7(2) of the Presidium decree enables them to examine: 'plans for the siting, development and specialisation of enterprises of local industry, everyday services, trade and public catering and of organisations and institutions of culture, public education and public health of higher subordination'.[58] Further, the Article notes that with regard to enterprises of higher subordination, plans for the expansion and construction of new enterprises must be placed before the soviets for their consideration and proposals.[59] Article 7(14) gives the soviets the right to grant and withdraw 'the use of tracts of land', and to exercise supervision 'over the utilisation of land'.[60]

But the lack of co-ordination between various branches of the economy and the separation of the planning of industrial zones and the communal sector render these rights useless. For example, as the chairman of Surgut Executive Committee complained:

> It is common knowledge that no department has the right to build on a city's territory without the permission of the soviet executive committee. Unfortunately, this rule is still broken frequently. The petroleum and construction workers of Surgut and Nizhnevartovsk, by-passing the Soviets are putting up production installations in future housing tracts.[61]

Although the city soviet had been instructed to examine every violation of the General Plan, and to arrange for the removal of installations erected illegally, '*it had failed to do so*' (my emphasis). One may speculate that the reason for this was that the city soviet was too frightened to challenge organisations on whom it depended for much of its finance.

The unplanned development of enterprises is clearly seen in the inadequacies of the soviets 'General Plans'. These are long-term plans for construction in the city covering 25–30 years, usually worked out by the Committee for Civil Constuction (Gosgrazhdanstroi) attached to Gosstroi USSR. Thus, for example, in Volgograd 79 new enterprises not envisaged in the General Plan of the city were sited there.[62] In Orenburg there are even cases in which state farms have been taken over by enterprises.[63] Usually the development of the city outstrips the calculation of the General Plan by three to four times or more. Since the war in the RSFSR there have been General Plans for 720 cities (by 1979) of which 370 (57 per cent) have had to be renewed.[64] Novokuznetsk has had eight General Plans, Volgograd six, Kkar'kov three.[65] In Kiev the prediction of population for 1990 was passed in 1975.[66] In Leningrad the forecast of 4 million by 1985 was reached in 1971.[67]

Sverdlovsk Gorispolkom on 2 July 1976 passed a decision on 'the Siting and Development of Enterprises in the City not Stipulated by the General Plan'. The ispolkom noted that the rate of growth of the city had significantly surpassed that envisaged in the plan, the 1980 population target having been met in 1975, 'because of the formation and siting of enterprises and organizations which had not been stipulated in the general plan, and the wide range of work undertaken by the ministries without the prior agreement of the gorispolkom'.[68] Once again, in 1977, the ispolkom passed a further decree on 'The Illegal Use of Land and Unwarranted Construction in Sverdlovsk'.[69] In this decision the ispolkom noted that several enterprises in the city had infringed the land-use codes of the RSFSR and other construction laws.

Unlike residential buildings, which are planned by the state committee for civil construction and architecture and the Union-Republic state construction committees, production facilities are the province of 700 institutes under dozens of ministries and departments. Thus, as Bocharov and Lyubovny note, it is not surprising that the industrial zones which occupy 30 to 40 per cent of all urban land are not planned in detail.[70]

Libkind writes of Sartov that it 'reminds one of a layer cake. Industrial buildings alternate with apartment houses.' The reason for this was that, 'in erecting its enterprises each of the ministries was only concerned with its own interests, creating a "city within a city"'. The basic problem, he notes, is that 'the composition and spatial organisation of the industrial zones' are not taken into account when urban ensembles are created. The city executive committee, having no uniform planning documents for such zones, is 'compelled to agree to the piecemeal siting of enterprises . . . giving rise to a patchwork arrangement'. Of the chief architects and their staffs, whose function it is to conduct the implementation of the general plans, Libkind notes that they 'cannot influence the pace and quality of industrial buildup. Their authority extends only to "the plant's gates"'.[71]

The expansion of enterprises places greater demands on the city soviets for housing, labour, energy, water and other raw materials. A.P. Botvin, a deputy to the USSR Supreme Soviet, speaking at the December 1975 session, noted the fact that many ministries and agencies decide upon the expansion of enterprises in the city of Kiev without the required co-ordination with the local planning commissions. No account is taken of the new expenditure imposed on the city for the increase in supplies of water lines, sewage pipes, electricity, gas and heating installations and the great outlays on road and street maintenance and other parts of the infrastructure.[72] As we have seen, enterprises seeking to expand their facilities in the city often promise to help with the provision of such social and cultural buildings and networks, only to break these promises once they have completed the initial outlay on the production facilities.

It is interesting to read part of the text of an interview that the chairman of Kiev City Soviet gave to a correspondent from *Komsomol'skaya Pravda* as reported on 25 July 1976.

Question: Where in fact do all the newcomers find jobs, inasmuch as construction of new enterprises in large cities is forbidden?
Answer: This is a touchy subject, because ministries 'make exceptions' and disobey the ruling. Indeed, they site their enterprise with very little regard for the extremely difficult problems they are causing a city.
Question: Could one say that the enterprises that are unable to attain high labour efficiency and that grow out instead of up are ignoring their cities' capabilities and, in effect, 'punishing' their own workers outside the factory gates?
Answer: It turns out that way. The disproportion between the rate of industrial development and that of municipal services and social and trade facilities is quite evident. We calculated that to overcome the lag in Kiev, Union ministries would have to give the city more than 100 million rubles in the course of the five-year plan.[73]

The chairman also noted that one of the largest enterprises in the city, whose employees have 1,200 children of pre-school age, had never constructed a kindergarten. In 1974 representatives of the soviet went to the minnistries to demand 4 million roubles for the construction of the kindergartens. They agreed — but the city received only 400,000 roubles. Once again they objected, and 14 ministries at last responded favourably. However, as the chairman pointed out, 'Going to the ministries for each clinic, store and municipal improvement we need is hardly efficient. Large cities need coherent overall planning of capital investments'.[74]

Thus the soviets have had little success in their attempts to control land use. Departments anxious to save money site their enterprises in large cities where they can plug into existing utility lines (water, sewage, electricity and transport). The soviets, dependent on those enterprises for funds, soon find that they are paying out large sums for these additional services, which reduces the very revenue they had hoped to gain. The uncontrolled expansion of enterprises renders the General Plans of soviets useless as indicators of enterprise expansion, and thus of population growth. Thus requirements for social facilities, housing and infrastructure are badly co-ordinated with plans for industrial production, causing the former to lag behind; and enterprises are under no compulsion to provide the additional services which are needed as a result of their expansion programmes.

Delay in the construction of the infrastructure

As we have seen, one of the commonest complaints of chairmen of executive committees is that the 'departmental' approach to planning leads to the unplanned build-up of cities and consequently a lag in the development of the infrastructure. Thus Kochetov shows there has been a significant delay in the development of the social, cultural and service spheres throughout the Soviet Union. He notes that by the beginning of the 1970s kindergartens were only 60 per cent, trade organisations 63 per cent, catering and service establishments 56 per cent and cinemas 42 per cent of established norms.[75]

As one member of Leningrad City Soviet's Chief Trade Administration observed in 1977, 'Lags in the development of the urban infrastructure — transportation, communications, municipal and consumer services, public health, education — have almost become the rule today'.[76]

The dispersal of funds through hundreds of ministries and thousands of enterprises accelerates the unco-ordinated development of the infrastructure. These problems are seen most clearly in the development of new cities in the Soviet Union. The situation in the city of Arkalyk is fairly typical of that in new Soviet cities. Although this oblast centre is half built, in 1977 it had virtually no construction base as there was no money for it. The major problem is that its development is being directed by outside construction organisations. As Myasnikov notes, 'Dozens of apartment houses have been erected, but nothing has been said about repair and maintenance facilities for them. Cultural and service construction lags behind housing construction, which in turn lags behind population growth'.[77]

A similar situation is to be found in Surgut, whose city soviet chairman observed, 'It could perhaps be called a model for the departmental approach to city planning.' In the centre is an old village with its ancient log-cabins. Next, there are the hastily thrown-together wooden buildings of the geologists; then comes a settlement of two-storey flats for the oil workers, followed by a five-storeyed residential district built for the power industry workers. In 1975 there was an acute housing shortage and the city soviet had continually to fight against these various agencies and endure attacks by construction outfits that were in a hurry to report job completion. Departmentalism had taken root. Thus the chairman remarked:

> Many problems could be avoided altogether if every department would show a greater interest in the future of its city and join forces with others in achieving common goals. For example, our city has 43 boiler plants built by various agencies. There are plans to build still more. Why? Surgut has a large central electric power plant . . . It could more than supply the city with heat, but we haven't managed to convince high officials in the USSR Ministry of Power of the expediency of using the plant to heat the city.[78]

In Nizhnevartovsk the lack of a clear plan for social and economic development has brought a number of serious social problems and has led to disproportions between industrial construction and the construction of housing. Although there is an acute labour shortage in the city, 3,700 women must stay at home because there are not enough kindergartens. The basic problem for Tyumen Oblast, as for the Soviet Union in general, is, as a *Pravda* correspondent noted in 1979, that: 'Everything stems from the complex's disproportionate, inharmonious development. Departmental politics often gains the upper hand, and there is no unified strategy for the formation and management of industry'.[79]

The history of the development of the city of Stary Oskol (Central Black Earth Region) shows clearly the stamp of 'departmentalism'. As a Soviet authority notes, the first stage in the formation of most cities is the construction of water, sewage, heat and gas, roads and power factories. Yet, 'while aware of this, the builders of Stary Oskol proceeded otherwise, on the basis of individual agency-oriented interests'.[80] In the city, housing foundations had been laid before the preliminary engineering work had even begun. This was at a time (1976) when it was necessary to lay more than 55 kilometres of water and sewage lines, 10 kilometres of concrete roads and 5 kilometres of heat mains. As Pokrovsky remarks:

> In other words when the buildings open for tenancy, they will have no running water, gas, sewerage lines and shops. What has happened here is the disproportion between the planning of capital investments and the organisation of work.[81]

The reason for this, as Pokrovksy reveals, is that Stary Oskol:

> has *three bosses*. The directorate of the USSR Ministry of Ferrous Metallurgy's future electrometallurgical Combine; secondly, the USSR Ministry for Construction of Heavy Industry Enterprises' electrometallurgical construction combine; and finally, the Stary Oskol City Soviet Executive Committee. Each of them in allocating funds for the city's development, 'forgets about creating the engineering facilties that will be used by all' . . . The whole construction project needs a single, general planner and a single inter-agency general client.[82] (my emphasis)

And what about the role of the local party committees? With regard to Tyumen oblast, a reporter from *Pravda* notes that while the local soviets cannot cope with departmental narrow-mindedness, the Party agencies have to a greater extent taken on the role of co-ordinators. 'But even they have neither the *authority* nor the *capability* to solve large-scale inter-branch problems'[83] (my empahsis). While they may appeal to their superiors, the slowness of the bureaucratic system allows the ministries and through them the enterprises to dominate the development of local economies.

Variations in the provision of social/cultural and other public amenities

The last two sections have shown that because of the lack of co-ordination of branch and territorial plans, there has been an unplanned development of many cities, and consequently a lagging-behind in the development of the non-production sphere in relation to the production sphere. The phenomenon of 'departmentalism', and the weakness of the pro rata system for pooling of funds, have left widely different provisions of social and cultural services from Republic to Republic and within oblasts and cities themselves. Table 4.2 shows the variations in a number of indices of capital cities in the USSR and cities with a population of over one million. The variation in the provision of housing stretches from a low of 9.7m^2 in Dushanbe to 15.9 in Baku and 16.4 in Moscow. The number of hospital beds per 10,000 inhabitants is 97.3 in Erevan and 176.3 in Alma-Ata.

As we have already seen, there are many raiony, cities, etc., where the provision of social and cultural facilities are well below

Table 4.2: Level of development of the infrastructure of capital cities and cities of population, 1 million + in 1978

City	Housing per inhabitant; in m²	Retail trade per 10,000 pop.	catering per 10,000 pop.	Number of hospital beds per 10,000 pop.	No. of books and journals in libraries per person	Cinema places per 1,000 pop.	Theatre places per 1,000 pop.
USSR	12.7	27	11	122.0	6.6	95.5	1.3
Alma-Ata	12.1	21	11	176.3	7.1	34.1	3.9
Ashkhabad	10.3	19	9	166.1	15.2	54.5	5.8
Baku	15.9	24	11	133.3	9.8	65.6	4.2
Vilnyus	13.2	14	12	175.7	11.1	20.8	5.4
Gorkii	12.5	15	9	145.1	7.3	29.0	2.6
Dushanbe	9.7	19	11	135.6	9.1	36.5	3.6
Dnepropetrovsk	13.6	15	9	144.1	6.1	30.0	2.6
Donetsk	14.1	12	11	166.7	3.0	38.2	1.9
Erevan	10.4	18	10	97.3	9.8	18.6	3.6
Kiev	14.2	15	10	140.2	6.2	28.4	2.8
Kishenev	12.4	18	12	169.9	12.1	21.9	3.8
Kiubyshev	12.2	13	10	132.9	7.1	35.4	2.3
Lenigrad	15.7	15	10	111.8	7.4	28.5	3.7
Minsk	12.9	11	9	105.4	9.6	18.2	2.6
Moscow	16.4	13	10	137.7	6.0	27.7	4.5
Novosibirsk	12.7	11	9	139.2	5.5	33.5	3.8
Odessa	12.3	20	11	120.5	7.7	56.4	4.6
Omsk	12.3	13	11	144.6	6.2	26.6	2.4
Riga	14.9	22	11	150.0	10.7	23.9	7.1
Sverdlov	12.9	13	10	159.7	5.9	27.3	3.9
Tallin	15.7	18	14	125.6	11.0	18.6	7.7
Tashkent	9.8	18	9	140.3	5.1	33.2	3.0
Tbilisi	12.8	18	12	137.6	8.9	25.3	7.2
Frunze	10.2	13	10	176.8	12.5	31.9	5.3
Khar'kov	14.1	16	12	143.1	8.1	29.1	2.8
Chelyabinsk	13.0	14	11	147.7	6.8	33.9	2.4

Source: A.V. Stepanenko, *Goroda v Usloviyakh Razvitovo Sotsializma* (Kiev, 1981) pp. 174–5.

the established norms. These differences, as we have stressed throughout this work, are related *primarily* to the industrial base of the soviet and only *secondly* to overtly political factors such as patronage, etc.

WHAT SHOULD BE DONE

Over the last decade there has been a vigorous debate in the Soviet press and scholarly journals with regard to the above problem. It is interesting to follow these discussions and note which solutions are being offered.

The views of A. Myasnikov, a Soviet sociologist, are fairly typical of those who want to see more power placed in the hands of the local soviets. He writes:

> There is only one way out of this situation — funds allocated to cities should be distributed centrally, through the State Planning Committee. Only then can a city count on getting its money. And when it comes to money the cities receive from departmental organisations' profits, the city Soviet executive committees should have the final say in determining how these funds should be used.
>
> *Legally the soviets have the powers of a master. Let them use these powers.* If a department decides to build in a city, it should go to the local Soviet, which would state the conditions under which a road or an enterprise could be constructed.
>
> When the soviets' legal authority is enhanced by financial powers; when new norms are developed that clearly define the way a city's funds are formed; when the city receives its share of profits through the State Planning Committee — *then city administrative agencies will be full-fledged masters of their cities.* (my emphasis)[84]

While members of the Republic and All-Union planning commissions do not go so far as to advocate the transfer of all funds to the soviets, they do support the need for stronger territorial planning of the infrastructure and of social and cultural amenities, etc. Thus V. Mozhin (Director of RSFSR State Planning Committee's Central Research Institute) and V. Savelyev (the Deputy Director) advocate that:

The entire regional production infrastructure should be subject to territorial planning. The comprehensive territorial planning of the infrastructure will increase its efficiency, improve the quality of service and create economic barriers against the tendency for industrial ministries and departments to establish their own 'self-sufficient economies'.[85]

D. Khodzhayev (head of a sub-department of the USSR State Planning Committee) calls for the planning of the infrastructure to be co-ordinated with that of production expansion. Ministries and their enterprises should provide indices for housing requirements alongside plans for the development of their enterprises. The USSR Bank should, he stresses, only finance construction projects in a comprehensive fashion. Thus 'production and non-production facilities should be financed simultaneously'. And ministries, in submitting lists of construction projects to Gosplan:

> should bear just as much responsibility for observing the guidelines for number of employees . . . and for providing these employees with housing and necessary services without undue delay as they do for fulfilling the plan for commissioning new capacities and for observing estimated cost figures and construction schedules.

It is remarkable to note that:

> At present, however, there are no confirmed, validated rules according to which ministries and departments can calculate capital investments in housing construction, even though the ministries must file a special form giving an estimate of housing needs along with the draft plans they submit to the USSR State Planning Committee.[86]

Turning to the views of a member of Leningrad Ispolkom's Department of Trade, and a dean of economic planning, we find much more detailed suggestions as to how the enterprises should pay for the facilities of the infrastructure. Thus they propose:

> (1) That the entire social infrastructure and much of the production infrastructure be made subordinate to territorial administrative agencies; (2) that special methods be developed to determine how much each major enteprise in the city should contribute to the creation and development of the infrastructure; (3) that rates

for various services be set so as to enable them to pay for themselves and to make a profit sufficient to finance the development of the infrastructure; and (4) that reductions in rates paid by the public be made up not out of the state budget but by the city's major enterprises, in proportion to the labour resources they use and the services they receive.[87]

The above examples show that at present the method of financing the non-production sphere is being given a public airing in the press, indicating that the need for change is well appreciated by the top leadership. However, while it is possible that territorial planning will be strengthened in this area, there are no signs that the ministries will have to relinquish their hold over these facilities, or that they will, as suggested above, have to pay more directly for the services they use.

THE PLANS, THE PLANNING COMMISSIONS AND THE PLANNING PROCESS

The plans

At present there are many different plans, worked out both at All-Union and Republic level, which touch upon the development of the oblasts and cities: (1) the General Scheme of Development and Siting of Industry; (2) the General Scheme of Settlement for the Country and Republics; (3) Regional Plans; (4) General Plans of Cities.[88]

The General Scheme of the Development and Siting of Industry is worked out by Gosplan USSR and other central organs for a 15-year period (with 5-year breakdowns). In a very general way it covers the basic industrial development of cities, population growth and standard of living. The General Scheme of Settlement, which is worked out by the State Committee for Civil Construction and Architecture attached to Gosstroi USSR, deals in more detail with civil construction in the cities. Regional plans worked out by Gosplan, Gosstroi USSR and at Republic level also deal with many of the same questions. These cover the siting of enterprises and the development of city infrastructure, the development of transport and architectural planning structures as well as ecological questions.

The general plans of cities are drawn up by the State Committees for Civil Construction at All-Union and Republic levels. Gosplan USSR's Department of Housing and the Communal Economy is also involved. Here a wider approach is taken to the planning of cities as a whole, but only in one area, that of construction. These plans also contain social-economic aspects, population forecasts and indices about the infrastructure. But these are far from being considered on the all-city scale. The essence of the General Plan is to provide for the development of the architectural lay-out of the cities. All other factors are only considered in the light of this over-riding aim.

Thus from above, at Republic and All-Union levels, the cities are planned with regard to the siting of industry and the development of large-scale construction works. However, one of the main problems for the soviets is that these plans are not co-ordinated with each other and they cover different time periods, use different statistical methods and often overlap each other. Nor are they synchronised with the plans composed at the local level by the oblasts and city soviets.

The oblast and city soviets participate only in the working out of five-year and yearly summary plans for the development of the economy. These are the plans which the soviets ratify in session each November or December. In general, these cover only those enterprises subordinate to the soviets, with the exception of details about the production of consumer goods. The local planning commission may also draw up summary plans on an *ad hoc* basis from figures given to them from non-subordinate enterprises for the development of housing and public amenities.

In recent years, however, there has been a positive trend towards comprehensive planning, with many cities compiling 'Complex Economic and Social Plans'. These allow for the integrated and balanced development of the cities covering all enterprises regardless of subordination. At first, in the early 1970s, these plans were confined to the large Republic capital cities, but more recently they have spread to smaller cities. The 1977 Constitution approved such developments, saying, 'In the framework of their powers local soviets ensure the complex economic and social development of their territories'.[89] As we have already noted, such developments have been fully supported at all the Party congresses of our period. Planning the development of the city as a whole and including a wide range of social indices which cover the infrastructure, these plans are the latest attempt to co-ordinate branch and territorial planning and put an end to 'departmentalism'.

At the beginning of the 1970s complex plans for economic development were worked out without the addition of social indices. For example, Riga's 1971–5 'Complex Economic Plan', ratitified by the soviet on 31 March 1972, included the following sections. (1) Industrial production. This outlined the volume of gross output for all the enterprises of the city regardless of subordination, for the city as a whole and for each raion. (2) Housing construction. This allowed for a forecast of all housing and kindergartens to be constructed in the city by all enterprises regardless of subordination.

A more complex approach is found in Complex Economic and *Social* Plans which provide for a wide number of indices with regard to the development of the infrastructure. Thus the Complex Economic and Social Development Plan of Daugavpils (Latvia) 1971–5 included such indices as, 'changes in the social makeup of the workforce', the cultural level of the workers and the development of political education.

The development of complex planning began in 1967 at Republic level, when the Republics were granted the right to plan for the all-round development of their territories including the basic indices of enterprises of Union and Union-Republic subordination. Soon afterwards such plans were adopted by the oblasts. To further this development, departments of territorial planning were formed in the Republic state planning committees. In the Ukraine by 1971 complex plans were adopted by all 25 oblasts and were implemented in many large cities and other oblasts throughout the Soviet Union.[92] However, their development has been erratic and there is still no single method of composing such plans or laying down the way in which they should be ratified. For large cities they may be ratified by Gosplan USSR or Republic Gosplan. For smaller cities they will usually be ratified by a joint session of the city Party and soviet bodies.

Thus, although the development of these plans provide for a greater degree of horizontal planning, it also pushes the composition and ratification of the plans upwards to Republic or All-Union level. In order to co-ordinate the development of cities, planning has to be directed from the centre; only these higher authorities can control the development of the large ministries and their enterprises. Thus the decision-making process has become more centralised as it has sought to achieve greater co-ordination. Similarly, the role of the Party is greater here.

In order to improve the co-ordination of planning, new committees have been set up attached to the Party and the soviets to oversee the composition and implementation of these plans. The membership of these committees is made up of Party secretaries, members of the executive committees of the soviets, heads of departments, members of the planning commissions of the soviets, Party activists, sociologists, economists and others. As we have noted, the Party is very active in all stages of this planning process. As one Soviet scholar notes, 'Soviets need the direct support and help of the Party as there is no direct mechanism which facilitates the interrelation of the soviets with these bodies [i.e. enterprises of higher subordination].'[93] Here the role of the Party as 'super co-ordinator' is paramount, as it is the only organisation which cuts across all other groups in society.

Leningrad's Council of Economic and Social Development, attached to the oblast Party committee, is regularly engaged in analysing the development of industry and social facilities in the region. In Kalinin Raion, Leningrad, a Council for Economic and Social Planning is attached to the Party committee of the raion. In its presidium in 1975 were the secretary of the raikom (chairman), the chairman of the raiispolkom, the chairman of the planning commission of the soviet, heads of the departments of the executive committee, heads of the Party, scientific workers, economists, jurists, doctors, teachers, psychologists and trade union and komsomol workers.[94]

To a large extent, then, the actual composition of such plans and the control of their implementation has been moved from the executive committee of the soviets to these special co-ordinating councils, which are firmly under the control of the Party. Noting the increased role of the Party in planning, one Soviet scholar writes:

A study of a number of local Party and soviet organs shows that at present, in the majority of cases, Party committees are entrusted with composing the plans of the social and economic development of the cities. In the first epoch this was necessary. In the present period, when the composition of plans for the complex development of the cities is widespread, work for the implementation and control of these must in our opinion be carried out by the city soviets. That is their function.[95]

Thus the development of the complex plans and the moves towards integration of the planning system have demanded, at the same time, more centralisation in the planning process and greater Party involvement in the whole planning procedure. However, there are still wide variations throughout the Soviet Union in the kinds of complex plans adopted.

Undoubtedly the development of these plans has done much to stem the further development of departmentalism and to bring greater harmony to branch and territorial plans. However there is as yet one serious flaw: the ministries and enterprises may still draw up their branch plans without taking account of the new 'Complex Plans'. As the Soviet scholar, Stepanenko, points out, there is an urgent need to give these planning documents greater legal status, making them obligatory for all enterprises.[96]

The planning commissions

One of the major inadequacies of recent legislation on planning is that it has failed to equip local soviet planning commissions with enough staff, wages and resources to exercise the new rights that have been given to the soviets.

As with finance departments, there is a lack of clearly-defined norms for the staff size of the planning commissions. Thus in Krasnodar in 1940, when it had a population of 200,000, there were nine members of the planning commission, whereas when the population in 1979 was 500,000 it had only seven members. In Saratov in 1952 the population was 470,000 and there were 24 members, while in 1976, with a population of 800,000 there were only 11 members.[97] Laptev, Lebedev and Pavlovich, in their study of cities in the RSFSR, have shown that because of the lack of cadres in some cities there are often no departments of transport and daily services. Thus in Murmansk the already overworked planning commission has taken over the work of these departments, while in Novgorod the commission deals with daily services and local industry.[98] For Sukhomlin the number of workers should be based on: (1) the population of the city; (2) the volume and speciality of its territory; (3) the size of the housing fund; (4) the social structure of the population.[99]

To cope with the work-load many planning commissions have to draft in volunteer workers. As P. Tsitsin, chairman of Voroshilov Raion Soviet, Moscow notes:

> The small borough planning commissions as currently constituted are incapable of handling all the work involved in preparing comprehensive plans for borough development and exercising full control over their implementation. In view of this, our borough Soviet set up a 19-member planning commission.[100]

Kalinin City Soviet Planning Commission is very weak, consisting of a chairman and three members of staff. According to the latest statute it should consist of a chairman plus six members of staff. The city soviet has often turned to higher authorities to raise the staff levels but without success. In order to supplement the deficiency, the city has ten volunteer workers. As the chairman of Saratov City Soviet Planning Commission pleads:

> The time has come to reinforce the staffs of local planning agencies with highly qualified specialists in various branches of the economy, and at the same time to increase these specialists' salaries . . . One of the city planning commission's basic functions should be the drafting of long-range and current plans for the city's social and economic development, but, because of staffing deficiencies, the commissions are unable to do as much of this work as they ought to.[101]

Kutafin, an expert in this field, reports that because of staffing difficulties the soviets cannot carry out a new right granted to oblasts in 1974 to compose fuel balances for their territory as a whole;[102] while Lebedev and Malyshev, in their study, found that 90 per cent of the workers in planning commissions considered that they were overworked, and that they often had to carry out extra work not directly related to their own departments.[103]

Like the finance departments and the majority of other departments of the soviet, the planning commissions are under dual subordination. There is some possibility that the vertical lines are not as strong here as in the finance administrations. It was only in 1966 that the commissions formally came under such dual control.

The power of appointment of the chairmen of the oblast and city planning commissions remains, however, within the ambit of the central planning agencies. Thus the chairmen and deputy chairmen of oblast soviets are appointed by Gosplan of the Republic, while the chairmen of city soviet commissions are appointed by the oblast in consultation with the Republic Gosplan; the members of the commissions are appointed by the corresponding soviet on the advice of the chairman. Of course all of these appointments will have to be approved by the relevant Party committees.[104] The commission work on plans produced each quarter. City planning commissions meet not less than once a month, current work being carried out by the apparat.

The membership of the planning commission varies from one

soviet to another, and generally encompasses a large number of specialists and heads of departments.

Moscow Oblast Planning Commission has the following membership: chairman, four deputy chairmen, heads of the departments of the commission (summary planning, agriculture, industry and daily services), head of the Design Buro of the oblast, deputy head of the Oblast Finance Department, chairman of Lyubertsy City Planning Commission and an economist from the department of summary planning.[105]

The city planning commissions are usually smaller, with fewer departments. Thus Ivanovo City Soviet Planning Commission has the following membership: chairman,, deputy chairman, chairman of the planning commissions of the raiony in the city, deputy head of the City Finance Department, head of the Industrial Transport Department, head of the planning sector of the Department of Capital Construction of the city, an inspector from the city Statistics Department and the Deputy Chief Architect of the city.[106]

The size and membership of the commissions will depend on the size of the city or oblast and its administrative status. The most complex structure is to be found in Moscow City Planning Commission which has 23 departments.[107]

For planning commissions of oblast level, standing orders were adopted by the RSFSR Council of Ministers in 1957[108] and 1966[109] The 1966 standing order widened their rights over housing, social and cultural plans and services. Since 1966 they have been entrusted with working out balances of labour supply, income and expenditure of the population, and summary plans for cultural and service facilities for the oblasts as a whole. In addition they were given the task of composing draft summary plans for housing and the communal economy. With regard to trade and services these were to cover all enterprises regardless of subordination.[110] And in 1974, as we noted, they were entrusted with working out balances for fuel as well as local building materials.

City-level standing orders were ratified by the RSFSR Council of Ministers in 1958,[111] 1968[112] and most recently 1974,[113] and the 1981[114] legislation has called for a new standing order to be drawn up. The 1968 standing order widened the rights of the planning commissions over the fields of housing, the communal economy and social services. Over these areas they were given the right to compose summary plans for all enterprises regardless of subordination. The latest standing order (28 March 1974) for city soviets in the RSFSR continued the path of strengthening their rights over enterprises of higher subordination. They were given the additional rights to receive from non-subordinate enterprise planning indices about the development of housing and the communal economy, construction of roads, social and cultural facilities, local building materials, trade, catering, education, health, conservation, production of consumer goods and training of youth.[115]

With regard to the development of the cities and oblasts it would appear that the oblast level has now taken over many of the functions of city planning. Lebedev and Malyshev in their study of 23 cities in the RSFSR note that the centre of gravity in relation to planning work has been removed to the branch departments of the city and oblast executive committees and the planning organs of the ministries, so that 'Gorplan fulfils only the function of summarising and transferring information for a number of objects of the cities' subordinate economy'.[116] Thus the departments of capital construction of the cities have their own planning bodies which by-pass the city level and report directly to the planning organs at oblast level.[117] For Lebedev and Malyshev, not only do the planning commissions fail to play a leading role in planning work, but they cannot even fulfil basic planning tasks: 'The key questions about the long-term development of cities are decided by the Party organizations or the oblast executive committee and the planning organs of the ministries and departments.'[118]

Composing the plans

As can be seen from Appendix 4, the planning process follows a similar pattern to that of the budget, and indeed the budget is really only one part of the National Economic State Plan.[119] As in budget planning, control figures are handed down from above. These are worked out jointly by the Council of Ministers of the USSR and Gosplan USSR, taking into consideration figures sent to them from Republic and oblast-level administrations. The oblasts and cities are totally dependent on the indices and norms worked out from above and on the development plans of the many enterprises situated on their territory. But as we have already noted, often the enterprises refuse to hand over their development plans, and seldom take into consideration the opinions of executive committee members when they are drawing up their plans for ratification by the Council of Ministers. However, in recent years, especially since the new legislation of 1979 and 1981, the local soviets have been given a greater say in the planning process, and enterprises are now obliged to consider the views of soviets before they ratify their draft plans in the Council of Ministers.

Moscow City Soviet is able to plan for the development of all enterprises in its territory, regardless of subordination, in its 'Complex and Economic and Social Plans'. These are worked out in three stages.

(1) Draft plans are worked out for enterprises subordinate to Moscow City Ispolkom 30 to 40 days before the draft plans of enterprises subordinate to All-Union ministries.

(2) Plans for the development of enterprises subordinate to RFSFR ministries are presented to the ispolkom 15 to 20 days before those of All-Union subordination.

(3) Finally, the proposals of All-Union-subordinated ministries and their enterprises are presented to the ispolkom. A 'Summary Plan of the Complex Economic and Social Development of Moscow City' is then composed and is normally completed 15 to 20 days after the receipt of figures from the All-Union enterprises.

This method of planning allows for a greater degree of co-ordination and the exchange of views between the All-Union and RSFSR ministries and Moscow City Executive Committee. Further co-ordination and modification take place when Moscow's complex plan is placed before Gosplans USSR and RSFSR. These commissions check that the city's plan is in line with central norms and the plans of the ministries. After the approval of Gosplan USSR, Moscow's draft plan is ratified by the USSR Council of Ministers. The draft plan of Moscow City Soviet is not simply the sum of enterprise plans. Gosplans USSR and RSFSR with the relevant Party bodies will act as arbiters, alongside the Council of Ministers, to decide on the final composition of the plan.[120]

CENTRALISATION OF THE PLANNING PROCESS

The above outline of the planning process shows, as does that of the budget process, the dominance of the central bodies at All-Union and Republic level. The process works from the top downward, each level having to base its plans on control figures worked out above. However, there have been some moves over our period which have enabled city and oblast soviets to make greater inputs into the decision-making process. The development of complex economic and social plans has given the soviets the ability to inject some

Table 4.3: Departmental structure of the ispolkomy of city and raion soviets in Vologda, Kostroma, Kaluga, Yaroslavl', Novgorod and Murmansk (late 1970s)

	Vologda C R	Kostroma C R	Kaluga C R	Yaroslavl' C R	Nogorod C R	Mumansk C R
Chairman of the ispolkom	+ +	+ +	+ +	+ +	+ +	+ +
Deputy chairman, secrt.	+ +	+ +	+ +	+ +	+ +	+ +
Assistant to chairman	+ *	+ *	+ *	+ *	+ *	+ *
General department	+ +	+ +	+ +	+ +	+ +	+ +
Planning commission	+ +	+ ''	+ +	+ +	+ +	+ *
Finance department	+ *	+ *	+ *	+ *	+ *	+ +
Organisation-Instr.	+ +	+ +	+ +	+ +	* +	* +
Capital construction	+ +	+ *	+ *	+ *	+ *	+ *
Communal economy	+ +	+ +	+ +	+ +	+ *	+ +
Housing	* +	+ +	+ +	+ +	+ +	+ +
Allocation of housing	+ +	+ *	+ *	+ *	* +	+ *
Education	+ +	+ +	+ +	+ +	+ +	+ +
Culture	+ *	+ *	+ *	+ *	+ *	+ *
Health	+ +	+ +	+ +	+ +	+ +	+ +
Physical culture/sport	* +	* +	* +	* +	* +	* +
Social insurance	+ *	+ *	+ *	+ *	+ *	+ *
Registry office	* +	+ +	+ +	+ +	* +	* +
Internal affairs	+ +	+ +	* +	* +	+ +	+ +
Trade	+ +	+ *	+ *	* *	+ *	* *
Transport	+ *	+ +		* *	* *	* *
Daily services and local industry	+ *	+ +	+ +	+ *	+ *	* *
Architect	+ +	+ +	+ +	+	+	+

C = City   R = Raion
+ shows that department is present   '' means no information   * means that the department is absent
Source: B.A. Pavlovich, 'Raspredelenie Kompetentsii mezhdu Gorodskim i Raionnymi (v Gorodakh) Organami Upravleniya', in P.N. Lebedev, *Sistema Organov Gorodskovo Upravleniya*, (1980), pp. 53–60, (p. 54).

measure of 'horizontal planning' into the system and to co-ordinate the various branch plans of the ministries and organisations of non-subordination, but this has been achieved only by pushing the composition of the plans and their ratification upward to Republic and All-Union level. Some Soviet scholars have suggested that all cities with a population of 500,000 upwards should have such complex plans ratified by Gosplan of the Republic.[121] Also, as we have noted, the role of the Party in composing complex plans has been very active, the co-ordinating councils attached to these bodies moving the decision-making process away from the planning commissions of the soviets to the councils.

One of the basic problems for the development of local soviets has been the dominance of outdated personnel norms which are worked out by Gosplan USSR, Gosstroi USSR, the USSR Ministry of Finance and others. Thus, as we noted, the size of departments of planning, finance and housing is often based on norms which are clearly unrelated to the population and industrial base of the territory.

Table 4.3 shows the variations in departmental structure which are present in cities and raiony of the RSFSR, and the effect of centrally prescribed norms on departmental structure. Because of staff shortages, in some raiony there are no departments of capital construction, transport or local industry, and at city level departments of social insurance, local industry, internal affairs, transport and organisation-instruction are missing. The degree of centralised leadership from above must be increased in those cities where no such departments exist.

A similar situation exists for norms which define the number of kindergartens, the amount of housing and other social and cultural facilities. For example, although the birth-rate in Voronezh is one-third of that in Bratsk, and Voronezh has more pensioners than Bratsk, nevertheless norms for the construction of kindergartens are identical in both cities. Consequently, as Myasnikov observes:

> the number of places in schools, children's combines, clubs and hospitals in Bratsk is close to or exceeds official norms, but the schools there operate in three shifts per day, there is not enough kindergarten space, and the hospitals are overcrowded.[122]

The basic problem is, he notes:

that the norms do not take account of a city's distinctive geographic features, its nationality characteristics or the population's social-demographic structure. Instead, they are based on nationwide averages that are not really applicable to individual communities.[123]

The norms are particularly bad with regard to the infrastructure. Thus the chairman of Kuibyshev City Soviet points out:

> The city soviet still receives insufficient allocations for the development of transport arteries, the water mains, telephone services and so on. For example we are given only 10% or 100,000 roubles per 1 million rubles of capital investments, and this plainly is too little. Calculations show that for a city with a population of 1 million or more the norm for municipal construction must be raised to at least 25%.[124]

In the city of Omsk there are severe shortages of asphalt, tar and cement. The city, with a population of over 1 million, still receives these allocations according to norms worked out when it was much smaller.[125] Indeed, norms for construction and transport have become a serious handicap to the development of Siberian cities. V. Obraztsov, the deputy chairman of Omsk City Soviet, writes of these norms:

> They make no allowance for the harsh climate of our region or its specific features. Why, for example, is the established construction cost per square meter of housing the same for us as for cities in the European part of the country? Allocations for housing maintenance are of equal size for industrial centres of regions that differ greatly in their natural conditions.[126]

One reason for the tenacity of these norms is the scarcity of resources. Each city has to compete for the all-too-few materials and resources that are available, and each will jealously guard its allocations even if it no longer requires them. Furthermore, as Myasnikov observes:

> the practice of resources distribution is fraught with disproportions, which lead to outright losses. Unprofitable cultural centers, theaters, stadiums . . . as well as empty schools, kindergartens and nurseries, can be found in large older cities, while these same

facilities are lacking in Bratsk, Kachkanar, Arkalyk . . . and other new cities.[127]

The centralisation of the planning process is well illustrated by the number of stages a plan for housing construction must go through before it reaches the drawing board. With the number of different ministries involved it is no wonder that co-ordination becomes impossible. DiMaio outlines the process in this manner. Before the city planning agency can confirm plans for capital construction:

(1) The State Committee for Civil Construction and Architecture, under Gosstroi USSR, must approve the housing designs.
(2) The Ministry of the Industry of Building Materials checks the technological details.
(3) In the case of the RSFSR, the RSFSR Ministry of the Communal Economy confirms the size of the labour force.
(4) The Ministry of Finance confirms the financial indicators, and ensures the city's plans are in accord with the national budget.
(5) Republic Gosplan sets the limits on capital investments which come down from USSR Gosplan.
(6) Funds for materials and equipment are confirmed by the Chief Administration for Material and Technical Supplies (Glavsnabsbyt) and the Republic Ministry of the Communal Economy.
(7) Plans for the actual allocations of materials and for credits and financing are drawn up with the collaboration of the state bank and the construction bank.[128]

The amount of centralised control will depend on the amount of money involved in the particular construction project. Thus Usenko notes that cities of Republic subordination such as Moscow and Leningrad can ratify the construction of any housing regardless of cost, cities of oblast centres up to 500,000 roubles, cities of oblast subordination 300,000 and of raion subordination 50,000 (figures are for cities in the Ukraine since the 1971 legislation). When the construction exceeds the soviets' maximum allowance they pass it up to the next level for ratification.[129]

One of the most serious limitations on the work of the soviets is that they cannot redistribute capital investments of the branch industries to improve the state of affairs in their territories, even when they can see on the spot the mistakes of the central planners.

Thus as Khodzhaev observes:

> Appeals made by local agencies to the government and to planning agencies usually contain requests for additional investments for lagging sectors of the municipal economy rather than for the redistribution of money within already allocated capital investments. It would be a good idea to consider removing existing restrictions and granting Union republics, ministries and departments — and through them, local Soviets and enterprises — the authority to make partial adjustments in plan assignments for the commissioning of new facilities in individual branches of the municipal economy (housing, utilities, schools), within the limits of the total capital investments allocated for this purpose.[130]

He adds:

> since local Party and Soviet agencies are most familiar with the acute problems of their cities and have the greatest stake in their solution, it seems reasonable that there should be a further expansion of the authority of republic and local Soviets to distribute allocated funds to the individual branches of the non-production sphere.[131]

As yet, however, there have been no moves in this direction and local soviets are still restricted in their ability to distribute such funds.

Over our period there has been a steady increase in the activities of the oblasts at the expense of the city soviets. In the late 1970s, Laptev, Lebedev and Pavlovich, in a study of the cities of Murmansk, Novgorod, Yaroslavl', Vologda, Kaluga, Kostroma and others, found that they had lost the following departments or administrations, transferred to the jurisdiction of the oblasts: local industry, city transport, communications, daily services, public catering, distribution and utilisation of labour, water supply and electrification.[132]

The transfer of departments to the oblast level has resulted in poor co-ordination of control over various areas of the city economy. In the cities, services are often split arbitrarily between city and oblast administrations. Laptev, Lebedev and Pavlovich found that the vast majority of leaders of city isopolkomy agreed that the absence of one unified system of services under the jurisdiction of the city executive committees had led to serious malfunctions and inefficiencies.[133]

These developments have naturally led to greater centralisation of functions and a reduction in city inputs. Thus the department of trade of a city soviet has little power over the daily running of shops in its territory, or over their specialisation and siting. In fact, city departments of trade have only the minimal right to define the opening hours of such outlets and to oversee their general compliance with central legislation. The real masters are the oblast administrations of trade, which are hardly in a position to know what is best for a district in a city far from the oblast administrative centre. In Khar'kov the City Executive Committee has jurisdiction over only 10 to 12 per cent of the enterprises engaged in the communal economy and daily services, while 75 per cent of such agencies are directly subordinate to the oblast level, and a further 10 to 13 per cent to ministries. The Department of Daily Services of Khar'kov City Soviet carries out only minor functions in the area of control and does not engage in the ratification of planning indices or the distribution of credit. All the major organisational activities for services in the city are carried out by the Oblast Adminstration of Daily Services.[134] According to Laptev, Lebedev and Pavlovich, a similar situation is also to be found in the planning commissions, administrations of capital construction and administrations of the municipal economy.[135]

Finally, Gorbachev, in his speech to the 27th Congress, noted that local soviets found difficulties in running their municipal economies and he urged, 'We should not be blind to the fact that for the time being their ability to tackle many of the local problems is limited; there exists *excessive centralization* in such matters which are not always clearly visible from the centre'[136] (my emphasis).

Thus, at present the local soviets are still dominated from above and restricted by centralised norms.

NOTES

1. See Taubman, Cattell, Leningrad and Frolic, 'Decision-making' and 'Municipal Administrations'.
2. See Sternheimmer 'Running Russian Cities' and Lewis and Sternheimer, *Soviet Urban Management*.
3. See Introduction, n. 15.
4. Frolic, 'Decision-making' and 'Municipal Adminstrations'.
5. See Introduction, n. 10.
6. G. Mil'ner, 'Voprosy Territorialinovo Planirovaniya Urovnya Zhizni Naseleniya', *Planovoe Khozyaistvo,* April 1974, 55–62 (p. 57).

7. Resolution of the Central Committee of the CPSU and the Council of Ministers of the USSR, 31 July 1957, 'O Razvitii Zhilishchnovo Stroitel'stva v SSSR', in *KPSS v Rezolyutsiyakh*, VII, 1955-9 (1971), 278-94.

8. 1971 City Resolution, *CDSP*, pp. 2-3.

9. Constitution, Article 147, in Lane, p. 581.

10. Resolution of the Central Committee of the CPSU, 12 July 1979, 'O Dal'neishem Sovershenstvovanii Khozyaistvennovo Mekhanizma i Zadachakh Partiinykh i Gosudarstvennykh Organov'; Resolution of the Central Committee of the CPSU and the Council of Ministers of the USSR, 12 July 1979, 'Ob Uluchshenii Planirovaniya i Usilenii Vozdeistviya Khozyaistvennovo Mekhanizma na Povyshenie Effektivnosti Proizvodstva i Kachestva Raboty', in *KPSS v Rezolyutsiyakh*, XIII, 1978-80 (1981), 405-7 and 408-51, respectively.

11. 1981 Resolution Soviets.

12. See Chapter 2, n. 11.

13. See Chapter 2, n. 11.

14. See Chapter 2, n. 12.

15. 1980 Oblast Law.

16. 1971 City Decree.

17. Decree of the Presidium of the USSR Supreme Soviet, 28 November 1978, 'Ob Osnovnykh Pravakh i Obyazannostyakh Gorodskikh i Raionnykh v Gorodakh Sovetov Narodnykh Deputatov', in *Sovety Narodnykh Deputatov: Status Kompetentsiya,, Organizatsiya Deyatel'nosti. Sbornik Dokumentov* (Moscow, 1980), pp. 313-22.

18. 1981 Resolution Soviets.

19. *Materialy XXIV S"ezda KPSS* (Moscow, 1971), p. 67.

20. *Materialy XXV S"ezda KPSS* (Moscow, 1976), p. 171.

21. *Materialy XXVI S"ezda KPSS* (Moscow, 1981), p. 125.

22. 'Political Report 27th Congress', translated in *Soviet Weekly*, 8 March 1986, p. 9.

23. See (e.g.) A.V. Stepanenko, *Goroda v Usloviyakh Razvitovo Sotsializma* (Kiev, 1981), p. 242.

24. A. Emel'yanov, 'Planu Byt' Kompleksnym', *Pravda*, 25th July 1974, p. 2; translated as 'The Plan should be Integrated', *CDSP*, 26, no. 30 (21 August 1974), 16.

25. P.N. Lebedev and B.P. Malyshev, 'Sushchestvuyushchaya Praktika Planirovaniya v Gorode', in *Sistema Organov*, edited by Lebedev, pp. 92-102 (p. 99).

26. V. Grigor'eva and V. Lagushkin, 'Rol' Planovykh Kommissii v Razvitii Gorodskovo Khozyaistva', *Planovoe Khozyaistvo*, October 1976, 85-6 (p. 85); abstracted as 'The Role of Planning Commissions in Developing the Urban Economy', *CDSP*, 28, no. 46 (15 December 1976), 10-11 (p. 10).

27. A.I. Kazannik, *Koordinatsionnaya Funktsiya Mestnykh Sovetov Deputatov Trudyashchikhsya* (Irkutsk, 1974), p. 15.

28. S.V. Solov'eva, 'Organizatsionno Pravovoi Mekhanizm Koordinatsionoi Deyatel'nosti Mestnykh Sovetov', *Sovetskoe Gosudarstvo i Pravo*, July 1974, 59-65 (p. 61).

29. K. Sheremet, E. Korenevskaya, S. Solov'eva, N. Starovoitov and

Yu. Todorskii, 'Koordinatsiia: Sushchestvo i Praktika', *Sovety Deputatov Trudyashchikhsya*, May 1976; translated as 'Coordination: its Essence and Practice', *Soviet Law and Government*, 15, no. 3 (Winter 1976–7), 24–37 (p. 28).
30. Sheremet *et al.*, ibid., p. 28.
31. N.A. Sukhomlin, 'Problemy Sovershenstvovaniya Planirovaniya Ekonomicheskovo i Sotsial'novo Razvitiya Gorodov' (unpublished Kandidat dissertation, Moscow M.V. Lomonosov State University, 1979), p. 25.
32. Sheremet *et al.*, 'Koordinatsiia', p. 29.
33. Myasnikov, 'There should be One Master', p. 8.
34. M. Mezhevich, 'Kompleksnoe Planirovanie Krupnykh Gorodov', *Planovoe Khozyaistvo*, March 1978, 110–15 (p. 111); abstracted as 'Comprehensive Planning of Large Cities', *CDSP*, 30, no. 15 (10 May 1978), 14–15 (p. 14).
35. Mezhevich, 'Comprehensive Planning', p. 14.
36. Ibid., p. 15.
37. Grigor'eva and Lagushkin, 'The Role', p. 10.
38. Ibid., pp. 10–11.
39. See Chapter 2, n. 12.
40. Klinetskaya, 'Funktsiya Finansirovaniya', p. 130.
41. Stepanenko, *Goroda*, p. 267.
42. Ibid., p. 267.
43. G. Melikyants, 'Zhiloi Dom, evo Khozyaistvo', *Izvestia*, 26 June 1976, p. 2; condensed as 'Housing and its Management', *CDSP*, 28, no. 26 (28 July 1976), p. 31.
44. Sheremet *et al.*, 'Koordinatsiia', p. 24
45. Ibid., p. 24
46. Ibid., p. 24
47. V. Azan, 'Gorodu-Kompleksnoe Razvitie', *Sovety Deputatov Trudyashchikhsya*, June 1975, 55–60 (p. 60).
48. Ibid., p. 60.
49. *CDSP*, p. 30.
50. M. Kovalev, 'Zaboty Goroda', *Izvestia*, 6 August 1975, p. 3; condensed as 'The City's Concerns', *CDSP*, 27, no. 31 (27 August 1975), p. 9.
51. Ibid., p. 9.
52. Yu Bocharov and V. Lyubovny, 'Gorod — Kompleks Edinyi', *Pravda*, 13 November 1976, p. 3; condensed as 'A City is a Single Complex', *CDSP*, 28, no. 46 (15 December 1976), 8–9 (p. 8).
53. Ibid., p. 8.
54. D. Khodzhaev, 'Kompleksnost'-Glavnoe Napravlenie v Zastroike Gorodov', *Planovoe Khozyaistvo*, August 1976, 43–52 (pp. 47–8); abstracted as 'Comprehensiveness is the Main Thrust of Urban Building', *CDSP*, 28, no. 40 (3 November 1976), 10–12 (p. 12).
55. A. Libkind, 'Arkhitektura Zavodskoi Zony', *Pravda*, 5 August 1975, p. 3; condensed as 'The Architecture of the Factory Zone', *CDSP*, 27, no. 3 (27 August 1975), 8–9 (p. 8).
56. Mezhevich, 'Comprehensive Planning', p. 15.
57. Polyak, *Byudzhet Goroda*, pp. 7–8.

58. *CDSP*, p. 27.
59. *CDSP*, p. 27.
60. *CDSP*, p. 27.
61. V. Beshkil'tsev, 'Kak Stroit' na Severe?', *Izvestia*, 14 February 1974, p. 2; condensed as 'How to Build in the North?', *CDSP*, 26, no. 7 (13 April 1974), 13–14 (p. 13).
62. V. Mozhin and V. Savalev, 'Napravleniya Sovershenstvovaniya Territorial'novo Planirovaniya', *Planovoe Khozyaistvo*, August 1976, 24–32 (p. 26); abstracted as 'Guidelines for Improving Territorial Planning', *CDSP*, 28. no. 40 (3 November 1976), 9–10 (p. 9).
63. Bocharov and Lyubovny, 'Gorod', p. 8.
64. Sukhomlin, 'Problemy', p. 42.
65. Ibid., p. 42.
66. Ibid., p. 42.
67. DiMaio, *Soviet Urban Housing*, p. 33.
68. S.A. Avak'yan, *Gorodskoi Sovet i Predpriyatiya Vyshestoyashchevo Podchineniya* (Moscow, 1979), p. 25.
69. Ibid., p. 46.
70. Bocharov and Lyubovny, 'Gorod', p. 8.
71. Libkind, 'Arkhitekture', p. 8.
72. Sheremet *et al.*, 'Koordinatsiia', p. 34.
73. N. Bodnaruk and R. Zaitsev, 'Chelovek i Gorod', *Kommsomolskaya Pravda*, 25 July 1976, pp. 2–3 (p. 3); abstracted as 'Person and City', *CDSP* 28, no. 36 (6 October 1976), 14–15 (p. 15).
74. Bodnaruk and Zaitsev, 'Person and City', p. 15.
75. A. Kochetov, 'Sotsial'no-Ekonomicheskii Aspekt Gradostroitel'stva', *Voprosy Ekonomiki*, October 1975, 23–4 (p. 26).
76. B.S. Vasil'ev and A.G. Stolbov, 'Puti Podema Infrastruktury Goroda', *Ekonomiki i Organizatsiya Promyshlennovo Prozvodstva*, 1977, no. 4, 133–7 (p. 133); abstracted as 'Ways of Building Up the Infrastructure', *CDSP*, 29, no. 35, 9.
77. Myasnikov, 'There should be One Master', p. 128.
78. Yu. Melikhov, 'Gorod Smotrit v Zavtra', *Izvestia*, 5 September 1975, p. 3; condensed as 'City Looks to Tomorrow', *CDSP*, 27, no. 36 (1 October 1975), 24– 5 (p. 25).
79. S. Vtorushin and V. Sevastyanov, 'Tyumen': Vtoroi Etap. — 3. Chtoby Idti Dal'she', *Pravda*, 17 May 1979, p. 2; condensed as 'Tyumen — the Second Stage. — 3. In Order To Go Futher', *CDSP*, 31, no. 20 (13 June 1979),, 7–8, 20 (p. 8).
80. V. Pokrovskii, 'Zven'ya Kompleska', *Pravda*, 14 July 1976, p. 2; condensed as 'Links of the Complex', *CDSP*, 28, no. 28 (11 August 1976), 17–18 (p. 17).
81. Ibid., p. 17.
82. Ibid., p. 17.
83. Vtoruskhin and Sevastyanov, 'Tyumen', p. 8.
84. Myasnikov, 'There should be One Master', pp. 8–9.
85. Mozhin and Savelev, 'Guidelines', p. 10.
86. Khodzhaev, 'Comprehensiveness', p. 10.
87. Vasil'ev and Stolbov, 'Ways of Building Up', p. 9.
88. Stepanenko, *Goroda*, p. 263.

89. Constitution, Article 147, in Lane, *Politics and Society*, p. 581
90. E.I. Korenevskaya, 'Gorodskie Sovety i Kompleksnoe Planirovanie Razvitiya Gorodov', *Sovetskoe Gosudarstvo i Pravo*, September 1973, 64–72 (p. 66).
91. Ibid., pp. 66–7.
92. *Sovershenstvovanie Territorial'novo Planirovaniya v Soyuznoi Respublike*, edited by A.S. Emel'yanov (Moscow, 1976), p. 6.
93. E.I. Korenevskaya, 'Mestnye Sovety i Territorial'novo Sotsial'noe Planirovanie', *Sovetskoe Gosudarstvo i Pravo*, July 1975, 82–8 (p. 87).
94. Ibid., pp. 85–6.
95. Sukhomlin, 'Problemy', p. 96.
96. Stepanenko, *Goroda*, p. 272.
97. Sukhomlin, 'Problemy', p. 91.
98. Yu. A. Laptev, P.N. Lebedev and B.A. Pavlovich, 'Analiz Vzaimodeistviya Oblastnykh i Gorodskikh Ispolkomov', in *Sistema Organov*, edited by Lebedev, pp. 47–53 (p. 50).
99. Sukhomlin, 'Problemy', p. 94.
100. P. Tsitsin, 'Iz Opyta Raboty Mestnovo Soveta po Razvitiyu Khozyaistva Raiona', *Planovoe Khozyaistvo*, July 1976, 79–95 (p. 82); abstracted as 'From a Local Soviet's Experience in the Economic Development of a Borough', *CDSP*, 28, no. 46 (15 December 1976), 9–10 (p. 10).
101. Grigor'eva and Lagushkin, 'The Role', p. 10
102. O.E. Kutafin, *Mestnye Sovety i Narodnokhozyaistvennoe Planirovanie* (Moscow, 1976), p. 52.
103. Lebedev and Malyshev, 'Sushchestvuyushchaya', p. 102.
104. D. Ya. Bykovskii and E.I. Kolyushin, *Mestnye Sovety i Planirovaniye Kompleksnovo Razvitiya Territorii* (Moscow, 1982), p. 72.
105. Ibid., p. 74.
106. Ibid., p. 72.
107. Kutafin, *Mestnye Sovety*, p. 42.
108. Resolution of the Council of Ministers of the RSFSR, 5 October 1957; cited in Kutafin, ibid., p. 46.
109. Resolution of the Council of Ministers of the RSFSR, 15 August 1966; cited in ibid., p. 46.
110. See ibid., p. 46.
111. Resolution of the Council of Ministers of the RSFSR, January 1958; cited in ibid., pp. 49–50.
112. Resolution of the Council of Ministers of the RSFSR, 9 October 1968; cited in ibid., pp. 49–50.
113. Resolution of the Council of Ministers of the RSFSR, 28 March 1974; cited in ibid., pp. 49–50.
114. See ibid., p. 50.
115. See ibid., p. 50.
116. Lebedev and Malyshev, 'Sushchestvuyushchaya', p. 101.
117. Ibid., p. 101.
118. Ibid., p. 101.
119. O.E. Kutafin, *Planovaya Deyatel'nost' Sovetskovo Gosudarstva* (Moscow, 1980), pp. 203–38.
120. V.V. Bitunov, E.G. Chistyakov and V.A. Shul'ga, *Metody Planirovaniya Khozyaistva Goroda* (Moscow, 1981), pp. 42–3.

121. Stepanenko, *Goroda*, p. 273.
122. Myasnikov, 'There Should be One Master', p. 8.
123. Ibid., p. 8.
124. A. Rosovskii, 'Kak Rasti Gorodu', *Pravda*, 30 July 1974, p. 3; condensed as 'How is the City to Grow?', *CDSP*, 26, no. 30 (21 August 1974), 31–2 (p. 31).
125. V. Obratsov, 'Oblik Goroda', *Pravda*, 24 May 1979, p. 2; condensed as 'City's Appearance', *CDSP*, 31, no. 21 (20 June 1979), 19–20 (p. 19).
126. Ibid., p. 19.
127. Myasnikov, 'There should be One Master', p. 8.
128. DiMaio, *Soviet Urban Housing*, pp. 63–4.
129. M.I. Usenko, *Pravovye Voprosy Deyatel'nosti Gorodskikh Sovetov Narodnykh Deputatov po Razvitiyu Zhilishchnovo Khozyaistvo* (Kiev, 1978), pp. 13–15.
130. Khodzhaev, 'Comprehensiveness', p. 12.
131. Khodzhaev, 'Comprehensiveness', p. 12.
132. Laptev, Lebedev and Pavlovich, 'Analiz', p. 48.
133. Ibid., p. 49.
134. A.I. Nedogreeva, *Koordinatsionnaya Deyatel'nost' Gorodskovo Soveta Narodnykh Deputatov* (Kiev, 1981), p. 123.
135. Laptev, Lebedev and Pavlovich, 'Analiz', p. 52.
136. 'Political Report 27th Congress', translated in *Soviet Weekly*, 8 March 1986, p. 12.

5
Local Soviets and the Planning of Housing

INTRODUCTION

Western literature with regard to housing in the USSR has largely addressed itself to the economic aspects of this industry and the growth of the housing sector in various republics and regions of the Soviet Union. Morton and DiMaio[1] have devoted considerable attention to these aspects. Others such as Lewis and Sternheimer[2] have touched upon the subject in their various works on budgets and planning. In particular they have stressed the wide variation in the provision of housing in cities throughout the USSR.

As with the study of planning, the principal writers who focus on the work of the *local soviets* and housing are Taubman and Cattell.[3] More recently Morton[4] has provided a general overview of the work of the soviets in this area, with particular reference to the 1970s. Morton, like Cattell and Taubman, underlines the weakness of the soviets before the enterprises.

While generally supporting the conclusions of these writers as regards the weak position of the soviets, I shall also emphasise that at times, problems arise because of the unwillingness of the soviets themselves to take on new responsibilities or to assert their rights. Because of the many structural problems (outlined in the Introduction and Chapter 1) such as shortages of staff and difficulties of co-ordination between Party bodies and state organs, local soviets often cannot take over new areas of the housing economy, even if they have the full support of the enterprises in their territories.

In this chapter we shall be particularly concerned with the following areas of housing policy: (1) the process of housing transfer from the enterprises to the jurisdiction of the soviets; (2) the role of the soviets in taking on the role of client (zakazchik) for housing construction; (3) the implementation of the Orel system of planning, which spread throughout the Soviet Union in the latter half of the 1970s.

A close look at the work of the soviets in planning the development of housing and the communal economy clearly illustrates the dominance of the ministries over this area of the economy, the wide dispersal of funds and thus the urgent need for territorial planning and greater powers to be given to the soviets over these enterprises. The ability of the ministries to thwart legislation in 1957,[5] 1967,[6] 1971,[7] 1978[8] and more recently in 1981[9] clearly demonstrates their political status in Soviet society. Once again we shall stress variations throughout the Soviet Union in the transfer of housing and the implementation of zakazchik rights. Just as there are some soviets who are more willing to press for their rights, there are some enterprises who are less willing than others to carry out transfers — for example, oil, gas, chemical and other heavy industries have been more reluctant than enterprises of light industry. At the local level such factors as the availability of labour and the role of the local Party bodies will be of some importance.

However, as we shall show, there are many cases when the soviets themselves are reluctant to take on the extra responsibility that comes with such transfers, or to act as zakazchik. Often we will meet 'psychological barriers' and a lack of faith on the part of the soviets that they can carry out such work. In a sense the political culture of the society is out of step with the new rights which have been given to the soviets, and thus with the new roles they are now expected to play. The long dominance of the enterprises in Soviet society, going back to the industrialisation drive of the 1930s, and their association with the heart of the 'revolutionary ideal', make any real challenge to their authority extremely difficult.

After outlining the statistics showing the percentage of housing under the control of the soviets and the ministries, we shall go on to discuss (1) the reasons for the slow transfer of housing to local soviets; (2) the difficulties the soviets have in taking on the function of zakazchik; and (3) problems in implementing the Orel system.

ENTERPRISE/SOVIET HOUSING

On 17 August 1981 local soviets in the USSR, as reported in *Pravda*, controlled only 40 per cent of the general housing in stock,[10] while in 1979 local soviets in the RSFSR controlled the even smaller figure of 35 per cent.[11] There are, however, wide variations. A 1976

Table 5.1: Percentage of housing and communal economy facilities belonging to city and settlement soviets according to plans of oblasts Ukraine, 1971–5

Oblasts	Housing	Water	Sewage	Gas
Ukraine Republic	45.6	49.2	50.3	53.4
Vinitskaya	42.3	49.1	50.0	62.2
Volynskaya	52.8	47.9	47.7	76.7
Voroshilovgradskaya	16.1	19.9	21.1	31.6
Dnepropetrovskaya	33.2	34.7	34.8	38.9
Donetskaya	26.4	32.3	33.9	50.2
Zhitomirskaya	54.7	63.7	65.0	74.1
Zakarpatskaya	69.4	70.5	71.2	84.7
Zaporozhskaya	40.9	44.8	45.1	47.7
Ivano-Frankovskaya	59.2	48.4	49.2	62.7
Kievskaya	31.9	34.1	35.3	45.8
Kirovogradskaya	41.5	49.1	50.0	57.3
Krymskaya	47.5	53.9	54.4	55.8
L'vovskaya	71.2	69.4	70.0	75.8
Nikolaevskaya	42.3	40.3	39.6	52.4
Odesskaya	70.5	75.3	76.1	79.7
Poltavskaya	40.1	37.8	38.8	50.7
Rovenskaya	62.6	61.9	63.2	77.3
Sumskaya	38.5	35.1	37.3	43.0
Ternopol'skaya	74.1	70.7	71.2	80.7
Khar'kovskaya	56.1	59.1	59.7	62.8
Khersonskaya	31.9	43.1	42.7	43.9
Khmel'nitskaya	61.3	65.9	68.8	77.2
Cherkasskaya	49.3	50.7	51.7	60.5
Chernovitskaya	85.2	86.1	86.0	90.3
Chernigovskaya	54.4	53.7	53.8	65.3
City Kiev	76.9	77.2	77.5	77.8

Source: L.M. Mushketik, *Kompleksnyi Territorial'nyi Plan v Usloviyakh Otraslevovo Upravleniya* (Kiev, 1974), p. 58.

report from the Standing Commissions of the USSR Supreme Soviet noted:

> the proportion of housing administered by local soviets at the present time is 74% in Moscow, 84% in Leningrad, 78% in the Armenian Republic, 67% in the Latvian Republic, 70% in the North Ossetian Autonomous Republic, and 65% in the Bashkir Autonomous Republic.[12]

Table 5.1 shows the wide variation in the housing stock that belongs to the city and settlement soviets in the oblasts of the Ukraine, according to plans of the oblasts for 1971–5. The table also shows variations in other communal economy facilities. Thus in

Table 5.2: Donetsk oblast, 1974

Departments/Housing	Thousands of M²	% of total
Local soviets	10.345	25.8
Donetsk railways	1.085	2.85
Ministry of Coal Ukraine Republic	13.241	27.9
Ministry of Energy and Electricity Ukraine Republic	1.119	3.0
Ministry of Metallurgy Ukraine Republic	3.540	9.55
Ministry of Heavy Industry Ukraine Republic	1.017	2.75
Total for five departments and soviets	30.349	81.8

Source: N.A. Sukhomlin, 'Problemy Sovershenstvovaniya Planirovaniya Ekonomicheskovo i Sotsial'novo Razvitiya Gorodov' (unpublished Kandidat dissertation, University of Moscow, 1979), p. 23.

Voroshilovgrad Oblast the soviets control only 16.1 per cent of the housing fund, while in Chernovtsy Oblast the figure is 82.2 per cent.

Table 5.2 shows the distribution of housing between the local soviets of Donetsk Oblast and five of the chief ministries situated in the oblast. As can be seen from Table 5.2, the Ministry of Coal of the Ukranian Republic controlled more housing than the local soviets. Sukhomlin notes that while these five departments and the soviets controlled 81.8 per cent of the housing stock:

> in the authority of the remaining 44 ministries was nearly 7 million m² of housing or 18.2 per cent. Here each enterprise controlled only a small amount, from 200 to 900 m². In all, the soviets controlled only 25.8 per cent of the housing stock; thus the remaining 74.2 per cent was effectively outside their jurisdiction.[13]

Table 5.3 shows a similar picture for Karaganda Oblast (Kazakhstan). This time the figures are for the planned development of the oblast 1981–5. As can be seen, the greatest part of the housing stock and other facilities lies under the control of the ministries. The oblast soviet controls only 361,000 m² to the ministries' 1,875,000, and indeed the amount of housing under one ministry, that of the coal industry, is three times that belonging to the oblispolkom. Another large controller of housing is the USSR Ministry of Metallurgy, which owns 550,000 m². The soviet controlled only

Table 5.3: Karaganda oblast: Plans, 1981–5

Committee	Oblast Executive USSR	Ministry of Coal USSR	Ministry of Metallurgy USSR	Ministry of Chemicals	Ministry of Oil and Chemicals	Ministry of Machinery USSR
Housing thousands of m^2	361	1065	550	60	120	80
Kindergartens number of places	4120	4060	840	560	840	1280
Schools number of places	8232	4064	2352	1176	1176	–
Hospitals number of beds	1040	880	1000	250	250	300
Polyclinics Number of patients per surgery	500	1300	300	500	600	600
Houses of culture, 'Pioneer' camps and sport facilities	–	11	5	3	4	2
Engineering and communication networks, Kms	134	110	20	–	–	–

Source: M.T. Baimakhanov, M.A. Binder and N.I. Akuev, *Oblastnye Sovety i Promyshlennye Predpriyatiya Vyshestoyashchevo Podchineniya* (Alma-Ata, 1982), p. 237.

4,120 out of 11,700 kindergarten places, and 1,040 out of 3,720 hospital beds. The figures in Table 5.3 show the extent of ministerial dominance over the control of housing and the wide variations that exist across the country. The dispersal of the housing stock throughout the branch administrations makes it extremely difficult to plan at territorial level. Often the amount of housing controlled by each enterprise is very small, as we saw with Donetsk. It is very uneconomical to disperse housing funds and materials in this way, and in fact there is much evidence to show that housing under the management of soviets is kept in better condition, has more facilities and is easier to run. Enterprises may want to maintain control of housing in order to attract workers, but they are not interested in spending money on its upkeep.

Thus the plans for capital repairs to the housing stock of the ministries 1976-8 were only fulfilled on average by 92 per cent, and of 3,000 million roubles granted for this purpose only 235 million were used. Not one single ministry fulfilled its plan for repairs in 1978, whereas the soviets, over the period of the 10th Five-year Plan, fulfilled their plans for repair by 102 to 103 per cent.[14] Indeed economists have worked out that if all housing were transferred to the authority of the soviets, 300 million roubles would be saved every year.[15] By uniting all the housing and repair facilities under one administrative roof the whole process could be planned more effectively, but as we have already noted, such proposals have been under discussion for nearly 30 years. We can now turn to examine the details of the transfer process.

THE TRANSFER OF HOUSING FROM THE ENTERPRISES TO THE SOVIETS

The protracted history of the policy to transfer housing to the jurisdiction of the local soviets clearly reveals both the power base of the ministries and their ability to drag their feet over this important issue. Taubman's study demonstrates the failure of this policy over the period 1957-72. We shall turn our attention to the period of the late 1970s, and particularly to the developments that took place after the adoption of major legislation in 1978.

In September 1978 the USSR Council of Ministers passed a resolution on 'Measures for Further Improving the Maintenance and Repair of the Housing Funds'.[16] In this resolution the soviets were once again called upon to speed up the transfer process; all such work was to be completed by 1985. As we shall note in our case-studies, the 1978 resolution contained an important provision that would appear to have helped this process. The new resolution recommended that when enterprises transfer their housing stock to the soviets the first choice of such housing should remain with these enterprises. As we have stressed (see Chapter 4), the greatest barrier to such transfers was the fear of the enterprise directors that such moves would lead to their losing workers. This new provision ensures that no such loss will take place.

However, there are still a number of serious problems which are blocking the transfers, and indeed over the period 1975-9, the amount of housing actually transferred has been disappointingly small. During this period the amount transferred to the local soviets grew only from 543.3 million m^2 or 39 per cent to 632.2 m^2 (40 per cent). Variations in growth in some other republics were: RSFSR 34 to 35 per cent, Ukraine 44 to 46 per cent, Kazakhstan 31 to 32 per cent, Tadzhikistan 48 to 52 per cent.[17]

We can now turn to a number of case-studies of republics, regions and cities, and examine in more detail the question of housing transfer.

The RSFSR

In the RSFSR there are now plans for the cities to complete the transfer of all housing by 1985; and while, over the period of the 9th Five-year Plan, 17.5 million m^2 were passed over to the soviets, during the period of the 10th Five-year Plan this was increased to 23.4 million.[18] However, as we have noted, at the end of 1979 only 35 per cent of the housing stock belonged to the soviets.

According to Butusov, the RSFSR Minister of Housing, the process was particularly slow in Archangel, Vladimir, Kemerovo, and Kamchatka Oblasts, and throughout the Republic the Ministries of Gas, Oil and Chemicals were particularly slow in making the necessary arrangements for their housing to be passed to the soviets.[19] In 1980, nearly half of the total housing stock was divided among thousands of small enterprises who controlled 10,000 m^2 and less. Because of the poor state of repair of enterprise housing, each year in the RSFSR, 1.5 million roubles has to be spent on maintaining such housing.[20]

The dispersal of repair organisations and equipment leads to the badly co-ordinated planning of repair work throughout the Republic and there is no one territorial plan which can cover such work. With regard to supplies for repair of housing the minister notes that, in spite of norms ratified by Gosplan USSR, Gosstroi USSR and Gosnab USSR for expenditures on housing maintenance, the supply position is so bad that it prevents soviets from accepting new housing. Thus the funds granted by Gossnab in 1981 for repairs were half the established norms, providing only 30 per cent of the required amounts of piping and other equipment.[21]

The city of Komosol'sk-on-Amur (1981 pop. 270,000)

This city at the beginning of the 1960s was beset by 'departmentalism'. Komsomol'sk-on-Amur had been constructed in the 1930s 'without a general scheme of construction', and soon a number of enterprises took control of housing construction with little co-ordination between one another. Thus at the beginning of the 1960s there was a total housing stock of 700,000 m^2 in the city, of which the soviet controlled only 49,000. The rest was under the authority of more than 30 enterprises and organisations. A similar picture was to be found with regard to the communal economy, water, heating, gas, etc.[22]

However, in 1963, the city soviet turned to the RSFSR Council of Ministers with a request for help to transfer departmental housing. The council responded favourably, and by 1965 the city ispolkom had successfully taken over the housing and communal base of 18 enterprises controlling 640,000 m^2.

The success of the city continued, so that by 1981 almost 90 per cent of the housing stock (2,600,000 m^2) was under its jurisdiction.[23] The 1978 Housing Resolution gave a further boost to their morale; a number of new repair trusts and an administration of housing maintenance in the ispolkom were formed. The city now acts as a 'single client' for most housing construction. Enterprises, on receiving funds for building, transfer them to the gorispolkom. At the beginning of each year the gorispolkom works out a plan which states how much housing space each enterprise will receive and what further grants are required, if any. Such a concentration of funds under the Department of Capital Construction of the gorispolkom allows for a greater degree of co-ordination in planning; and indeed the general plan for this city has been successful.

The city soviet has been prepared to accept all housing regardless of its condition and by 1975 it had successfully demolished all the run-down buildings formerly belonging to the enterprises. As the head of the Housing Maintenance Administration remarks, their success in transferring housing has been due in part to the policy, long in practice, whereby 'We have established a procedure that in those cases when a person leaves his accommodation for another city, somebody from them same enterprise will occupy it.'[24] As we have noted, this was formally written into the 1978 Housing Resolution.

The history of housing transfer in this city shows that the soviets can be successful if they persevere and are willing to take on the extra responsibilities and work that accompany such transfers.

The city of Voroshilovgrad (1980 pop. 500,000)

In 1980 the total housing fund comprised 6,427,500 m^2, of which the city soviet controlled 2,494,000 and the ministries 1,776,500. From 1976 to 1980, as in other areas throughout the country, there was a slow rate of transfer, the city soviet receiving only 40,000 m^2. After the 1978 legislation, however, as A. Taranuhka, the chairman of the gorispolkom, noted, 'things began to speed up'. In 1980 the gorispolkom was due to receive 65,000 m^2 and in the next few years plans had been drawn up for a further 1.2 million from 53 departments and organisations. When these have been effected, as the chairman remarks, 'practically all the housing will be in one hand'.[25]

However, the city has one major problem — a chronic shortage of repair materials. Thus in 1979, of 19 listed items essential for the maintenance of the housing fund, the city soviet received only two in full. The remainder faced serious shortages. Thus instead of 510 tons of sewage pipes they received 19.3; instead of 153 tons of bitumen, 23; of the requested 3,900 m of central heating radiators, only 315; and instead of 28,000 kgs of calcium carbide for welding gas piping, a mere 500 were recieved.[26]

Moreover, all requests for special repair equipment for the citys' blocks of high-rise flats were turned down by the Ukranian Republic Ministry of Housing and Communal Economy because of 'lack of funds'. Again, the chairman notes the absence of a territorial plan, and the dispersal of such supplies amongst a vast number of ministries and enterprises. With regard to the Housing Ministry's job of co-ordinating such funds, the chairman complained, 'At present the Ministry of Housing, and to some extent the state civil construction committee attached to Gosstroi USSR, which are occupied by this problem, are too weak to solve such major issues.'[27]

Saratov oblast

In 1980 Saratov Oblast controlled 3,649,700 m^2 of housing, while the much larger figure of 10,685,400 was under the authority of the ministries. Over the period 1976–80 the soviet agreed to accept 452 blocks comprising 320,330 m^2, and by the beginning of 1980 they had successfully transferred over 200,000. A new agreement was being drawn up to cover the period up to 1985.[28]

However, many of the raiony were experiencing difficulties over such work, the workers' settlement of Stepnoe being typical. Here the majority of workers are engaged at one of the branches of the large production association 'Saratovneftgaz' which is engaged in oil and gas exploration. In this raion the majority of the housing still remains in the hands of the production association and the raion soviet has done little to take it over. The reasons for this have been forcefully stated by the chairmen of the raion soviet:

> I am prepared only to accept capital housing. The eight-storey housing, of which the majority is badly in need of repair — not under any circumstances. The five-storey housing demands serious repairs. Besides, the production association has no funds or technical supplies for servicing these houses. Until we have all of these things it is out of the question.

He goes on:

> We will accept only housing in ideal conditions; by the way, the soviet has 15–20,000 roubles in all for capital repairs, but [the production association] has several times that amount — let it do the repair work and then we will see.[29]

However, the housing official of the production association's branch in Stepnoe gives a different view. On hearing the words of the chairman of the raion soviet, he remarked, 'I am simply at a loss to know what to do. We have been talking about this problem for *ten years*' (my emphasis). He produced a number of documents which showed that the enterprise had for some time been prepared to transfer 162 houses, comprising 60,000 m^2, with the appropriate communal economy facilities, gas, water, etc., 'but they [the raion soviet] will not accept them'. In reply to the chairman's remarks about the lack of funds for repairs and their attempts to pass over badly-repaired housing, he pointed out that in 1978 a joint commission of the soviet and the enterprise had drawn up an agreement about repair work. This had been fulfilled by the enterprise but still the soviet refused to accept the housing. Indeed he remarked, 'We cannot detect a keen interest on the part of our soviet in these affairs'.[30]

With regard to payments, the housing official noted that the exact funds and staff and repair facilities were ready to be transferred to the jurisdiction of the soviets. Each year, for maintaining their housing stock, the enterprise pays out 216,000 roubles, and for repairs 70,000 all of which they had agreed to transfer to the soviet.[31]

But what was stopping the soviet from accepting such funds and housing? Fetisov, the specialist correspondent from *Sovety Narodnykh Deputatov* who conducted these interviews, notes that for the soviet to accept this housing would be slightly risky, as it involved new responsibilities. He stressed, 'It is not easy for them to overcome their doubts and to prepare themselves . . . for this'.[32] Finally, the correspondent met the general director of the production association, who informed him that other raiony had successfully accepted housing. He remarked, 'Our chief concern is excavating oil and gas. We are not specialists in the housing economy'.[33] As regards Stepnoe he further stated, 'It is beyond our power; the ispolkom stubbornly holds its ground and unfortunately the Oblast Department of the Communal Economy is not persistent enough about this question'.[34]

We can see that at times the soviets do not feel morally and psychologically equipped to enforce their rights, even when the ministries are in favour of such transfers. The difficulty of receiving supplies for maintenance is obviously a major reason for the slow transfer of ministerial housing at present.

In the 1979 session of Saratov City Soviet, a deputy from Frunze raion noted another important stumbling block: the complicated procedure for transferring houses, staff and repair facilities to the soviets. According to a 1969 'Instruction' of the Ministry of Finance and the Ministry of Housing of the RSFSR, all documents concerning such transfers must be agreed by the deputy chairman of the soviet and the deputy minister of the particular ministry concerned. But the latter is normally in Moscow; and thus, as the deputy notes, for every unit of housing one has to visit the capital, and a large volume of paper must pass back and forth. This delays the whole process.[35] As Fetisov asks, 'Why cannot the agreement be made with the head of the enterprise in the territory?'[36]

Bashkir ASSR

The Bashkir autonomous Republic has vigorously pursued a policy of transferring housing to the soviets, and indeed was one of the first in the RSFSR to take this path. By 1980, 63 per cent of the total housing fund had been passed to the soviets. In 1977, the Minister of Municipal Services noted that 'housing has been transferred to the soviets in 10 out of 17 cities', but he also remarked that the transfers were taking place slowly:

What stands in the way? Many factors. One is that enterprise-owned buildings are usually in a run-down condition. But once the enterprises have signed the documents to transfer them to the Soviet executive committees, they completely abandon all concern for housing.[37]

Thus in the cities of Kumertau, Belebei, Ishimbai and Tuimazy, where housing is completely under the jurisdiction of the soviets, the executive committees have received no help from the Ministries of Petroleum and Coal in renovating the buildings and demolishing old buildings. The major drawback, the minister states, is that:

Unfortunately there is still no all-Union regulation that would define the conditions and procedures for receiving and transferring apartment buildings and would be binding not only on the local Soviets but also the enterprises and agencies.[38]

Not all soviets are as fortunate as Stepnoe where the enterprise promised to pay for the necessary repairs and maintenance, and agreed to pass over not only housing but communal economy facilities, staff and equipment. With regard to repair work in the Bashkir ASSR, the minister remarks:

The increase in available housing has sharply increased the need for capital repairs and made it necessary to set up new municipal-service facilities. It would seem that the money allocated for these purposes should be increased, but this is by no means what has happened. For many years this money has amounted to only 13% of the total capital investments for housing construction, which is considerably lower than the Russian Federation average. The result is that available supplies are not even in keeping with existing norms, which have long been obsolete and need to be revised.[39]

Another problem frequently reported is the shortage of staff to carry out the additional work. As the minister observes:

> We think it is high time the Russian Republic Ministry of Finance and Ministry of Housing and Municipal Services drew up staffing guidelines for the branch administrations of city Soviet executive committees. Sometimes the number of employees in them is set arbitrarily. Consider one of our republic's big cities — Sterlitamak. It has 215,000 inhabitants. All the municipal-service enterprises there are under the administration of the city Soviet executive committee, but the municipal services adminstration consist of only nine persons. The administrations are bigger in other cities, even though they have substantially less to do.[40]

Moscow oblast

A study of the *Bulletin of the Executive Committee of Moscow Oblast Soviet* shows the frustration and the struggles which the soviet had to undergo in order to get housing transfers under way. On 22 February 1977 the ispolkom passed a decision on 'The Work of the Ispolkomy of the Oblast, Cities, and Raiony in Improving the Maintenance of the Housing Stock in the Oblast'.[41] This decision was passed in order to carry out the demands of the Buro of Moscow Oblast Party Committee in its resolution of the same name passed on 24 August 1976.[42]

In Article 2 of the decision the transfer of a total of 1,819,000 m^2 of housing to the soviets of the cities and raiony was demanded. With such transfers the oblast administrations of energy, water, gas and electricity were to ensure the additional acceptance of the necessary engineering networks for the communal economy. In the Oblast Administration of Housing a control department was created to oversee the transfers.[43]

However, in a further decision on 30 December 1977 concerning the fulfilment of the February decision, the soviet noted that progress in carrying out the transfers was very slow. Poor work had been carried out in the cities of Shchelkovo, Lyubertsy, Kolomna and Orekhovo-Zuevo. Of the planned transfer of 17,000 m^2 to Shchelkovo City Soviet not a single metre had been passed over; and the Oblast Departments of the Communal Economy had not carried out the required work to ensure the provision of gas, electricity, water, etc.[44]

On 23 February 1979 the soviet had to pass another decision with regard to the non-implementation of the transfer of housing. This time it noted that although between 1976 and 1979 a total of 2,331,000 m^2 had been transferred, little had been done to further this process in the cities of Voskresensk, Egor'evsk, Klin, Khimki and Shchelkovo.[45] As we shall show later, the oblispolkom had similar problems in persuading its subordinate soviets to act as 'single clients' for housing construction, and to change to the 'Orel system' of planning. The oblast may pass a large number of decisions without any positive results. Its ability to implement and control such work would appear to be much more limited than Western scholars have realised (see Chapter 6).

From our case studies five conclusions may be made:

(1) Enterprises that do finally agree to transfer try to pass on their old housing which is badly in need of repair.
(2) Local soviets have a chronic shortage of materials, money and manpower to cope with the transfers, and this is one of the chief reasons for their inability to accept enterprise housing.
(3) The dispersal of repair equipment through the various ministries and the ministers' attempts to try to provide everything for themselves leads to the badly co-ordinated distribution of such funds. The ministry of housing of each republic is itself in a weak position in the face of ministerial 'departmentalism' and cannot ensure the distribution of enough materials for the maintenance and repair of the soviets' housing stock. At the same time, the ministries fail to utilise millions of roubles each year granted to them for such work.
(4) The procedure for the transfer of housing is unduly centralised, involving protracted negotiations between ministry chiefs in Moscow and local representatives of the soviets. This wastes time on both sides and causes unnecessary expenditure on business trips to and from the capital.
(5) The problem of slow transfer does not always rest with the

ministries. Some soviets are unwilling to take on the extra responsibilities and work involved with such transfers.

ZAKAZCHIK RIGHTS

As we have noted, one of the major problems for the soviets is the wide dispersal of state funds for the construction and maintenance of housing among the different enterprises, and the inefficient and selfish use of such funds. One of the main areas which shows the absurdity of this state of affairs is that of housing construction. In any city there will often be many different construction agencies, belonging to different enterprises, engaged in the building of housing. The soviets will have little control over the work of these agencies, and in many cities there are no comprehensive plans for the development of such housing. This, as we have seen, leads to the unco-ordinated development of the production and non-production spheres.

Of crucial importance, then, for the soviets in their attempts to co-ordinate the work of these organisations has been their right to act as 'single client' (zakazchik) for the construction of all housing. Rather than having the chaotic system whereby enterprises build their own housing, the soviets' departments of capital construction would concentrate all funds for such buildings under one roof. Then, all construction in the territory of the soviet has to be approved by this department, allowing for greater integration of planning in the territory as a whole.

As with the right to transfer housing, the soviets were first granted zakazchik rights in 1957,[46] and these rights were emphasised again in 1971.[47] Most recently the 1978 housing legislation[48] reiterated the need for soviets to take on this function. Throughout the Soviet Union there are again variations in the implementation of this new right, and both successes and failures on the part of the soviets to adopt this method of planning.

In 1976 Vilnius City Soviet found some measure of success in co-ordinating the development of housing construction in its territory. The reason for this was that in Vilnius, housing construction involved only one client (the city executive committee), one designer (the institute of planning of urban construction), and one contractor (a residential construction combine). Thus:

The procedure is simple. Enterprises transfer to the executive committee all funds allocated for construction and a short time later they pick up the keys to the new apartments . . . the prime benefit that derives from having a single client, or chief construction agent, is realisation of the principle of integrated development.[49]

Both Moscow and Leningrad have acted positively with regard to zakazchik rights. It was announced that by June 1968 all state capital investment in Moscow's housing would be transferred from the ministries to the city soviet. Before the change took place Moscow had more than 500 different clients for housing construction.[50]

By 1965 Leningrad controlled 87 per cent of all housing on its territory. Cattell's study shows that from a very early stage the Leningrad City Soviet took steps to control the construction of its housing. All plans for construction had to be submitted to the city's Architecture Department by 1 September for construction during the following year. Such housing, unlike that in other city soviets, was not turned over to the enterprises but was maintained by the Leningrad Soviet.[51]

Both Leningrad and Moscow pioneered the formation of construction combines, which were to have full responsibility for the entire process of housing construction, from obtaining raw materials to the finished house. This allowed for a higher degree of co-ordination between the various agencies involved. In Moscow the Main Administration of Construction by the late 1960s was building 85 per cent of Moscow's housing.[52] These two cities, like Vilnius, have used the system of one client — one designer — one contractor, thus achieving greater integration of planning.

In 1975 Yu. Tsygankov (Instructor in the Construction Department of the Central Committee of the CPSU) noted the spread of the 'single client' system:

> Whereas at the beginning of 1974 the volume of housing and civil construction performed by city Soviet executive committees' capital construction administrations was 48% of total construction, this index has risen to 85% in Karaganda, 80% in Komsomolsk-on-Amur, 74% in Tallin and 70% in Yaroslavl'. In Murmansk and Ryazan, for instance, almost all urban construction has been transferred to the jurisdiction of the city Soviet executive committee.[53]

Laptev and Malyshev note that while in the cities of Tol'yatti,

Table 5.5: Kaluga city soviet: Plans for the department of capital construction and contractors for construction of housing and the communal economy, 1978-9

	Plans of ispolkom		Plans of contractors		Express of plan of ispolkom over that of the contractors (in %)	
	1978	1979	1978	1979	1978	1979
All	12683	11271	11157	10388	13.6	8.0
Including:						
Housing	8428	8928	7898	8582	6.6	4.0
Communal economy	1323	609	1069	543	23.8	12.2
Education	1946	1221	1550	835	25.5	46.2
Health	201	236	152	230	32.2	2.6
Culture	186	no figure	150	no figure	24.0	no figure
Others	559	277	388	198	44.1	39.9

Source: Yu. A. Laptev and B.P. Malyshev, 'Vzaimodeistvie Mezhdu Gorispolkomami i Nepodvedomstvennymi im Predpriyatiyami i Organizatsiyami pri Sozdanii Sotsial'noi Infrastruktury Goroda', in *Sistema Organov Gorodskovo Upravleniya*, ed. P.N. Lebedev (Leningrad, 1980), pp. 68-80 (p. 70).

Naberezhyi and Chelny, the departments of capital construction act as a single client, in other smaller cities where the majority of enterprises are of higher subordination, a large ministry will act as client; this is the case in Chernovtsy, Rybinsk and others.[54]

The city of Sverdlovsk passed a decree on 30 July 1976 'Reducing the Number of Construction Agencies for Housing Construction in the City of Sverdlovsk', which marked the beginning of its campaign to act as zakazchik.[55] Before this resolution there were 160 clients, and only 40 per cent of construction passed through the soviet. In the decree 41 enterprises were granted the right to construct housing. The city soviet obliged a number of organisations to choose one zakazchik for housing construction. The remainder had to arrange their programmes with the Department of Capital Construction.[56]

However, not all soviets have been so successful in taking on the function of single client. Thus in Kiev, as late as 1976, there were still 132 clients,[57] in Krasnodar in 1974, 140,[58] and in 1978 30 each in the cities of Novgorod and Kaluga.[59]

The unco-ordinated planning of construction work has created major discrepancies between the planned volume of work of the departments of capital construction of the soviets and the actual plans of the construction agencies. This leads to many unfinished buildings. Thus, in 1977 alone, the value of uncompleted construction for the country as a whole was 92.4 million roubles, or 85 per cent of the total planned capital investment.[60] Table 5.5 shows the effect of poorly co-ordinated plans in the city of Kaluga over the period 1978–9. In 1978 the Department of Capital Construction of the ispolkom planned to spend 1,526,000 roubles in excess of the planned construction work of the contractors. In 1979 the figure was 883,000 roubles. As can be seen, most of the badly co-ordinated work was in the field of the communal economy and amenities.

Often the ministries refuse to comply with the requests of the soviets and do not acknowledge the departments of capital construction as zakazchiki. The following examples illustrate the need to give the soviets greater rights over this area.

The city of Chernovtsy

Here, in 1980, the Soviet was still not acting as single client. The city had managed to concentrate only 10 per cent of capital investment for the construction of housing, of which 80 per cent of the contractors were small, non-subordinate enterprises. The main zakazchik for housing construction is the 'Metallurgicheski' combine. The city soviet tried in vain to take over the function of zakazchik for housing while leaving education, health and the communal economy in the hands of the enterprise, but the combine refused, for the familiar reason that it wanted to retain total control over the housing process in order to attract workers. The city is further weakened by the fact that it has a poor production base for such construction and lacks the personnel to carry out such work. Thus it has not been able to state its rights with any real conviction.[61]

The city of Surgut

Surgut, as we noted earlier, is a new town which has suffered greatly from departmentalism. In 1979 the city had still not been successful in its attempts to take on the function of zakazchik. At first it attempted to give this function to the Ministry of Petroleum, the other ministries being instructed to transfer to this agent's books their central allocations; but as the chairman of the executive committee pointed out, 'No matter how hard we campaign and cajole, they either do not do this at all, or they put it off for a long time'. This results in the usual delays in the construction of housing and public amenities and trade facilities. In March 1979 Surgut still had 30 clients for housing construction.[62]

The city of Angarsk

In 1978 Angarsk was still struggling againt departmentalism and the city soviet had failed to take on the function of single client. The USSR Ministry of Petroleum and the Petro-refining Industry, which owns the bulk of housing in the city, had refused point blank to co-operate.[63]

THE OREL SYSTEM OF PLANNING

One new planning method which has done much to further the spread of the single-client system is the Orel method of housing construction. This new system was given official approval in a Central Committee Resolution of 1974 on 'The Experience of the Work of the Orel Oblast Party Committee in Organising the Regular Commissioning of Housing and Civil Facilities in the City of Orel'.[64] Thus the resolution stated:

> The party, soviet and economic organizations have been able to concentrate capital investments, which are now in the hands of a single client — the city Soviet executive committee. This has made it possible virtually to put to an end the scattering of capital investments, to reduce by one third the number of apartment houses under construction simultaneously, to channel the released funds into the creation of carryover reserves, and to improve the provision of design documentation to the construction projects.[65]

Construction time for housing has been cut by an average of 20 per cent and the labour productivity of the construction workers increased by 16 per cent. In this way, 'In two years time the economic effect has been about 1 million roubles'.

As a result:

> It has been recommended that the Union-republic Communist Party Central Committees, territory and province Party

committees and ministries and departments utilize the experience of the organisation of housing and civil construction in the city of Orel.[66]

But what exactly is the system? As the instructor of the Central Committee's Construction Department explains:

Essentially, it boils down to the creation, on a citywide scale of a continually operating design and construction conveyor for the construction of facilities, regardless of their departmental affiliation.[67]

The adoption by the city soviet of the function of a single client is an essential part of this process. As Bocharov and Lyubovny write:

In a number of the country's cities Party and Soviet officials and economic managers have brought order into the client-constructor-designer system by concentrating capital investments in the hands of the city Soviet executive committees. In Orel for example, the scattering of capital investments has been ended and the number of buildings simultaneously under construction has been cut by one third. The evenly placed opening for occupancy of housing and civic buildings, with the inclusion of the construction of housing and industrial enterprises in a continuous two-year plan, makes possible the city's comprehensive development and the timely co-ordination of construction assignments with material and technical resources and the preparation of the territory where construction is done.[68]

The new planning method has, since the 1974 Central Committee Resolution, quickly spread throughout the Soviet Union. By 1976 it was in operation in more than 30 cities of the Russian Republic as well as in the Ukraine, Byelorussia, Azerbaidzhan and Armenia.[69] Moreover, plans were under way for 5 million m^2 of housing, one-third of the entire programme for 1976, to be built in this way.[70] By 1979 the Orel System was in operation in 120 cities of the USSR.[71]

It is instructive to look at the development of the new system in Orel from its outset in 1971. The initiative probably came from above, as it involved the USSR Ministry of Industrial Construction from the beginning, and was under the close direction of the Party bodies at both oblast and city levels. As M. Mironov, secretary of the Orel City Party Committee, remarks, 'the elaboration and introduction of the system of continuous planning and continuous flow construction was headed *directly* by the province and city Party committees'[72] (my emphasis). Thus a co-ordination group was set up in the oblast Party committee to see to the implementation of the system, while a commission to prepare materials was formed under the city Party committee. At the suggestion of the Party agencies in October 1971 the Orel Oblast Soviet Executive Committee empowered the Capital Construction Administration of the City Soviet Executive Committee to act as single client for housing and civil construction. Here we see the flow of power coming from the oblast Party committee to the oblast soviet, who then gave instructions to the city soviet.[73]

Before such a move, however, intensive discussions had taken place between all the organisations concerned; there was no question of enforcing a central policy on the agencies at local level, for in the beginning there were many doubts about the new system. As Mironov remarks of the various interested parties:

> They did not dispute the advantages of having a single client. But they also had major doubts. 'If we deprive the building clients of their independence,' they said, 'this could cause sudden cutbacks in the capital investments allocated by ministries and departments to enterprises and organizations under their jurisdiction. And what if the single client refuses to take into account the participating enterprises' interests with respect to the siting of housing within the city limits?'[74]

When the project finally got under way, the Party bodies still had to cope with some officials who were against the system:

> We also found some economic managers who tried to retain the customary methods of organizing construction and buildup work in the city. They beseiged the Party and Soviet agencies and under the slogan of 'the interests of our collective', tried to obtain special privileges for themselves. Of course, we didn't allow them to get away with it.[75]

These quotations show the difficulties that members of soviets will face when, unlike their counterparts in Orel, they do not have the support of the central Party and state bodies with regard to their acting as zakazchik.

Finally, 'a harmonious design and construction conveyor was created'. The single client is the city executive committee, the single designer the Orel State Urban and Rural Construction Design Institute, and the single construction organ the Orel Construction Trust's Construction Adminstration. As Mironov concludes:

> Practice has completely swept aside the arguments of the skeptics. Apart from drawing up official documents on the transfer of capital investments to the city Soviet executive committee's Capital Construction Administration and distributing housing space among the members of their collectives, the executives of economic organizations now perform virtually no functions related to the construction of housing and civil facilities.[76]

However, as with the transfer of housing, the Orel system has not been successful in all areas, and the ministries have maintained the upper hand. The history of Moscow Oblast's attempts to implement the Orel system will be typical for many other soviets.

Moscow oblast soviet

Immediately after the 1974 resolution which recommended the Orel system, Moscow Oblast, in a decision of 12 August 1974 (Article 1), instructed the Department of Construction, the Department of Construction and Building Materials, the Administration of Capital Construction, the Oblast Planning Commission, and departments and administrations of the soviet, to transfer to the Orel system of planning from 1975.[77] All funds for the development of housing and amenities were to be concentrated in the Administration of Capital Construction. In Article 3 the city and raiony soviets were instructed to carry out such work, forming control commissions to oversee the move to two-year planning of capital construction. A similar commission was formed at oblast level consisting of a chairman and five members.[78]

But more than a year later, in December 1975, the oblispolkom noted that the Department of Capital Construction of the oblast had not taken enough measures to concentrate housing and cultural services constructed by the Department of Construction and to implement the Orel system of two-year planning.[79] Again, in its decision of 15 March 1976 on the implementation of the Orel system, the oblast noted that the Department of Construction had failed to fulfil its yearly plan for housing construction and amenities. Along with the Oblast Planning Commission, the Department of Capital Construction and the executive committees of the city and raion soviets, it had not carried out enough work to concentrate capital investments under a single client. The oblispolkom commented, 'little attention has been devoted to ensuring the regular commissioning of facilities and their maintenance.'[80] As a result, in 1975, as in the previous year, 42 per cent of the construction was carried out in the fourth quarter and almost 30 per cent in December.[81]

Despite Moscow Oblispolkom's decision of August 1974, a number of city and raion soviets had still by March 1976 failed to form control commissions to check on the implementation of the new system. Thus in its March 1976 decision the oblispolkom sought to tighten up its control procedures. The Department of Construction was instructed to report to the oblispolkom each month on the progress of construction work. Again it urged the necessity of speeding up the formation of the single-client system. In the construction plans for 1977 no buildings were to be constructed by the clients of the ministries.[82] However, Article 9 of the decision laid down that the oblispolkom could only *suggest* to the ministries that they transfer their investments for housing to the Department of Capital Construction. The oblispolkom did not have the right to instruct the ministries to carry out such transfers.[83] Here lies the root of the problem. The soviets still do not have the right to demand that enterprises participate in the single-client system, and they have few sanctions to wield against those enterprises who break contracts.

On 16 July 1981 the oblast executive committee was again noting the slow progress made in assuming the function of single client, and in changing to the Orel system of planning. Once again the agencies involved were all instructed or advised to implement these policies. A further co-ordinating council was formed to see the implementation of such work.[84]

Seven years had passed and very little seemed to have been achieved. The introduction of radically new methods such as these obviously entail a large number of changes in the working methods of large organisations, the uprooting of long-established practices, and the consequent creation of new political relations. The Moscow example illustrates the difficulties of initiating such radical changes across the many branch administrations of the oblast, cities and raiony, and the resistance by ministers and other central officials to changes which may threaten their power bases; for the implementation of the Orel system results in the movement of funds away from the ministries and enterprises and the concentration of them in the oblast, city and raion soviets.

The history of housing legislation over the period 1957–82 illustrates the battle by some central factions to bring more efficiency into the planning and implementation of housing construction and its maintenance. A struggle is being waged to prevent the resources for this area being dispersed throughout the branch administrations. The traditional view that the ministries and their enterprises should control housing and other amenities has been challenged, but the ministries have jealously guarded their control of housing in the fear that such a loss of control would lead to a loss of workers. A promise of housing is still a strong inducement to workers, who in areas of labour shortages are free to choose their place of employment from competing enterprises.

As many Soviet scholars stress, until all housing and municipal facilities are under the direct authority of the soviets, and the staffs and wages of the departments of the soviets are increased, the real masters of the oblasts and the cities are not the soviets nor even the Party, but the *ministries*.

NOTES

1. See Morton 'Housing Problems' and 'The Soviet Quest', and DiMaio, *Soviet Urban Housing*.
2. See in particular Lewis and Sternheimer, *Soviet Urban Management*.
3. See Taubman, *Governing Soviet Cities*, and Cattell, *Leningrad*.
4. Morton, 'Local Soviets'.
5. 1957 Legislation (Housing).
6. 1967 Legislation (Housing).
7. 1971 City Decree.
8. Resolution of the Council of Ministers of the USSR, September 1978, 'O Merakh po Dal'neishemu Uluchsheniyu Ekspluatatsii i Remonta Zhilishchnovo Fonda', *Sobranie Postanovlenii Pravitel'stva SSSR, Otdel Pervyi*, 1978, no. 22, statute 137.
9. 1981 Resolution (Soviets).
10. *Pravda*, 17 August 1981.
11. T. Fetisov, 'Zaboty ne Tol'ko Saratovskie', *Sovety Narodnykh Deputatov,* January 1980, 56–62 (p. 56).
12. G. Melikyants, 'Zhikloi Dom, evo Khozyaistvo', *Izvestia*, 26 June 1976, p. 2; condensed as 'Housing and its Management', *CDSP*, 28, no. 26 (28 July 1976), 31.

13. Sukhomlin, 'Problemy', p. 23.
14. Fetisov, 'Zaboty', p. 56.
15. D. Kolotilkin, 'Effektivnost' Zhilishchnovo Khozyaistva', *Voprosy Ekonomiki,* July 1979, 94–101 (p. 98); translated as 'The Effectiveness of Housing', *Problems of Economics,* 22, no. 7 (November 1979), 37–51 (p. 45).
16. See n. 8.
17. Fetisov, 'Zaboty', p. 56.
18. S. Butusov, 'Zhil'yu Odnovo Khozyaina', *Sovety Narodnykh Deputatov,* March 1982, p. 28.
19. Ibid., p. 29.
20. Ibid., p. 29.
21. Ibid., p. 33.
22. A. Taranuka, 'Pol'za Nalitso', *Sovety Narodnykh Deputatov,* May 1981, 36–40 (p. 37).
23. Ibid., p. 37.
24. Ibid., p. 38.
25. G. Petrov, 'Nazrevshaya Problema', *Sovety Narodnykh Deputatov,* March 1980, 57–61 (p. 57).
26. Ibid., p. 58.
27. Ibid., p. 59.
28. Fetisov, 'Zaboty', p. 57.
29. Ibid., p. 57.
30. Ibid., p. 57.
31. Ibid., p. 58.
32. Ibid., p. 58.
33. Ibid., p. 58.
34. Ibid., p. 58.
35. Ibid., p. 60.
36. Ibid., p. 60.
37. R. Zakirov, 'Kak Upravlyat' Domami?', *Pravda,* 20 November 1977, p. 3; condensed as 'How should Apartment Houses be Managed?', *CDSP,* 29, no. 47 (21 December 1977), 21–2.
38. Ibid., p. 21.
39. Ibid., p. 22.
40. Ibid., pp. 21–2.
41. Decision of 22 February 1977; *Byulleten' Ispolnitel'novo Komiteta Moskovskovo Oblastnovo Soveta Narodnykh Deputatov* (hereafter *Byulleten'*), 1977, no. 7, 1–3.
42. *Byulleten'* (1977), p. 1.
43. *Byulleten'* (1977), p. 1.
44. Decision of 30 December 1977; *Byulleten',* 1978, no. 6, 18–19.
45. 'O Merakh po Dalneishemi Uluchsheniyu, Ekspluatatsii i Remonta Zhilishchnovo Fonda v Oblasti', *Byulleten',* 1979, no. 7, p. 10.
46. 1957 Legislation (Housing).
47. 1971 City Decree.
48. See n. 8.
49. V. Chekanauskas, 'Zametki Arkhitektora Gorod Raduet Cheloveka', *Pravda,* 21 May 1976, p. 3; condensed as 'City Makes People Happy', *CDSP,* 28, no. 20 (16 June 1976), 25.

50. DiMaio, *Soviet Urban Housing*, p. 158.
51. Cattell, *Leningrad*, p. 124.
52. Frolic, 'Decision-making', p. 46.
53. Yu. Tsygankov, 'Geografiya 'Nepreryvki'', *Pravda*, 28 September 1975, p. 2; condensed as 'Geography of the "Continuous-Planning System"', *CDSP*, 27, no. 39 (22 October 1975), 6–7 (p. 6).
54. Yu. A. Laptev and B.P. Malyshev, 'Vzaimodeistvie Mezhdu Gorispolkomami i Nepodvedomstvennymi im Predpriyatiyami i Organizatsiyami pri Sozdanii Sotsial'noi Infrastruktury Goroda', in *Sistema Organov*, ed. Lebedev, pp. 68–80 (p. 73 (n. 12).
55. Avak'yan, *Gorodskoi Sovet*, p. 60.
56. Ibid., p. 60.
57. Yu. Makarov, 'Gorplan: Puti Sovershenstvovaniya', *Sovety Narodnykh Deputatov*, August 1980, 88–92 (p. 92).
58. M. Gerashchenko and V. Tsingalenok, 'Kam Stroim Goroda', *Pravda*, 3 March 1974, p. 2; condensed as 'How We Build Cities', *CDSP*, 26, no. 9 (27 March 1974), 27–8 (p. 28).
59. Laptev and Malyshev, 'Vzaimodeistvie', p. 72.
60. Ibid., p. 70 (n. 7).
61. Ibid., p. 75.
62. Yu. Melikhov, 'Gorod Smotrit v Zavtra', *Izvestia*, 5 September 1975, p. 3; condensed as 'City Looks to Tommorow', *CDSP*, 27, no. 36 (1 October 1975), 24–5 (p. 25).
63. V. Brovkin and V. Ermolaeev, V. 'Vstrechaya Novoselov', *Pravda*, 29 May 1978, p. 3; condensed as 'Greeting New Setters', *CDSP*, 30, no. 22 (28 June 1978), p. 11.
64. Resolution of the Central Committee of the CPSU, 13 August 1974, 'Ob Opyte Raboty Orlovskovo Obkoma KPSS po Organizatsii Ritmichnovo Vvoda v Ekspluatatsiyu Zhilishchno-Grazhdanskikh Obektov v g. Orle', in *KPSS v Resolyutsiyakh*, XI, 1972–5 (1978), 431–3.
65. 'Ob Opyte Raboty', p. 432.
66. Ibid., p. 432.
67. Tsygankov, 'Geography', p. 6.
68. Bocharov and Lyubovny, 'A City is a Single Complex', p. 8.
69. Stepanenko, *Goroda*, p. 277.
70. Yu. Tsygankov, 'Novyi Etap "Nepreryvki"', *Pravda*, 2 August 1976, p. 2; condensed as 'New Stage of the "Continuous-Planning" System', *CDSP*, 28, no. 31 (1 September 1976), 15–16 (p. 16).
71. Stepanenko, *Goroda*, p. 227.
72. M. Mironov, 'Orlovskaya "Nepreryvka" Nabiraet Silu', *Ekonomicheskaya Gazeta*, 24 March 1975, p. 9; condensed as 'The Orel "Continuous-Planning System" Gathers Momentum', *CDSP*, 27, no. 15 (7 May 1975), 8–9 (p. 8).
73. Ibid., p. 8.
74. Ibid., p. 8.
75. Ibid., p. 9.
76. Ibid., p. 9.
77. 'O Perekhodye na Neperyvnoe Planirovanie i Potochnoe Stroitel'stvo Obektov Zhilishchnovo i Kul'turno-Bytovovo Naznacheniya', 12 August 1974, *Byulleten'*, 1975, no. 23, 9.

78. *Byulleten'* (1974), p. 2.
79. 'O Povyshenii Kachestva Zhilishchnovo i Kul'turno-Bytovovo Stroitel'stva Inzhenernovo Oborudovaniya i Blagoustroistva v Gorodakh i Selakh Oblasti', *Byulleten'*, 1975, no. 23, 9.
80. 'Ob Obespechnenii Ritmichnovo Vvoda Zhil'ya i Kul'turno-Bytovykh Obektov v Komplekse s Blagoustroistvom i Ozleniem i O Bolee Shirokom i Effektivnom Vnedronii Orlovskovo Metoda Potochnovo Stroitel'stva i Nepreryvnovo Planirovaniya', *Byulleten'* (1976), no. 10, 1.
81. *Byulleten'* (1976), p. 1.
82. *Byulleten'* (1976), p. 4.
83. *Byulleten'* (1976), p. 4.
84. *Byulleten'* (1981), no. 15, 25.

6

Problems of Implementation and Control in Soviet Local Government

For a number of years the deeds and actions of party and government bodies trailed behind the needs of the times and of life — not only because of objective factors, but also for reasons of a subjective order . . . The inertness and stiffness of the forms and methods of administration, the decline of dynamism in our work, and an escalation of bureaucracy — all this was doing no small damage. Signs of stagnation had begun to surface in the life of society.

The situation called for change, but a peculiar psychology — how to improve things without changing anything — took the upper hand in central bodies and, for that matter, at local level as well. (Gorbachev's speech to the 27th Congress of the CPSU, 25 February 1986).[1]

INTRODUCTION

The previous chapters have outlined the problems the Soviet leadership faces in trying to co-ordinate branch and territorial planning and to introduce comprehensive planning in the cities and oblasts. At the beginning of the 1980s the Soviet Union still faced the problem of a fragmented administrative structure and the dispersal of its economic resources through tens of ministries and thousands of enterprises.

Undoubtedly the principles of 'democratic centralism' and 'dual subordination' have been used by the central leadership to support the development of a centralist ethos within the various bureaucracies of the Party and state. Our study of the budget and planning processes has underlined the excess of centralisation within these bodies. However, our research has also shown the inability of both Party and state agencies at the centre to co-ordinate the implementation of central policies in the oblasts and cities and to cut across the autonomy of the various ministries in order to integrate policy implementation.

In order to appreciate the underlying administrative problems which have led to this situation, it is necessary to take a closer look at the Soviet bureaucratic system and the work of officials in implementation and control.

In this chapter I shall outline the basic theories of classical and modern sociologists of bureaucracy with particular regard to the study of implementation and control. Then I shall move on to an assessment of Soviet bureaucracy in the light of these theories, to a case study of Moscow Oblast Executive Committee, and finally to a discussion of implementation and control in local soviets throughout the Soviet Union. My aims will be to show: (1) that the Soviet leadership faces serious problems in implementing its policies in the localities and controlling the work of subordinate agencies; and (2) that such problems are not primarily the result of the active participation of 'interest' or 'bureaucratic' groups at the local level, but rather are more often related to bureaucratic defects, problems of processing and co-ordinating information and other *universal* bureaucratic distortions, which are *magnified* in the Soviet setting. Taking account of the conclusions we reached in earlier chapters on the budget, planning and housing, and evidence about control work outlined in this chapter, I shall stress both the centre's concern with improving control work and the failure of the central leadership to enforce many of its policies in the localities.

CLASSICAL AND MODERN THEORIES OF BUREAUCRACY

Max Weber's pioneering study of bureaucracy emphasised its positive and rational aspects; more recent theorists have stressed its dysfunctional and negative tendencies. Modern sociologists have disagreed with the Weberian view of the local bureaucrat as a passive implementer of orders, and of bureaucracy as a purely rational, machine-like system, with bureaucrats themselves expressing no normative or culturally-conditioned views. For Weber, the bureaucrat 'is only a simple cog in an ever-moving mechanism which prescribes to him an essentially fixed route of march'.[2] However Albrow emphasises, 'The official has characteristics as a social being beyond those which the administrative code specifies. Like other men he has interests, prejudices and fears. He forms friendships and cliques'.[3] Merton points to the dysfunctional aspects of Weber's theory of bureaucracy, with its strict observance of rules, whereby service to clients takes second place to the observation of administration procedures.[4]

Other theorists such as Downs,[5] Sleznick,[6] Crozier[7] and more recently Dunsire[8] and Pressman and Wildavsky,[9] have stressed the ability of bureaucrats to change and mould policies as they pass down through the administrations from idea to reality. Thus Dunsire writes:

> Government . . . may devise a policy to solve a problem, meaning that they envisage an output from governmental agencies which, if produced, would in their estimation solve it: but it is a common experience that the output actually produced is not that which was envisaged. Either no output is produced at all (the policy intentions never reach the point of being transformed into action upon the environment), or else an output different in quantity, quality or direction from that intended is produced.[10]

Scholars have argued that there are two principal factors which contribute to these dysfunctional aspects:

(1) motivational — the conscious moulding or manipulating of central policies to meet the interests of the bureaucrats.
(2) structural — implementation problems will exist because of the complexity of modern bureaucratic structures. Bureaucratic dysfunctions and difficulties of control and co-ordination will be present regardless of the motivational factors and the self-interests of the bureaucrats.

Downs stresses the 'motivational aspect' but also recognises the importance of structural problems. Thus in his classic book *Inside Bureaucracy*, he stresses that there are two types of distortion inevitable in any bureaucracy. The first is the 'winnowing process', the screening and witholding of information by officials during the upward transmission of information. The second, the 'leakage of authority' which takes place in the downward passing of orders. Downs writes, 'whenever rational officials have the power to make the choices they will use that power to achieve their own goals'. Each official will have a different goal depending on 'the four basic causes of conflict in bureaus', which are, 'differential self-interest, differential modes of perceiving reality, differential information and uncertainty'. Thus:

> because individual officials have varying goals, and each uses his discretion in translating orders from above into commands going downward, the purpose the superior had in mind will not be the precise ones his subordinate's orders convey to people further

down the hierarchy. The resulting diversion constitutes a leakage of authority.[11]

Downs also contends that the very transmission of orders involves an act of translation and interpretation. Commands must be made intelligible to the various officials at different levels of the administration and this will normally mean they have to be 'expanded', and at the same time made more 'specific', as they pass towards the implementation point.[12] Dunsire, following this line, adds that officials within each area of an administration have their own '"universe of discourse", sphere of interests, concepts, working vocabulary and style of going about things'.[13] He adds:

> The nature of the 'interpretation' is illumined by the appreciation that each office in a bureaucracy, although subordinate in rank, is to be seen as possessing a degree of autonomy. The officeholder inhabits a niche that does not exist anywhere else in the organisation. The office is the collecting centre and storage point for information about the area of task at that level.[14]

Downs concludes, 'the result is that the policies of any organisation are defined at all levels, not just the top'.[15] However it is important to stress, as Downs himself does, that authority leakage is not necessarily the result of self-interest on the part of the officials, but rather is, in Hammer's words, 'a cumulative misunderstanding of what the regime intended'.[16]

Similarly, Selznick and Crozier look to the interests of the bureaucrats to explain distortions of policies during implementation.

Selznick also regards goal variance as an essential attribute of officialdom but he develops this further into the concept of 'goal displacement',[17] whereby departments and sub-groups promote their own interests to the detriment of central policies. The complexity of organisations makes delegation of responsibility inevitable, but as sub-departments grow they begin to promote their own sub-goals. 'In this way subgoals from simple means become ends in themselves'.[18] Similarly Crozier, in his study of two French government agencies, shows how highly cohesive occupational groups can manipulate the rules of a bureaucracy to suit themselves.[19] Mouzelis outlines Crozier's theory thus:

> The strategy consists in the manipulation of rules as means of

enhancing group prerogatives and independence from every direct and arbitrary interference from those higher up. But as rules can never regulate everything and eliminate all arbitrariness, areas of uncertainty always emerge . . . In such cases the group which, by its position in the occupational structure can control the unregulated area, has a great strategic advantage which is naturally used in order to improve its power position . . .[20]

Pressmen, Wildavsky and Michael Hill, on the other hand, stress structural problems. Thus Pressman and Wildavsky draw our attention to the arithmetic of implementation and the mechanics of the decision-making process. They note that policies may fail to be implemented even when all the major political groups support them. The sheer number of decisions to be taken and agreements reached may contribute to delays and distortions. Thus they write:

The reader should be conscious of the steps required to accomplish each link in the chain. Who had to act to begin implementation? Whose consent was required to continue it? How many participants were involved? How long did they take to act? Each time an agreement has to be registered for the programme to continue we call a decision point. Each instance in which a separate participant is required to give his consent we call a clearance.[21]

The greater the number of decision points and clearances within a bureaucracy, the greater the likelihood of distortion taking place.

Micheal Hill, in his study of local government in Britain, also notes the importance of structural factors and identifies a number of different centre-periphery relations depending on the structural make-up of the bureaucracy. Thus he observes:

The simplest model is clearly that in which the centre and the periphery belong to the same organisation. The most complex occurs when policy information depends upon co-operation between separate autonomous organisations, and particularly where responsibility at the periphery is (a) delegated to several organisations with separate territories and (b) depends upon co-ordinated actions between two or more organs.[22]

Unlike Downs, whose theory was designed for a single

hierarchical organisation, Pressman and Wildavsky, as well as Michael Hill, provide us with a 'multi-organizational' approach. Thus, as Dunsire notes, writers such as Downs:

> spoke of 'distortion' and the 'leakage of authority', but they assumed that the chief at the top did have the authority to command . . . In the multi-organisational context, in contrast, actions cannot be commanded. There is no hierarchy of officials in a single line of command who can be directed toward a set of predetermined objectives . . . Into the activity of interpretation . . . there is injected a new element, a decision about whether or not to comply or co-operate with what are, effectively, the wishes of someone in another organisation — someone else's boss, with other interests, other political supports, other constraints on resources.[23]

Hill gives two models of policy-making with particular reference to the implementation process. The first he calls the 'top-down' model, which is based on the assumptions that (1) 'policy-making and administration can be neatly separated'. Policy made at the top can be implemented without any problems 'about a dynamic implementation-policy interaction' and the implementers are 'in no sense concerned with policy making'. (2) There are 'explicit policy goals so that the implementation process can be interpreted in terms of success or failure in the achievement of these goals'.[24]

Hill stresses that the top-down model presents an unrealistic picture of the implementation process as seen from the bottom. There local officials will have to respond to situations in which there are 'unclear' or 'unrealistic' policy inputs from the top. Thus, he stresses:

> The process of policy making is a complex one in which a multiplicity of actors are seeking to influence the final outcome, the policy. The process involves making of compromises and deals so that the eventual policy may not be satisfactory to any single 'party'. Moreover, it will be likely to be a complicated and ambiguous phenomenon, open to multiple interpretation and specifying more than one policy goal. At worst contained within what we may regard as a single policy may be conflicting goals.[25]

A further problem for the top-down model is the difficulty of evaluating the failure or success of a policy by the simple judgement that it has or has not been implemented. For Hill, 'Most success is only partial, and most failure is not total.' Rather what happens during the implementation process is that delays occur, objectives are modified, some parts of policies receive more emphasis than others.[26]

All these ambiguities about the nature of policy lead Hill to suggest a 'second complentary perspective':

> This alternative view of the implementation process takes what is done as central, and sees policies as attempts to influence that process . . . A great deal of government activity occurs without any clear view of what policy is.[27]

This second picture:

> recognizes the variety of public (and private) sector agencies, all of which adhere to differing administrative procedures, differing rules, reflect conflicting interests, etc. The objectives of policy therefore become lost (or become muddy) and the only clear empirical observations are about what in practice happens. Implementation is in this sense the operation of development control, the management of the housing stock, the delivery of health services, . . . with the focus of study being upon what may be presumed to be the purposive action at the bottom end.[28]

For Hill, development control:

> thus is not seen as the implementation of structure and local planning policies but rather as coping with a range of day to day problems. In consequence local environmental policy evolves from practice rather than vice-versa.[29]

Hill's criticisms of the top-down model are particularly useful for our study of Soviet bureaucracy. As we shall stress in our case-study of Moscow Oblast, structural problems have led to cases of ambiguity and confusion on the part of local-level bureaucrats as to the precise nature of their work. Decision-making within the executive committees and their departments varies from area to area and there are many unregulated procedures related to the collation of information and implementation of local decisions. The role of the local Party and state official must in many instances involve dealing with problems where there are no clear policies, or, as we noted in Chapter 1, where conflicting instructions may be handed down from above.

In essence any bureaucracy consists of actors, organisations and policies, all of which are set in a social and political environment. Each of these variables will condition the implementation process and will vary from country to country. An important theoretical study of the implementation process by Van Meter and Van Horn postulates seven variables that are crucial for the understanding of implementation in any society:

1. *The nature of the policy to be carried out, according to*
   (i) The amount of change involved
   (ii) The degree of consensus upon its goals present among actors
2. *The standards by which performance is to be measured*
3. *The resources and incentives made available*
4. *The quality of inter-organisational communication and control*
5. *The characteristics of the implementing agencies, according to*
   (i) Size and competence of staff
   (ii) Degree of hierarchical control
   (iii) Amount of political support available
   (iv) The vitality of the organisation
   (v) Openess of internal communications
   (vi) Kind of linkages with policy-making body
6. *The economic, social and political conditions*
7. *The disposition of the implementors made up of*
   (i) The cognition (comprehension, understanding of the policy)
   (ii) The direction of their response (accept, neutral, reject)
   (iii) The intensity of their response.[30]

Webb and Wistow postulate that:

Policy implementation encompasses at least three major tasks: the *explication* of policy intentions and the *communication* of policy intentions or sub-goals to relevant 'actors' (individuals, organisational sub-units . . .); obtaining the *compliance* of these actors; and *securing* an environment conducive to implementation (e.g.

ensuring that actors have appropriate material resources and authority to act and that different actors are related to one another by appropriate organisational structures and processes).[31]

With regard to compliance, Webb and Wistrow use the classic study of Etzoni, who drew attention to three approaches: (1) the offering of incentives; (2) the application of sanctions for non-compliance; (3) the moulding of the normative structure within which people operate.[32]

We shall turn in the next section to an assessment of Soviet bureaucracy and the implementation process in the light of the above discussion.

THE NATURE OF SOVIET BUREAUCRACY

In this section I shall outline the distinctive features of Soviet bureaucracy and the major factors which contribute to implementation problems at the local levels.

(1) Unlike Western nations, the Soviet Union has not one bureaucracy but three, those of the Party, soviets and ministries. Thus many of the ailments that we have seen in the administrations of the West will be magnified, and there will be the additional problem of achieving co-ordination between these three bodies. This we saw clearly in our discussion of branch and territorial planning. Problems of translation and interpretation will also be greater as instructions pass from Party to soviet or ministry as well as from top to bottom. Our discussion of Party-state relations has shown the problems of 'role ambiguity' and 'role conflict' for Party and state officials. The Party must lead and guide but not supplant the state bureaucracy; but in practice, as we have seen, Party leadership may range from guidance to 'petty tutelage'.

The different bureaucracies, as well as having their own internal implementation problems, will also suffer from the problem of 'multiple commands' or even conflicting instructions, leading to a state of confusion among such officials as to what constitutes a priority at any one time. As, we have seen, the timing of the planning and budget processes differ, leading to problems of co-ordination in these areas.

The structural problems outlined above are further exaggerated by the sheer size of the Soviet Union, with its 50,000 different administrative units divided amongst Union, Republic, okrug, oblast, krai, city, raion, settlement and rural soviets. Pressman's and Wildavsky's arithmetic is pertinent here; with such a large number of decision points and clearances neded, implementation will be a problem regardless of the motivational aspects of discretion. Similarly, Dunsire's remarks about multi-organisational bureaucracies are important, as policies must cut across the three bureaucracies. Selznick's concept of goal displacement can readily be seen in the 'self-sufficient economies' of ministries and enterprises and their ability to divert central funds away from the primary objectives into building up sub-sectors of these bodies. Thus the Ministry of Food of the Ukranian Republic had a faster rate of growth in these subsidiary concerns (i.e. housing construction, production of materials for infrastructure) than its primary function of food production. Similarly, the Ministry of Construction of the Ukraine produces less than one-third of construction materials in the Republic, the rest being produced by other ministries not primarily engaged in such tasks[33] (see Chapter 4). Thus the *explication* and *communication* of policies in the Soviet setting poses a large number of problems involving difficulties of translation and interpretation within the various adminstrations of Soviet society.

The criteria by which officials should be selected for promotion within the ministerial and soviet bureaucracies is also a major problem. Inefficient personnel will often be promoted because of political patronage or political considerations. Although the Party has introduced a large number of specialists into its ranks, the classic problem of 'red or expert' remains a dilemma for the leadership. A related problem which we shall note in the next section is the difficulty of dismissing an official for incompetence. Brezhnev's policy of 'stability of cadres' has led to a situation where serious mistakes are left unheeded and incompetence tolerated; thus political expediency has had to be bought with bureaucratic inefficiency.

(2) Problems of implementation are likely to be much greater in the Soviet Union because of the closed and secretive nature of the decision-making process, the absence of a 'free press' and the inability of interest groups to campaign openly for certain policies. Because of greater problems in making themselves heard at the input side, Soviet bureaucrats are more likely to turn their attention to the output side, the implementation process. The Soviet bureaucrat is also much more likely to have stronger ties with his bureaucracy than are officials in the West. He receives not only his salary from the administration, but a whole range of other necessities of life. Thus his accommodation, medical facilities, kindergarten and

education provision, as well as food supply, recreation and holidays will all be provided by his administration. As Smith states, 'there is thus a fusion of institutional and individual interests not found in the West'.[34] This is liable to make the Soviet bureaucrat a fierce opponent of any change in administrative procedures that would threaten his access to such privileges or distribute responsibility from one department to another. We have seen the difficulties faced by the central leadership over the implementation of the 'Orel system of planning', the introduction of zakazchik rights and the policy of transferring houses to the jurisdication of the local soviets.

(3) The problems of evaluation and control are also liable to be greater in the Soviet setting because of the fact that it is a non-market society. Both Downs and Rigby have noted the important point that, unlike commercial organisations, bureaucracies work in a non-market environment, and the problem is magnified in the Soviet Union by the fact that the social and political system is itself non-market. As Hammer notes, in a society where the regime is the central decision-maker, and where it must choose between competing programmes put forward by various bureaucracies:

> the underlying question is . . . How much are the bureaucracy's services actually worth? . . . When the factors are produced in a market economy, it is possible to develop at least an approximate idea of the actual cost of operating a bureaucracy. In the Soviet Union, the factors are not purchased at competitive prices but are themselves allocated among the bureaucracies by a non-market process.[35]

The setting of norms and targets, of yearly and five-year plans is fraught with difficulties for the central leadership. The inability to evaluate the performance of many different administrations and enterprises has led to a state of affairs where plans are set either too high or too low. We have noted formalism in reports of plan fulfilment, false reporting by finance officials of local conditions, the hiding and hoarding of resources and the inflexible role of central officials over the fixing of norms to meet local conditions. This means that information feedback will be very poor and the leadership will be unaware of the true state of affairs in any one locality, as information is distorted on its way upward. Hammer states this problem eloquently:

> Every regime must be concerned about authority leakage and will

develop tools to cope with the problem. But, in practice, these tools will often be themselves bureaucratic techniques and not totally effective. The regime will seek to obtain clear and accurate information about bureaucratic performance, but it can never be sure that the information is totally reliable. Inevitably, the regime will, to some extent, be dependent on the bureaucracy itself for information about bureaucratic performance and the accomplishment of the regime's goals . . . a Soviet bureaucracy, like its counterpart in the West, will seek to maximise the resources that are made available to it . . . The problem for the regime is to get access to independent information so that it is not totally dependent on the bureaucracy for data about performance.[36]

City and oblast soviets are almost totally dependent on the ministries and enterprises for information about industrial developments in their territories. Often the enterprises will not divulge details about their development plans (see Chapter 4).

Within the Soviet Union the Party, possessing as it does its own information supply, is to some extent an effective counterbalance. But even the Party must rely on the enterprises and other state organs for information. As we shall show, the existence of both Party and state control bodies leads to even greater confusion and further problems in co-ordinating control activities.

(4) *Compliance* is also a problem for the Soviet leadership. We have already noted the lack of local incentives, the poor wage structure in the departments of finance and planning, the shortages of staff — all of which lead to poor adminsitrative performance. Similarly, we have already noted the unwillingness to use sanctions. In the next section we shall note the inability of leaders of executive committees to implement their policies, as a result of the absence in Soviet administrations of both incentives and strict sanctions. This has led to a lack of morale within these bodies, which neither ideological appeals nor political persuasion from the Party can counter. We have seen the inability of the soviets to force enterprises to comply with contracts over the pooling of funds because of the absence of economic sanctions.

So far it would appear that all seven of Van Meter's and Van Horn's variables have negative connotations when applied to the Soviet Union. However, this is far from the case, for the negative features noted above are at least partly offset by more positive features not to be found in the West.

(1) The Soviet administrations are dominated by a single,

hierarchical organisation — the Party, which plays the key role in the selection, placement and control of all officials. The formulation and often the implementation of policies are carried out directly by the Party. This means that the formation of interest groups, as we know them in the West, is impossible in the Soviet Union. To a large degree it limits the articulation and promotion of the interests of bureaucrats to their own particular bureaucracies; hence the term 'bureaucratic groups' as put forward by Hough and others.[37]

(2) Soviet officials must work under an ideology and political culture which promotes a centralised political ethos. Marxism-Leninism, democratic centralism and dual subordination all give support to the formation of strong vertical ties within each administration, and, as we have seen, to poor horizontal and local ones. Thus officials within the Soviet administrations will find it much more difficult to call for a decentralisation of decision-making or reallocation of responsibilities within their bureaucracies. Officials from different departments will find it difficult to group together to promote local interests or the interests of their professions and there is only one trade union movement which is itself dominated by the Party. While undoubtedly cases are known where officials were able to achieve success by campaigning together at different levels (Khrushchev's Education Reform, for example), their ability to do so is much more restricted than in the West. In many ways the Soviet official is much more isolated and cut off from potential allies than his Western counterpart, who can campaign in the open and through his own trade union.

(3) In the age of the 'Scientific and Technological Revolution' the central leadership has paid increasing attention to the 'Scientific Organisation of Labour' and the 'Scientific Organisation of Management'. In June 1970 Brezhnev noted that the science of victory in building socialism is in essence the science of management.[38] While Khrushchev stressed a philosophy of 'the withering away of the state' and encouraged citizen participation in administration, Brezhnev sought to strengthen the state apparatus. Thus new and better techniques for controlling the implementation of policies have been experimented with. In his speech, to the 27th Party Congress, Gorbachev called for, 'Heightening the efficacy of centralized guidance of the economy, strengthening the role of the centre in implementing the main goals of the party's economic strategy and in determining the rates and properties of national economic growth'.[39] The growing complexity of society has called for improved analytical methods of administration. In the 1970s the

'systems approach' to management gained popularity. Cocks writes, 'The distinguishing feature of the systems approach is that it insists upon taking an integrated and total view of a problem rather than a fragmented and piecemeal approach'.[40] D. Gvishiani, a high Soviet official, notes of system analysis:

> What interests us . . . is the basic conclusions as to the need for a complex, all-round approach to management and the disclosure of its integrative function . . . This approach makes it possible to see the whole managed system as a complex set of interrelated elements, united by a common aim, to reveal the integral properties of the system, its internal and external links.[41]

The systems approach was given added impetus after the December 1973 Central Committee plenum in which Brezhnev spoke out against departmental pluralism and parochialism. The systems approach can be seen as a counter-measure to the fragmentation of the economic and administrative system that I outlined earlier. Volkov observes that:

> In the course of the NTR [the Scientific and Technological Revolution] technocratic and bureaucratic tendencies can arise . . . their neutralization should not be regarded as an easy or almost automatic matter . . . the more the impact of the NTR is felt in the sphere of management, the stronger and more effective must be the party and public control which ensures removal in good time of possible elements of the bureaucratic approach to social life.[42]

With reference to East European regimes, Cocks also stresses the importance of the systems approach as a counter-measure to bureaucratic interests:

> Through application of the systems approach the regimes seek to restore a sense of purpose and cohesion to government, to refocus and assert the general interest, and to reorient officialdom to new missions and roles. In contrast to the prevailing system of branch and departmental planning and management, a more 'programmed-goals approach' (programmno-tselevoi podkhod) is considered a more suitable means for promoting 'management by objectives' and 'control by results'. Such an approach, above all, facilitates the mobilization of commitment and discipline required to implement policy.[43]

As we have seen, a new stress has been given to 'corporate planning' and to solving inter-branch problems. Here Cocks notes:

> The concept of programming provides a device for integrating and ensuring the fiscal, technical, and human resources that are required to implement major interbranch projects. It facilitates emphasis on a more function-orientated and less department-oriented structure of planning as well as focus on outputs and results as opposed to inputs and items of expenditure accounting.[44]

Finally, we should note the development of computer technology in Soviet administrations. Gvishiani contends:

> Of major importance in present-day conditions is comprehensive technical re-equipment, specifically the overall mechanization and automation of the process of obtaining, storing, processing and using different types of information . . . Here a special part is played by automated and computerized management systems . . . creating a basis for a genuinely scientific approach to solving management problems.[45]

These new developments in the 'Scientific Management of Administration' must be seen as an important counterbalance to the fragmentation of the economic system as outlined in earlier chapters. The central leadership is involved in a struggle against bureaucratic dysfunctions and bureaucratic groups and is seeking to re-assert national priorities and policies over parochial interests. However, it is the conclusions of this study that such moves towards greater control over the bureaucracies have largely failed. The reason for this is that the three positive factors noted above are not enough to offset completely the negative ones mentioned earlier and because the Party itself suffers from bureaucratic problems.

IMPLEMENTATION AND CONTROL IN MOSCOW OBLAST EXECUTIVE COMMITTEE

How does the Soviet Union cope with the problems outlined in the previous section? Earlier theories of Soviet society, such as those of 'Totalitarianism' and 'the Administered Society', have stressed the ability of the central authorities, and particularly the Party, to control all aspects of the economy. However, a study of Moscow Oblast Executive Committee in its attempt to control the work of its own departments and those of lower soviets reveals a number of serious shortcomings in the areas of control.

First we shall examine the process of control and implementation within the oblispolkom before examining its relations with cities and raiony under its jurisdiction.

In 1973 the *Bulletin* of Moscow Executive Committee outlined a series of measures aimed at overcoming a number of shortcomings in control work.[46] All documents entering the apparat of the executive were to be automatically placed under 'control'; previously, only those specifically directed by the chairman and deputy chairman had been so placed. It had become increasingly apparent that the procedures for the processing and implementation of policies within the apparat were inefficient and clumsy. Although a complex set of procedures had been drawn up as early as 1960 there were still problems over defining the roles of the many departments and groups engaged in control. Problems of parallelism and duplication of functions and a lack of co-ordination between the various bodies dealing with control were widespread.[47] Badly staffed departments had to deal with an ever-increasing number of documents.

Each year 60,000 to 64,000 documents (which include 1,000 to 1,200 resolutions of Party and government) arrive at the offices of Moscow Oblast Ispolkom. Each year, moreover, the ispolkom passes between 1,200 and 1,400 decisions, of which on average 400 are under continuous control.[48]

The Presidium of Moscow Oblast Executive Committee plays a major role in the checking and verification of the implementation of decisions. Deputies of the soviet and lower soviets, heads of departments and other leading officials are often called before it to discuss problems of implementation and report on their work in executing the oblasts' decisions. Thus throughout 1972 and the first half of 1973 the Presidium adopted 33 decisions with regard to control.[49]

However, although a 'Public Inspectorate' of Control, headed by the former secretary of the oblispolkom, N.E. Petukhov, had been created to see to the smooth operation of control work, there were still serious problems. Thus a 1973 *Bulletin* report notes the widespread occurrence of decisions being taken within the administration of the oblispolkom without any real possibility of their being carried out. Many decisions were passed without those responsible for their implementation being named, and in others no date was stipulated by which they should be fulfilled.[50] In 1972 the oblispolkom passed a decision[51] which noted that 'often the preparation of decisions for the implementation of resolutions of higher organs was "dragged out", infringing the established dates for their fulfilment'. Thus in December 1972 it was noted that resolutions received by the oblispolkom in March, April and May of that year had still not been implemented. Often decisions drawn up by the departments and administrations had to be reworked because of poor preparation. And the decision noted, 'Several heads of departments and administrations had allowed elements of indiscipline in their work'.[52] By November 1973, of 410 decisions under control, 21 decisions had not been implemented although the dates for their completion had passed.[43]

In 1978 the oblispolkom, still alarmed by the difficulties over ensuring control within its apparat, decided to form a 'Group of Control'.

The *Bulletin* not only outlines the considerable problems of control within Moscow Oblast apparat, but gives a good deal of information with regard to the oblispolkom's inability to control decision-making within the executive committees of the cities and raiony of its territory.

Thus in its decision of 18 September 1975 on 'The Work of Domodedovo City Soviet in Organising Control and Checking the Execution of Resolutions of Higher Organs and their own Decisions',[54] Moscow Oblispolkom noted:

(1) Decisions were passed primarily on current problems, with little account of the long-term development of the city.
(2) Instead of implementing urgent policies, the city executive spent its time passing new decisions.
(3) The implementation of many decisions was 'dragged out', and many others were not even placed under the control of the executive.
(4) Fifty per cent of those decisions which are placed under control are still implemented late.
(5) Decisions of the city soviet are not 'concrete' and do not reflect an understanding of the factual state of affairs in the localities. They are often passed without giving dates by which they must be executed and naming the officials responsible.
(6) There is still no card index system for registering documents within the apparat of the city executive committee.

A similar decision regarding Bidnov City Soviet was passed on 22 August 1978. Here the oblispolkom noted:

(1) Of 79 decisions which had undergone control in the past one and a half years, 28 or 35.4 per cent had not been implemented on time; of 2,397 official documents taken under control over the last year, 883 (36.8 per cent) were implemented late; and in the first six months of 1978, each fifth document suffered a similar fate.
(2) Again the decisions of the city were not concrete, failed to name responsible officials, and instead of implementing urgent decisions the Soviet passed repeats of earlier decisions. Thus from 1972 to 1978 the ispolkom passed nine decisions on questions related to the work of cultural institutions, but the situation had not improved.[55]

This emphasises the degree of tolerance that members of the executive committees have of poor work by subordinate enterprises and departments, the absence of effective disciplinary measures and ultimately the lack of control.

A similar situation is to be found in the Department of Capital Construction of Moscow Oblast. Thus the oblast in its decision of 28 August 1974 noted a number of faults in the administration, stressing: (1) the absence in the administration of a clear system of control, the infrequency of checks on the implementation of higher decisions and the resulting delays in fulfilment of decisions; (2) a 'liberal attitude' to infringements of state and labour discipline.[56]

Not only do these examples show the poor state of implementation and control within the cities of Moscow Oblast but they reveal the inability of the oblast to bring about an improvement in their activites. The problems which are revealed are fairly similar from one example to another, yet throughout the period these same problems are revealed time and time again by various ispolkomy. Part of the job of the *Bulletin* is to show by these examples what are the most pressing problems and what should be done to remedy them, but in this area it appears that none of the subordinate bodies have been paying much attention to the oblast, and as a result the same problems were still widespread in 1981.

It is informative to look at the measures outlined by Moscow Oblispolkom with regard to improving control within the apparat of Balashikha City Executive Committee and its administrations. By its decision of 3 September 1981 the oblispolkom decided:

(1) To draw to the attention of the city soviet and its chairman the

serious shortcomings in the organisation of control over the implementation of resolutions of higher organs and its own decisions.
(2) To oblige the city soviet to remove the above shortcomings in the organisation of control in the departments of the city and in lower soviets.
(3) Systematically to examine questions of control in the sessions of the gorispolkom. To give in these sessions a 'fundamental assessment of the presence of indiscipline, formalism and red-tape'.
(4) Within a month to work out a clear system of control within the apparat of the gorispolkom.
(5) To oblige Balashikha City Soviet to report to Moscow Oblast about the implementation of this decision by 1 February 1982.[57]

There is no mention here of the dismissal of officials or even the imposing of fines or other administrative sanctions, nor are there precise statements as to what measures the city soviet should take to solve its problems. The oblast can only give general guidelines; it has no time to deal with such problems in more depth, and thus its own ability to control subordinate agencies is restricted.

IMPLEMENTATION AND CONTROL IN THE SOVIET UNION — LOCAL SOVIETS IN GENERAL

We have already seen that the problem of control with regard to the work of the Party is not new to the Soviet Union. Similarly, problems within the state bodies have been rife throughout our period, as can be seen in the many references to control in the statements of the Party congresses (see the quotation by Gorbachev at the beginning of this chapter). Thus the 23rd Party Congress in 1966 noted, 'The Congress attributes great significance to the correct organisation of control and verification of the implementation of Party and Government decisions.[58]

In 1967 an *Izvestia* editorial spoke out against 'irresponsibility', 'windbaggery' and 'indifference', emphasising that 'the Communist Party has waged and is continuing to wage an implacable struggle against manifestations of bureaucratism, which is profoundly alien to the basic nature of the Soviet apparatus, against red tape and an excessive devotion to petty formalities'.[59] The Resolution of 1971 on raion and city soviets which was adopted by the Central Committee once again raised the subject, remarking:

> In the practice of raion and city soviets one still comes across elements of formalism; the work of a soviet is frequently evaluated by the number of various types of measures, meetings and conferences, rather than by results achieved in the economic, social and cultural fields. Many soviets exercise insufficient control over the observance of legislation, are not conducting a proper struggle with violations of state discipline, and are doing a poor job of raising the responsibility of officials for the duties entrusted to them.[60]

More recently, at the 25th Party Congress in 1976, Brezhnev noted that the Politburo and Secretariat had 'devoted far more attention than in the past to control over the verification of the fulfillment of adopted decisions';[61] and in 1980 Hoffmann wrote:

> The policy-making procedures of the Brezhnev administration are proving to be less successful than anticipated. That is, the power of the present Politburo and Central Committee to make decisions is greater than their power to implement those decisions, and this gap appears to be widening.[62]

The 1967 *Izvestia* editorial was rather optimistic when it remarked that 'the past few years have infused the activity of the soviets and administrative agencies with a fresh spirit'.[63] In 1981, 14 years later, two resolutions were passed by central bodies noting the poor quality of control work within the ministries and executive committees.

Thus in its resolution of 14 April 1981 on 'Measures for Improving Control-Revision Work in the Ministeries and Departments and Other Organs of Administration', the Council of Ministers of the USSR admitted 'that in carrying out control work over finance and economic activities, associations, enterprises, organizations and institutions continue to exhibit serious shortcomings'.[64] Control was often carried out superficially and was 'formal' in character. Within the ministries and departments the work of organising control was not co-ordinated, allowing for 'parallelism and duplication'. The resolution called for the creation of a special 'control-revision' apparat within the ministries and administrations of the ispolkomy.

In August 1981 another resolution followed, this time from the

Central Committee, on 'Further Perfecting Control and Verification of Implementation in Light of the Decisions of the 26th Party Congress'. The resolution called upon the central committees of the Republics, krai, oblasts, cities and all other Party bodies, to direct the work of the soviets towards a more active engagement in control functions. The resolution stressed the lack of co-ordination at the local level in control work:

> Party committees are called upon to direct their activities towards unifying the power of the control organs and to removing the practice whereby several enterprises and institutions are exposed to a large number of checks and revisions, to working out measures aimed to removing parallelism and duplication in conducting check-ups, and to strengthening the ties between the organs of people's control, standing commissions of the soviets, members of the 'komsomol searchlight' and trade union organizations.[65]

The Soviet scholar Avak'yan, in a recent article, also highlights the problem of poor co-ordination in control work. He points to the fact that as many as 50 different control organisations may be active in oblasts and large cities. Thus Gosbank, the State Bank for Construction, technical inspectors, sanitary inspectors and others from the Department of Gas, Fire, Prices, Energy and from the organisations of People's Control, from the soviets and Party, and many more will be present.[66] Not only are there many different bodies but the same group is often un-coordinated between different levels. Thus one enterprise may be inspected by a number of different bodies in the same week or even by one organisation from two different administrative levels, e.g. oblast and city.

Control within the soviet executive committees

One of the main problems, which we have already noted with reference to finance and planning activities, is the overload of work on the poorly-staffed departments of the ispolkomy. This has led to many of the problems outlined above. It also leads to serious implementation problems because of the inability of local officials to take the time to adapt central directives to meet the specific conditions of their locality. In this way local officials are enforcing a centralisation that is not required by the directives of these policies. Fritskii has shown that overworked staff often simply copy, word-for-word, central decrees and resolutions and then send them out for implementation without specific commands and details which would facilitate their adaptation to the local environment. Indeed Fritskii asserts that 25 to 33 per cent of the decisions of several oblasts in the Ukraine are of this nature.[67]

Another problem caused by staff shortages and the low morale of personnel within the administration of the soviets is the poor preparation of decisions. Selivanov notes that often the work is so bad that it leads to the distortion of central directives.

There also appears to be some confusion among the members of the ispolkomy as to which decisions may be enacted by the chairman of the executive committee alone, and which require ratification by a vote of the majority of the executive. This has led to a situation whereby a large number of decisions are adopted without consultation with other members of the executive or with those who will be responsible for their implementation. This in turn makes implementation more difficult. In L'vov Oblast there has been an increasing tendency for the chairman to enact decrees without such 'collegial' discussion. Thus in 1977, of 515 decisions, 101 were passed in this manner (i.e. as decrees of the chairman).[68]

As we have seen in our case study of Moscow Oblispolkom, a major problem is the absence of a standard procedure for dealing with information within the apparats of the ispolkomy. In Donetsk Oblast Soviet a system has been introduced whereby all decisions have to be discussed by key personnel in a number of departments. Thus the secretary of the oblast observes:

> All questions of planning of capital investment, finance from the budget, and changes in the plans for the development of enterprises and organizations of oblast subordination must be agreed with the oblast planning commission, the finance department and the chairmen of the relevant standing committees.[69]

In a case of disagreement a document is written up listing those in favour and those against the particular proposal. Those drafts which have met opposition are examined by the chairman or deputy chairman before being discussed in a session of the ispolkom. In this way decisions, when passed, will have a far greater chance of being implemented without countless days being spent in reformulating and reworking them.

However, the main problems would appear to be the vast number

Table 6.1: Decisions and decres of Khar'kov and Donetsk oblasts, 1976-7

	1976		1977	
	1	2	1	2
Decisions passed including those jointly with obkom	703	736	736	791
Number of sessions of oblispolkom	24	26	25	25
Number of decisions passed at each session average	29	28	29	31
Total number of documents sent out to oblast orgs.	277	861	285	863
City and raion	993	559	866	337

1 = Donetsk oblast   2 = Khar'kov oblast
Source: A.F. Selivanov, 'Problemy Kachestva Reshenii i organizatsii ikh Ispolneniya', in *Ispolnitel'nyi Komitet Mestnovo Soveta Narodnykh Deputatov*, ed. I.F. Butko (Kiev, 1980), pp. 233-76, (p. 256).

of documents to be dealt with and poor staff provision. Table 6.1 shows the large number of decrees adopted by Khar'kov and Donetsk Oblast Soviets. In 1976 Khar'kov Oblast received 521 resolutions and directives from the Ukrainian Republic Government, 1,197 other documents from the Republic ministries and departments, and 6,946 letters and complaints from workers. In 1977 the corresponding figures were 526; 1,420; 7,534.[70] One answer to these problems has been the introduction of computers into the executive committees, the number of which increased dramatically over the 1970s. In 1981 the largest and most complex computers were to be found within the administrations of Moscow and Leningrad City Soviets. Thus Moscow City Soviet has at its service the computer 'Signal' which deals with 100,000 documents each year concerned with control.[71] At present all of the capital cities and most of the oblasts are using computers. In the Ukraine computers are active in Kiev, Dnepropetrovsk, Donetsk and Khar'kov Oblast Soviets. In Kiev, the ispolkom is provided with a detailed account of the implementation each week. The chairman of the gorispolkom recieves information about those decisions which have been implemented, and is also given a list of those decisions which ought to be fulfilled in the next few days.[72]

I have already discussed the greater attention paid to systems theory and computing within the Soviet administrations. Indeed, the 'computer revolution' could lead to the introduction of unified procedures and contribute further to the process of centralisation within the administrations. First, however, more co-ordination in the development of computers, the types of program they use and the departments which use them, will have to be achieved. Like other areas of the Soviet economy, the introduction of computers and the creation of programs has been unco-ordinated, both between Republics and within them. Thus Selivon notes that problems are caused by 'an absence of a general state policy (at the scale of the Republic and country) for the application of computers in the activities of the local soviets'.[73] At present each city and oblast works out its own system with the help of scientific workers and specialists. If a unified system is devised and standard procedures for the processing of documents are introduced, undoubtedly this will give the leadership greater potential to control the implementation of their policies and to check their fulfilment.

This chapter has outlined the serious problems which the Soviet leadership faces in enforcing its policies in the localities. I have outlined two principal reasons for such problems: (1) structural and (2) bureaucratic interests. I have maintained that those bureaucratic problems found in Western countries will be magnified in the Soviet setting because of the centralised and fragmented nature of the economic and administrative system and the existence of three major bureaucracies of the Party, ministries and soviets. In addition we have noted the enormous size of the country, containing as it does over 50,000 administrative units cutting across 15 Union Republics. Our chapters on budget formulation and on planning have outlined the problem of integrating planning at the local levels. Similarly, the problem of Party-state relations is peculiar to communist states. I have shown that problems of defining the boundaries between Party and state administrations have led to poor co-ordination and implementation of policies in the oblasts and cities.

My study of Moscow Oblast Executive Committee, and local soviets in general, has shown a surprising degree of laxity within these bodies over the control of the implementation of central policies. Within the various departments of the city and oblast soviets, there are still many unregulated procedures for the receiving, processing and storing of information. There also appears to be a general tolerance of bureaucratic inefficiencies and a low level of work by administrative personnel. In addition there is an unwillingness to enforce heavy penalties on officials who have failed to comply with executive decisions.

I have also stressed that bureaucratic groups in the Soviet Union are more likely to change and mould policies in the output stage, in the process of implementation, rather than at the input stage. Thus we have noted the power of the ministries to drag their feet over the transfer of housing to the soviets, their ability to build up 'self-sufficient economies', to break contracts for the pooling of resources and to thwart the introduction of the 'Orel system' of planning. The Party is, I contend, more successful in making policy than in implementing it.

In order to deal with the fragmented nature of the planning and economic systems, and the power of groups to mould or block policies, the central leadership has in recent years attempted to improve its management of society. Systems theory and computer technology have been introduced in order to reassert national objectives and to counteract the influence of bureaucratic interests. Brezhnev spoke out against 'parochialism' and emphasised the need to rationalise policy-making and implementation. For Holloway, the Soviet interpretation of rationalisation:

> stresses the hierarchical nature of administrative structures; it points to the possibility of optimal decision making; it emphasizes the role of information flows in administration . . . and the uses of new data processing technology; and it assumes that the self-regulation of Soviet society is to be achieved through the interaction of two subsystems: the controlling and the controlled.[74]

However, our study has also shown that the fragmentation of the system and other structural and motivational factors outlined above have prevailed over the leadership's renewed offensive to increase its control over policy implementation. Indeed, computer technology is itself a victim of the fragmented nature of the Soviet bureaucracy. As we have seen, it is being implemented in the localities in the absence of specific guidelines or a national policy. Different cities and oblasts are adopting a wide variety of systems and programs. While it is important to bring to light the leadership's concern with management and control, my study, in the end, shows the instability of both the Party and the soviets to overcome such fragmentation and to achieve policy integration.

NOTES

1. 'Political Report 27th Congress', translated in *Soviet weekly*, 8 March 1986, p. 3.

2. Cited in Nicos P. Mouzelis, *Organisation and Bureaucracy: an Analysis of Modern Theories*, revised edn (London, 1975), p. 41.
3. Martin Albrow, *Bureaucracy* (London, 1976), pp. 55–6
4. Robert K. Merton 'Bureaucratic Structure and Personality', in *Reader in Bureaucracy*, ed. Robert K. Merton, Ailsa P. Gray, Barbara Hockey and Hanan C. Selvin (Glencoe, Illinois, 1952), pp. 361–71.
5. Anthony Downs, *Inside Bureaucracy* (Boston, 1967).
6. Philip Selznick, 'An Approach to a Theory of Bureaucracy', *American Sociological Review*, 8 (1943), 47–54.
7. Michel Crozier, *The Bureaucratic Phenomenon* (London, 1964).
8. Andrew Dunsire, *The Execution Process*, vol 1: *Implementation in a Bureaucracy;* vol 2: *Control in a Bureaucracy* (Oxford, 1978).
9. Jeffrey L. Pressman and Aaron Wildavsky, *Implementation: How Great Expectations in Washington are Dashed in Oakland; Or Why it's Amazing that Federal Programs Work at all. This Being a Saga of the Economic Development Administration, as told by Two Sympathetic Observers who Seek to Build Morals on a Foundation of Ruined Hopes* (Berkeley, Los Angeles, and London, 1973).
10. Dunsire, *Execution Process*, vol. 1, p. 18.
11. Downs, *Inside Bureaucracy*, p. 134 (for all three quotations).
12. Ibid., p. 133.
13. Dunsire, *Execution Process*, vol. 2, p. 2.
14. Ibid., p. 5.
15. Downs, *Inside Bureaucracy*, p. 134.
16. Hammer, 'Inside the Ministry', p. 59.
17. Selznick, 'Theory of Bureaucracy' (esp. pp. 47–8), as summarised in Mouzelis, *Organisation and Bureaucracy*, p. 60.
18. Mouzelis, *Organisation and Bureaucracy*, p. 61.
19. See n. 7.
20. Mouzelis, *Organisation and Bureaucracy*, p. 160.
21. Pressman and Wildavksy, *Implementation,* p. xvi; cited in Dunshire, *Execution Process*, vol. 1, p. 70.
22. Michael Hill, 'Implementation and the Central-Local Relationship', in *Central-Local Government Relationships* (n. p., 1979), Appendix II (separately paginated).
23. Dunsire, *Execution Process*, vol. 1, p. 71.
24. M. Hill, 'Implementation', pp. 4–5.
25. Ibid., p. 5.
26. Ibid., p. 7.
27. Ibid., p. 9.
28. ibid., p. 8.
29. Ibid., p. 8.
30. D.S. Van Meter and C.E. Van Horn, 'The Policy Implementation Process: A Conceptual Framework', *Administration and Society*, 6 (1974–5), 445–88.
31. Adrian Webb and Gerald Wistow, 'Implementation, Central-Local Relations and the Personal Social Services', in *New Approaches to the Study of Central-Local Government Relationships,* ed. G.W. Jones (Westmead, 1980), pp. 69–83.
32. Amitai Etzioni, *A Comparative Analysis of Complex Organisations:*

Or Power, Involvement, and their Correlates, first edition (Glencoe, Illinois, 1961); revised and enlarged edition (New York and London, 1975).
33. Emel'yanov, 'The Plan Should be Integrated'.
34. Smith, 'Bureaucratic Politics', p. 4.
35. Hammer, 'Inside the Ministry', pp. 55–6.
36. Ibid., p. 59.
37. See Introduction, n. 17.
38. Paul M. Cocks, 'Retooling the Directed Society: Administrative Modernization and Developed Socialism', in *Political Development in Eastern Europe*, ed. Jan F. Triska and Paul M. Cocks (New York and London, 1977), pp. 53–92 (p. 56).
39. 'Political Report 27th Congress', translated in *Soviet weekly*, 8 March 1986, p. 9.
40. Cocks, 'Retooling', p. 62.
41. D. Gvishiani, *Organization and Management: A Sociological Analysis of Western Theories* (Moscow, 1972; a translation of *Organizatsiya i Upravlenie Sotsiol. Analiz Burzhuaznykh Teorii*, first edition (Moscow 1970); second edition (Moscow, 1972), pp. 140, 142; cited in Cocks, 'Retooling', p. 62.
42. Yu. Volkov, 'The System of Power and Democratic Institutions', *Social Sciences*, no. 3 1975, p. 123; cited in Erik P. Hoffmann, 'The Scientific Management' of Soviet Society', *Problems of Communism*, 26, no. 3 (May-June 1977), 59–67 (p. 63).
43. Cocks, 'Retooling', p. 63.
44. Cocks, 'Retooling', p. 60.
45. Gvishiani, *Organizastsiya i Upravlenie*, second edition, pp. 526–7; cited in Erik P. Hoffmann, 'Information Processing and the Party: Recent Theory and Experience', in *Soviet Society and the Communist Party*, ed. Karl W. Ryavec (Amherst, 1978), pp. 63–87 (p. 72).
46. *Byulleten'*, no. 16 (1973), 33–6.
47. *Byulleten'*, (1973), p. 33.
48. *Byulleten'*, (1973), p. 33.
49. *Byulleten'*, (1973), p. 35.
50. *Byulleten'*, (1973), pp. 35–6.
51. Decision, 2 November 1972, 'O Khode Vypolneniya Resheniya Ispolkoma Mosoblsoveta No. 992 ot 15 Oktyabrya 1971 goda 'Ob Uluchshenii Organizatsii Kontrolya i Proverke Ispolneniya''', *Byulleten'*, no. 23–4, (1972), 18–19.
52. *Byulleten'* (1972), pp. 18–19.
53. *Byulleten'* no. 2, (1974), p. 29.
54. *Byulleten'*, no. 21, (1975), 6–7.
55. *Byulleten'*, no. 20, (1978), 1–3.
56. *Byulleten'*, no. 19, (1974), 11.
57. *Byulleten'*, no. 19, (1981), 8–9.
58. 23rd Party Congress 1966, 8 April 1966, 'Rezolyutsii i Postanovleniya S"ezdas po Otchetnomu Dokladu Tsentral'novo Komiteta KPSS', in *KPSS v Resolyutsiyakh*, IX, 1966–8 (1972), 16–35 (p. 32); excerpts translated as 'On the Report of the Central Committee', in *Resolutions*, V, edited by Schwartz, 60–71 (p. 69).
59. Anon., 'Slovo i Delo', *Izvestia*, 7 June 1967, p. 1; translated as

'Words and Deeds', *CDSP*, 19, no. 23 (28 June 1967), 29-30 (p. 30).
60. 1971 City Decree, p. 2.
61. L.I, Brezhnev, 'Otchet Tsentral'novo Komiteta KPSS i Ocherednye Zadachi Partii v Oblasti Vnutrenei i Vneshnei Politiki', in *XXV S"ezd Kommunisticheskoi Partii Sovetskovo Soyuza . . . Stenograficheskii Otchet*, 3 vols (Moscow, 1976), I 26-115 (p. 92); cited in Erik P. Hoffmann, 'Changing Soviet Perspectives on Leadership and Administration', in *The Soviet Union since Stalin*, ed. Stephen F. Cohen, Alexander Rabinotitch and Robert Sharlet (London and Basingstoke, 1980), pp. 71-92 (p. 82).
62. Hoffman, 'Changing Soviet Perspectives', p. 82.
63. Anon., 'Slovo i Delo'.
64. Resolution of the Council of Ministers of the USSR, 2 April 1981, 'O Merakh po Uluchsheniyu Kontrol'no-Revizionnoi Raboty v Ministerstvakh, Vedomstvakh i Drugikh Organakh Upravleniya', *Sobranie Postanovlenii Pravitel'stva SSSR, Otdel pervyi*, 1981, no. 15, statute 89.
65 Resolution of the Central Committees of the CPSU, 11 August 1981, 'O Dal'neishem Sovershenstvovanii Kontrolya i Proverki Ispolneniya v Svete Reshenii 26 S"ezda KPSS', in *KPSS v Rezolyutsiyakh*, XIV, 1980-1 (1982), 441-8 (p. 447).
66. S.A. Avak'yan, 'Kontrol'naya Funktsiya Sovetov', *Sovety Narodnykh Deputatov*, March 1982, 17-26.
67. O.F. Fritskii, 'Sovershenstvovanie Form i Metodov Upravlenicheskoi Deyatel'nosti Ispolkomov Mestnykh Sovetov', in Butko, pp. 212-32 (p. 227 (n. 21)).
68. A.A. Selivanov, 'Sovershenstvovanie Stilya Deyatel'nosti Apparata Ispolkomov Mestnykh Sovetov', in *Ispolnitel'nyi Komitet*, ed. Butko, pp. 233-76 (p. 266).
69. D.F. Rassikhina, 'Iz Opyta Deyatel'nosti Ispolkoma Oblastnovo Soveta', in *Ispolnitel'nyi Komitet*, ed. Butko, pp. 277-97 (p. 284).
70. Selivanov, 'Sovershenstvovanie', p. 257.
71. Avak'yan, 'Kontrol'naya', p. 23.
72. N.F. Selivon, *Kontrol'naya Funktsiya Mestnyk Sovetov Narodnykh Deputatov* (Kiev, 1980), p. 100.
73. Ibid., pp. 98-9.
74. David Holloway, 'The Political Use of Scientific Models: The Cybernetic Model of Government in Soviet Social Science', in Lyndhurst Collins (ed.), *The Use of Models in the Social Sciences* (London: Tavistock, 1976), pp. 116, 121, cited in Hoffmann, 'Changing Soviet Perspectives', pp. 85-6.

Conclusion

This study has examined the work of city and oblast soviets over the Brezhnev period (1964–82), and has been primarily concerned with problems of control and implementation in Soviet local politics. The chapters on planning, housing and finance have outlined the difficulties faced by the central leadership in enforcing national policies in the localities. The chapters on Party-state relations and control have shown in more detail the bureaucratic nature of implementation problems. The overall aim of the study has been to provide an explanation for such problems. From the study two hypotheses may be put forward which account for the poor state of control and implementation within local Soviet administrations: (1) *structural/bureaucratic problems;* (2) *bureaucratic interests*.

(1) Throughout this work we have stressed the importance of structural defects within and across Soviet bureaucracies. At the national level, we have emphasised the vertical fragmentation of the Soviet economic and administrative system. Problems of co-ordination across the three bureaucracies of the Party, ministries and soviets have magnified the traditional bureaucratic problems which are to be found in the West. Locally, we have demonstrated that the executive committees of the soviets are unable to control effectively the work of subordinate bodies. Many of the procedures for the gathering, processing and storing of information are unregulated, departments often suffer from shortages of staff and there is poor continuity of structure between city and oblast levels. In addition, ill-defined boundaries of Party and state control have led to weak execution of central policies.

(2) Out study has also shown the power of bureaucratic groups to mould and adapt policies in their own interest or to drag their feet over the implementation of some policies. The implementation of the 'Orel system' of planning, and of 'zakazchik' rights, for example has varied substantially from area to area according to the strength of bureaucratic opposition; but the transfer of housing to the jurisdiction of the soviets provides the most instructive example of the delaying power of such interests. The ministries have continually dragged their feet over such transfers, so that as recently as 1981 they still controlled 60 per cent of all housing in the USSR.

My treatment of the output side of policy-making lends support to the view that within Soviet administration there is now a tendency to centralise decision-making and an attempt by the central leadership to regain control of the execution process. This trend is clearly seen in the Central Committee's resolutions aimed at providing for greater central Party control within the ministries, and in the new rights given in 1971 to PPOs to supervise and control state bodies. The centralisation of decision-making in the areas of finance, planning and housing has been described in Chapters 3, 4 and 5. We have also noted the movement of departments from the city level upwards to the oblast level. In its attempt to counteract the vertical fragmentation of the system, the centre has striven to achieve corporate planning at the local level, and the Party through its 'co-ordinating councils' has taken a leading role in such work; but with more integration has also come more centralisation, as corporate plans of cities now require ratification at Republic or central levels. The creation of the Industrial Production Associations has also pushed decision-making authority upwards from city to oblast level.

In opposition to those scholars who support 'interest group' or 'pluralist' models and who thus stress the input side of policy-making, I contend that policies are much more likely to be changed at the output side. Structural problems and bureaucratic interests certainly allow changes to be made to policies in the execution process; I would maintain, however, that the ability of bureaucratic groups to influence policies at the formulation stage is much less. The administrative principles of 'democratic centralism' and 'dual subordination', and indeed the Marxist-Leninist ideology itself, ensure a centralising tendency within Soviet administrations. Party control over policy inputs is greater than over outputs. Its monopoly of the means of communication and the appointment of cadres ensures its ability to direct the formulation of policy. Moreover, as we have seen, the Soviet bureaucrat is much more isolated within his bureaucracy than his Western counterpart, and he is unlikely to antagonise a body on which he depends for many of the necessities of daily life. Even the centrally-organised trade union is dominated by the Party.

Some of these problems have been recognised by Soviet leaders themselves. Brezhnev stressed the need, in the age of the 'Scientific and Technological Revolution', to create a more effective and efficient administration. He thus placed emphasis on better management techniques. The introduction of computer technology and systems theory, as seen in the 'Scientific Organisation of Labour' within Soviet administrations, must be viewed as an attempt by the leadership to gain control over local bureaucratic groups. More recently Gorbachev has stressed the need for greater central guidance of the economy. At the 27th Party Congress, he spoke out against 'departmental and parochial interests' and he declared 'a determined and relentless war on bureaucratic practices'.[1] This study, by looking at outputs, has uncovered a strong vertical and hierarchical system of decision-making, highly centralised in its mode of operation. However, my study of finance, housing and planning has also shown the vertical fragmentation of the system. Poor horizontal channels of communication have prevented the integration of planning at local levels. The strong vertical thrust of planning and the excessive centralisation of budget and plan formulation have been rendered impotent by the fragmentation of the system and the structural and bureaucratic interests outlined above.

Throughout the period the leadership has experimented with legislation aimed at providing greater horizontal co-ordination. The stress on corporate planning, and legislation giving the soviets greater powers of 'co-ordination and control' *vis-à-vis* the enterprises, can be seen as attempts by the central leadership to gain more control over the branch administrations, and to harmonise branch and territorial planning. While Khrushchev abolished the majority of the central ministries, Brezhnev, after their reinstatement, sought to dissipate their authority by creating the Industrial Production Associations which often cut across different ministries and territories.

However, the legislation aimed at improving the power and status of the soviets and their executive committees has been one-sided and badly planned. Many of the new rights and duties given to the executive committees cannot be implemented because of staffing problems (outdated norms for departmental size, poor wages and low morale). New legislation is needed to back up the existing rights given to the soviets in 1971, 1980 and 1981 and to deal with the problem of staff size and departmental structure. The local soviets have failed to implement many of their rights simply because they are overburdened with work and cannot take on extra responsibilities. We have seen, for example, that the transfer of housing would require extra work and responsibilities, which many soviets are reluctant to take on.

The political culture of Soviet society must also partly explain the failure of the soviets to carry out their rights. We have already noted the importance of ideology with its stress on the centralisation of administration. We should also remember the traditional authority of the ministries and enterprises in Soviet society. The Stalinist industrialisation drive of the 1930s was bound up with the revolutionary ideal of socialism, and the development of industry is seen as an essential part of the development of the Soviet Union towards full communism. The ministries have thus gained a great deal of authority through their association with such ideals and because of the historical development of cities and regions which were often built around new industries. From a very early stage, the ministries were engaged in building housing for their workers and providing other amenities such as polyclinics, kindergartens and clubs. While it may be more economical to transfer these amenities to the jurisdiction of the soviets, the high status of industry in the Soviet Union has allowed the ministries to block such developments.

The question, however, remains: Why has the central leadership not sought to deal with the structural problems mentioned above, which impede soviets from carrying out their new co-ordinating and controlling roles? Are the size of the bureaucracy and dysfunctions in the administration to blame — or is the leadership itself divided over such policies? We have always to bear in mind that the Soviet leadership has to consider the political consequences of economic decentralisation or administrative changes. It may be more rational to pass housing over to the soviets and to increase the soviets' authority in society, but politically this may create further demands for local and national autonomy and potentially dangerous and divisive developments in Soviet statehood. Hoffman has detected three competing Soviet perspectives with regard to the development of Soviet administration:

> one that seeks to rationalize centralized party leadership through the use of new techniques, technology, and incentives; another which advocates reducing CPSU supervision over the major non-party bureaucracies; and a third which calls for greater regional planning and decision making by party and state organs.[2]

He observes that the first of these perspectives dominates at present, but he also notes that 'there appears to be growing support among the Soviet bureaucratic elites for the second and third alternatives, or for some kind of synthesis'.[3] This study has shown that the first of Hoffman's alternatives is indeed squarely in the forefront of Soviet administrative practice.

Similarly, the 'red/expert' problem has been a continual source of worry to Soviet administrators for many years. Persons who are professionally competent may not be politically reliable — and vice versa. Change under Brezhnev was slow and consensual, as epitomised in the phrase 'stability of cadres'. Within Party and state bodies there was a low turnover of personnel. Khrushchev antagonised the Party by insisting on high levels of compulsory turnover; Brezhnev, however, expanded the Party and state organs and maintained loyal supporters in administrative posts for long periods of office. At the same time, in order to ensure loyalty to the Party and to the centre, Brehznev encouraged the promotion of personnel across the Party-state divide. This study supports the conclusion of Hill and others with regard to the existence of a 'unified leadership pool' which is under the nomenklatura of the Party.[4] As we have seen in case studies of Moscow Oblast and Moscow Obkom, officials move from within the Party apparat to executive posts within the soviets, and vice versa. To enforce loyalty to the centre and its values, soviet and Party officials are trained together in Moscow before being posted to senior positions at oblast or city levels.

But while Party officials may be loyal to central policies and values, their power over the development of enterprises in their territories is very limited. My chapters on housing and planning have demonstrated the inability of either Party or soviet officials to control the expansion of enterprises in the cities and regions of the Soviet Union. I have also shown the poor co-ordination between vertical Party control within the ministries at the top and local horizontal control over the enterprises from the obkoms and gorkoms in the localities. The large number of Central Committee resolutions devoted to control within the ministries indicates just how serious this problem is at present. The Party, like the soviets, seems to be defeated by the vertical fragmentation of the system.

A major finding of this study is the importance of the industrial base as a determinant of local budgets and the provision of housing and other amenities. The number, type, size and jurisdiction of enterprises to be found in different cities and oblasts is, I contend, more important than overtly political factors such as patronage or other representative ties of the local Party leaders with central bodies. Politics will be very different in a city such as Ufa where only 2 of the 400 enterprises are subordinate to the city soviet than in another city where the majority of enterprises are of local subordination.

The importance of the ministerial channel has increased over our period, as enterprises have been able to keep above-plan profits and other incomes. The amount of off-budget funds as a percentage of the total amount spent in any area has also increased. We have also noted the soviets' new rights to pool the funds of the enterprises for the provision of housing and other social facilities. I have stressed, however, that such participation by the ministries is voluntary, and the soviets are weakened here by the absence of economic sanctions to enforce the implementation of such contracts. It must be stressed that the ability of local officials to participate in the policy input stage and in bargaining over resource allocations will differ fundamentally according to the issue and the amount of involvement of local-level enterprises. As we have seen, local officials will be able to trade with enterprises over the provision of housing and social amenities and consumer products. Since the economic reforms of the mid-1960s, enterprises have had at their command considerable sums of money and materials, such as off-budget funds. Taubman has drawn our attention to the local conflict between Party, soviets and ministries, and I support his conclusions concerning the pluralism of interests to be found at the local level.[5] However, it must be added that a large proportion of other resources — such as funds for education, health, agriculture, heavy industry, defence and security — will come down through the state budget and thus will not be open to such 'bureaucratic bargaining'. It must be remembered that two-thirds of the income of cities comes from above with very small contributions from city executives. While Taubman is right to stress the importance of such local-level conflict, we must not ignore the other more centralised aspects of budget income.

My research has also shown that we must distinguish between Party guidance over the formulation of policies, and Party control over the implementation of policies. Their role in the fomer is much stronger than in the latter. It is true that the local Party bodies do not have the power to engage in major allocation decisions, which are made in the central ministries in Moscow. Thus they often have to deal with controlling the 'output side' of ministerial activities. To date they have failed to introduce horizontal co-ordination into the vertically fragmented economic system. But this should not lead us to see their role as being primarily that of an arbitrator of local disputes. This study has shown the Party's ability to act as the political boss of the locality. Central Party resolutions have noted the 'petty tutelage' of the Party over state bodies, and we have seen the widespread existence of 'podmena' in Party-state relations. The term 'political broker' is far too neutral for what I see as in fact, as well as in theory, the 'leading and guiding force in society'. The

Party's main tasks are to hand down priority policies to the state organs and to ensure the implementation of central policies.

Throughout this study I have been concerned with the relationships between cities and oblasts. The most important point to note is the marked degree of centralisation to be found at oblast level. Thus, as we have seen, many departments such as local industry, transport, services and water supply have been transferred from city to oblast level. Because of the shortage of staff in some cities there are no departments of transport or daily services and these are thus run directly by oblast departments.

With regard to finance a similar situation obtains. Here the new system of drawing up the local budgets utilising control figures have given the cities far less opportunity to bargain for greater revenues. In some oblasts the city budgets are drawn up with very little regard to the requests of the city finance departments and of members of the city executive committees. As we have seen, there has been a decline in the cities' secured income at the expense of a rise for the oblasts. Although cities received some service industries from Republic and oblast levels, the formation of the Industrial Production Associations in 1973 robbed the cities of many of their profitable enterprises and concentrated them at oblast level.

Thus at present two-thirds of all income for cities still comes from above. Turnover tax and income from profits, two major components of the local budget, depend totally on the industrial base of the soviet and thus will vary substantially from area to area. Even for oblasts the situation is not much better. As we noted, in 1974 not one single oblast in the RSFSR had a majority of its income as secured income.

Paradoxically, as the centre has opted increasingly for corporate planning, it would appear that the oblasts are being singled out as the chief co-ordinating areas. At this level central policies meet local ones and branch plans merge with territorial. This development of the oblasts will almost certainly lead to a further loss of local autonomy for the cities over finance and planning.

However, the system of planning local finance is over-centralised and counter-productive from the point of view of the leadership and its attempts to improve implementation programmes. The absence of local incentives and the top-down system of budget planning have led to the hiding and hoarding of funds by local-level officials. Similarly, local finance bodies have often overstated their need for federal revenues and have understated the amount of income generated at local levels. False figures are passed up the hierarchy

CONCLUSION

giving the central leaders an incorrect picture of the true state of affairs in the localities.

Western scholarly literature, in concentrating on the input side of decision-making, has, I feel, over-emphasised the power of groups in Soviet policy formation and failed to give adequate attention to the real problems that the Soviet leadership faces at the output side. Hough's theory of 'Institutional Pluralism', stressing group influences at the input side, an incremental style of decision-making and the role of the Party as a mediator of group interests, has failed to uncover the centralising trends within Soviet administrations, and the role of the centre in reasserting control over group activity (though it is only fair to add that Hough was engaged mainly in disproving the totalitarian model).[6]

This study has shown the structural and motivational aspects of implementation defects and the problems faced by the central leadership in enforcing its policies in the cities and oblasts. These problems do not spring (in the main) from group interests at the input side but rather from group blockage and bureaucratic influence at the output side. By focusing on the implementation process I have shown, (1) the real problems of policy implementation and control within Soviet bureaucracies, and (2) the renewed activity of the central leadership to assert its control over the execution process. However, any adequate model of Soviet politics should seek to explain both the input and output side of policy-making. My study of the output side must therefore finally be seen, not as an attack on those dealing with the input side, but as a complementary work which will, I hope, increase our knowledge of local-level implementation problems and contribute to a fuller understanding of Soviet politics.

NOTES

1. 'Political Report 27th Congress', translated in *Soviet Weekly*, 8 March 1986, pp. 10 and 18.
2. Hoffmann, 'Changing Soviet Perspectives', p. 88.
3. Ibid., p. 88.
4. For a discussion of this see Hill, *Soviet Political Elites,* pp. 167–8.
5. See Introduction, n. 12.
6. See Hough, *Soviet Prefects,* and Hough and Fainsod, *How the Soviet Union is Governed.*

Appendix 1

Occupation of Deputies who spoke at sessions of Moscow oblast soviet over the period December 1969-79 (40 Sessions)

First Party Secretaries/secretaries of cities, raiony and oblast levels	14.8%
Chairmen of ispolkomy of cities, raiony, rural and settlement soviets	13.1%
Heads of departments/administrations of the oblast, cities, raiony; heads of production associations	12.4%
Chairmen/first deputy chairmen, deputy chairmen and secretaries of the Oblast Executive Committee (Oblispolkom)	12.8%
Chairmen of the Standing Commissions of the Oblast	8.5%
Directors of enterprises and trusts, managers and chief engineers	10.8%
Kolkhoz and sovkhoz heads	4.5%
Brigade leaders, foremen	3.6%
Workers	9.7%
Chief agronomists, chief doctors, teachers, trade union officials, heads of cultural institutions, representatives from the army	7.8%
Central Committee Apparat/Council of Ministers RSFSR/ Gosplan Gosstroi and other central representatives	2.0%

Source: Complied by the author from *Byulleten'*, December 1969-December 1979.

Appendix 2

Occupation of Deputies who gave Reports and co-reports at sessions of Moscow oblast soviet over the period 1969–1979 (40 Sessions)

Chairmen of the Oblast Planning Commission	9.25%
Heads of the Oblast Finance Department	10.1%
Chairmen of the Standing Commission for Planning and the Budget	10.1%
Chairmen of the Oblispolkom	14.8%
First deputy chairmen	4.6%
Deputy chairmen	11.1%
Secretaries of the Oblispolkom	4.6%
Chairmen of the Mandate Commissions	4.6%
Chairmen of other standing commissions	20.3%
Chairmen of City Soviets	3.7%
Heads of the Oblast departments/administrations	4.6%
Other heads	1.8%

Source: Compiled by the author from *Byulleten'*, December 1969–December 1979.

Appendix 3

Occupations of Deputies who spoke at the Budget and Planning Sessions of Moscow Oblast Soviet over the Period December 1969–79

First Party secretaries of cities, raiony and oblast levels	10.0%
Chairmen of ispolkomy of cities, raiony, rural and settlement soviets	11.5%
Heads of departments/adminstrations of cities, raiony, heads of production associations	13.1%
Leading members of the oblast executive committee, i.e. chairmen, deputy chairmen, heads of planning commission, finance department and secretaries	29.2%
Chairmen of the standing commissions of the oblast	8.4%
Directors of enterprises, trusts, managers and chief engineers	5.1%
Directors of schools	3.1%
Kolkhoz and sovkhoz heads	3.1%
Leaders of brigades, foremen	7.0%
Workers	9.2%

Source: Compiled by the author from *Byulleten'*, December 1969–December 1979.

Appendix 4

The Planning Process

THE PROCESS FROM THE TOP

The USSR Academy of Science, the USSR State Committee for Science and Technology and Gostroi USSR work out a Complex Plan for Science and Technology for a 20-year period. This is then presented to the USSR Council of Ministers and Gosplan USSR. Every five years the plan is amended.

Gosplan USSR, on the basis of the above plan and recommendations from the Party Central Committee, works out jointly with All-Union ministries and councils of ministers of the Union Republics, a *Draft Plan for the Economic and Social Development of the USSR* which covers a ten-year period. This is then placed before the USSR Council of Ministers.

On the basis of the approved Draft Plan for Economic and Social Development, Gosplan USSR then works out 'control figures' and norms for each five-year period with breakdowns for each year. These are then placed before the councils of ministers of the Union Republics and the ministries.

Guided by the 'control figures', production associations, enterprises and organisations work out *Draft Five-year Plans of Economic and Social Development*, with yearly breakdowns of major economic indices.

Ministries and councils of ministers of the union republics, on the basis of 'Control figures' and the Draft Five-year Plans of enterprises and organisations, work out *Branch and Republic Five-year Plans* with yearly breakdowns, and present these to Gosplan USSR.

Gosplan USSR, after studying the draft plans of the ministries and of the councils of ministers of the republics, works out final balances for the *Draft Five-year State Plan of Economic and Social*

Development of the USSR, and presents these to the USSR Council of Ministers.

FROM THE VIEWPOINT OF THE OBLAST AND CITY SOVIETS

Enterprises and organisations present their economic and social plans to their superiors in the ministries and at the same time a number of basic indices to the oblast soviets (in theory). The six basic indices are industry, capital construction, labour, housing and the communal economy, education and material resources.

On the basis of such information, oblast soviets work out the necessary balances for the planning of industrial development and the provision of housing. Balances are also worked out for labour resources, local building materials and general income/expenditure.

At the second stage, ministries inform Gosplans of the Republics of the corrections to their draft plans for all their enterprises. These are then passed on to the planning commissions of the oblast soviets. The planning commissions then draw up their own plans for the complex development of their territories. On the basis of such information Gosplans of the Republics work out basic indices for the development of the regions with particular regard to the siting of industry.

In the concluding stage All-Union ministries give the councils of ministers of the Republics information about their most important indices, and oblasts are given information about the economic indices of enterprises of higher subordination (in theory). On the basis of such information and local balances, the planning commissions of the oblasts and cities work out final plans for the economic and social development of their territories, and these are finally presented to Gosplans of the Republics. Republic Gosplans then amend the plans of the oblasts in line with the 'control figures' handed down from USSR Gosplan and the Council of Ministers of the USSR.

Source: O.E. Kutafin, *Planovaya Deyatel'nost' Sovetskovo Gosudarstvo* (Moscow, 1980), pp. 213–15.

Selected Bibliography

WESTERN AUTHORS AND PUBLICATIONS

Cattell, David T., *Leningrad: A Case Study of Soviet Urban Government* (New York, 1968)
―――― 'Local Government and the Provision of Consumer Goods and Services', in *Soviet Local Politics and Government*, ed. Everett M. Jacobs (London, Boston and Sydney, 1983), pp. 172–85
Cocks, Paul M., 'The Policy Process and Bureaucratic Politics', in *The Dynamics of Soviet Politics*, ed. Paul Cocks, Robert V. Daniels and Nancy Whittier Heer (Cambridge, Mass. and London, 1976), pp. 156–79
―――― 'Retooling the Directed Society: Administrative Modernization and Developed Socialism', in *Political Development in Eastern Europe*, ed. Jan. F. Triska and Paul M. Cocks (New York and London, 1977)
DiMaio, Alfred John, Jr, *Soviet Urban Housing: Problems and Policies* (New York, Washington and London, 1974)
Dunsire, Andrew, *The Execution Process*, vol 1: *Implementation in a Bureaucracy;* vol 2: *Control in Bureaucracy* (Oxford, 1978)
Friegut, Theodore H., *Political Participation in the USSR* (Princeton and Guildford, 1979)
Frolic, B. Michael, 'Municipal Administrations, Departments, Commissions and Organizations', *Soviet Studies*, 22 (1970–1), 376–93
―――― 'Decision Making in Soviet Cities', *American Political Science Review*, 66 (1972), 38–52
Hammer, Darrell P., 'Inside the Ministry of Culture: Cultural Policy in the Soviet Union', in *Public Policy and Administration in the Soviet Union*, ed. Gordon B. Smith (New York, 1980), pp. 53–78
Harasymiw, Bohdan, '*Nomenklatura:* The Soviet Communist Party's Leadership Recruitment System', *Canadian Journal of Political Science*, 2 (1969), 493–512
Hill, Ronald J., *Soviet Political Elites: The Case of Tiraspol* (London, 1977)
―――― *Soviet Politics, Political Science and Reform* (Oxford, 1980)
Hoffmann, Erik P., 'Role Conflict and Ambiguity in the Communist Party of the Soviet Union', in *The Behavioral Revolution and Communist Studies*, ed. Roger E. Kanet (New York and London, 1971), pp. 233–58
―――― 'Information Processing in the Party: Recent Theory and Experience', in *Soviet Society and the Communist Party*, ed. Karl W. Ryavec (Amherst, 1978), pp. 63–87
―――― 'Changing Soviet Perspectives on Leadership and Administration', in *The Soviet Union since Stalin*, ed. Stephen F. Cohen, Alexander Rabinowich and Robert Sharlet (London and Basingstoke, 1980), pp. 71–92
Hough, Jerry F., *The Soviet Prefects: The Local Party Organs in Industrial Decision-Making* (Cambridge, Mass., 1969)

—— ed., *The Soviet Union and Social Science Theory* (Cambridge, Mass., 1977)
Hough, Jerry F. and Merle Fainsod, *How the Soviet Union is Governed* (Cambridge, Mass. and London, 1979)
Jacobs, Everett M. (ed.), *Soviet Local Politics and Government* (London, 1983)
Lewis, Carol Weiss, 'Politics and the Budget in Soviet Cities' (unpublished PhD dissertation, Princeton University, 1975; abstracted in *Dissertation Abstracts International*, 37 (1976–77), 570-A)
—— 'Comparing City Budgets, the Soviet Case', *Comparative Urban Research*, 1977, 46–57
—— 'The Economic Functions of Local Soviets', in *Soviet Local Politics*, ed. Jacobs, pp. 48–66
Lewis, Carol W. and Stephen Sternheimer, *Soviet Urban Mangement: With Comparisons to the United States* (New York and London, 1979)
Morton, Henry W., 'Housing Problems and Policies of Eastern Europe and the Soviet Union', *Studies in Comparative Communism*, 12 (1979), 300–21
—— 'Local Soviets and the Attempt to Rationalize the Delivery of Urban Services: The Case of Housing', in *Soviet Local Politics*, ed. Jacobs, pp. 186–202
Smith, Gordon B., 'Bureaucratic Politics and Public Policy in the Soviet Union', in *Public Policy*, ed. Smith, pp. 1–17
Sternheimer, Stephen, 'Running Soviet Cities: Bureaucratic Degeneration, Bureaucratic Politics, or Urban Management?' in *Public Policy*, ed. Smith (New York, 1980), pp. 79–107
Stewart, Philip D., *Political Power in the Soviet Union* (Indianapolis and New York, 1979)
Taubman, William, *Governing Soviet Cities: Bureaucratic Politics and Urban Development in the USSR* (New York, Washington and London, 1973)
Theen, Rolf H.W, 'Party and Bureaucracy', in *Public Policy*, ed. Smith (New York, 1980), pp. 18–52

SOVIET AUTHORS AND PUBLICATIONS

Avak'yan, S.A., *Gorodskoi Sovet i Predpriyatiya Vyshestoyashchevo Podchineniya* (Moscow, 1979)
—— 'Kontrol'naya Funktsiya Sovetov', *Sovety Narodnykh Deputatov*, March 1982, 17–26
Baimakhanov, M.T., M.A. Binder and N.I. Akuev, *Oblastnye Sovety i Promyshlennye Predpriyatiya Vyshestoyashchevo Podchineniya* (Alma-Ata, 1982)
Barabashev, G.V. and K.F. Sheremet, 'KPSS i Sovety', *Sovetskoe Gosudarstvo i Pravo*, November 1967, 31–41; translated as 'The CPSU and the Soviets', *Soviet Law and Government*, 7, no. 1 (Summer 1968), 7–16
—— *Sovetskoe Stroitel'stvo* (Moscow, 1981)

SELECTED BIBLIOGRAPHY

Butko, I.F., (ed.), *Ispolnitel'nyi Komitet Mestnovo Soveta Narodnykh Deputatov* (Kiev, 1980)
Emel'yanov, A., 'Planu Byt' Kompleksynym', *Pravda*, 25 July 1974, p. 2; translated as 'the Plan should be Integrated', *CDSP*, 26, no. 30 (21 August 1974), 16
Fedorinov, E.I., 'Rukovodstvo KPSS Sovetami-Obekt Istoriko-Partiinykh Issledovanii', *Voprosy Istorii KPSS*, 1974, no. 12, 86–95
Filimonov, V.I., *Sovershenstvovanie Sostavleniya Mestnykh Byudzhetov* (Moscow, 1976)
Il'yushenko, V., 'Partiiny Kontrol' v Ministerstve', *Partiinaya Zhizn'*, 1981, no. 3, 46–50
Kazanik, A.I., *Koordinatsionnaya Funktsiya Mestnykh Sovetov Deputatov Trudyashchikhsya* (Irkutsk, 1974)
Khakalo, G.V., 'Kommunist v Sovete', *Kommunist Byelorussii*, 1978, no. 2, 45–9
—— *Partiinoe Rukovodstvo Sovetami* (Minsk, 1981)
Khimicheva, N.I., *Byudzhetnye Prava Raionnovo Gorodskovo Soveta* (Moscow, 1973)
—— *Subekty Sovetskovo Byudzhetnovo Prava* (Saratov, 1979)
Kim, I.L., *Sovershenstvovanie Poryadka Sostavleniya Byudzheta* (Moscow, 1975)
Klinetskaya, N.V., 'Funktsiya Fiinansirovaniya v Mekhanizme Upravleniya Gorodom', in *Sistema Organov*, edited by Lebedev, pp. 112–31
Kutafin, O.E, *Mestnye Sovety i Narodnokhozyaistvennoe Planirovanie* (Moscow, 1976)
—— *Planovaya Deyatel'nost' Sovetskovo Gosudarstva* (Moscow, 1980)
Laptev, Yu. A., P.N. Lebedev and B.A. Pavlovich, 'Analiz Vzaimodeistviya Oblastnkyh' Gorodskikh Ispolkomov', in *Sistema Organov*, ed. Lebedev, pp. 47–53
Laptev, Yu. A., and B.P. Malyshev, 'Vzaimodeistvie Mezhdu Gorispolkomami i Nepodvedomstvennymi im Predpriyatiyami i Organizatsiyami pri Sozdanii Sotsial'noi Infrastruktury Goroda', in *Sistema Organov*, ed. Lebedev, pp. 68–80
Lebedev, P.N., ed., *Sistema Organov Gorodskovo Upravleniya (Opyt Sotsiologicheskovo Issledovaniya)* (Leningrad, 1980)
Mezhevich, M., 'Kompleksnoe Planirovanie Krupnykh Gorodov', *Planovoe Khozyaistvo*, March 1978, 110–15; abstracted as 'Comprehensive Planning of Large Cities', *CDSP*, 30, no. 15 (10 May 1978), 14–15
Mushketik, L.M., *Kompleksyni Territorialńyi Plan v Usloviyakh Otraslevovo Upravleniya* (Kiev, 1974)
Nedogreeva, A.I., *Koordinatsionnaya Deyatel'nost' Gorodskovo Soveta Narodnykh Deputatov* (Kiev, 1981)
Novikov, I., 'Partiinoe Yadro Soveta', *Sovety Deputatov Trudyashchikhsya*, December 1973, 14–18; translated as 'The Party Nucleus of a Soviet', *Soviet Law and Government*, 13, no. 2 (Fall 1974), 56–64
Piskotin, M.I., 'Ekonomicheskaya Reforma i Sovetskoe Byudzhetnoe Pravo', *sovetskoe Gosudarstvo i Pravo*, January 1969, 93–102; translated as 'The Economic Reform and Soviet Budgetary Law', *Soviet*

Law and Government, 7, no. 4 (Spring 1969), 27–35
Polyak, G.B., *Byudzhet Goroda* (Moscow, 1978)
────── 'O Pravovom Regulirovanii Finansovoi Deyatel'nosti Mestnykh Sovetov', *Sovetskoe Gosudarstvo i Pravo*, 1979, no. 2, 55–9; translated as 'Regulation of Law of Financial Operations of Local Soviets', *Soviet Law and Government*, 18, no. 2 (Fall 1979), 42–52
Rovinskii, E.A. and O.N. Gorbunova, *Byudzhet Prava Mestnykh Sovetov Narodnykh Deputatov* (Moscow, 1978)
Rozenbaum, Yu. A., *Formiorvanie Upravlencheskikh Kadrov* (Moscow, 1982)
Selivon, N.F., *Kontrol'naya Funktsiya Mestnykh Sovetov Narodnykh Deputatov* (Kiev, 1980)
Shakhnazarov, G.K., *Sotsialisticheskaya Demokratiya: Nekotorye Vorposy Teorii* (Moscow, 1972); translated as *Socialist Democracy: Aspects of Theory* (Moscow, 1974)
Sheremet, K., E. Korenevskaya, S. Solov'eva, N. Starovoitov and Yu. Todorskii, 'Koordinatsiia: Sushchestvo i Praktika', *Sovety Deputatov Trudashchikhsya*, May 1976; translated as 'Coordination: Its Essence and Practice', *Soviet Law and Government*, 15, no. 3 (Winter 1976–7), 24–37
Shevtsov, V.S., *KPSS i Gosudarstvo v Razvitom Sotsialisticheskom Obshchestve* (Moscow, 1974); translated as *The CPSU and the Soviet State in Developed Socialist Society* (Moscow, 1978)
Solov'eva, S.V., 'Organizatsionno Pravovoi Mekhanizm Koordinatsionoi Deyatel'nosti Mestnykh Sovetov', *Sovetskoe Gosudarstvo i Pravo*, July 1974, 59–65
Stepanenko, A.V., *Goroda v Usloviyakh Razitovo Sotsializma* (Kiev, 1981)
Usenko, M.I., *Pravovye Voprosy Deyatel'nosti Gorodskikh Sovetov Narodnykh Deputatov po Razvitiyu Zhilishchnovo Khozyaistvo* (Kiev, 1978)
Vinogradov, N.N., 'Partiinye Gruppy vo Vnepartiinykh Organizatsiyakh', *Voprosy Istorii KPSS*, 1973, no. 5, 39–51; translated as 'Party Groups in Non-Party Organisations', *Soviet Law and Government*, 12, no. 3 (Winter 1973–74), 21–46
────── *Kommunisty v Sovetakh* (Moscow, 1979)
────── *Partiinoe Rukovodstvo Sovetami v Usloviyakh Razvitovo Sotsializma* (Moscow, 1980)

Index

administrative structure of Soviet Union 6–9
authority leakage 183, 191

Brezhnev 3, 193, 194, 200, 210, 211, 213
budget 62–89, 90–109
  centralisation in planning 86–7, 91–2, 99, 101–3
  city-oblast relations 81, 99
  drawing up of 90–109; new system 983, 96–101; old system 94–6
  expenditure 70, 72–6; social and cultural 72, 74–6
  income 70, 76–87; regulated 70, 82–7; secured 70, 78–82
  legislation 66, 67–71, 81
  of cities 1, 72–85 *passim*
  of oblasts 74–85 *passim*, 95–101 *passim*
  off-budget funds 63–5
  see also profits, taxes
bureaucracy 2, 182–95
  distinctive features of Soviet 189–95
  in ministries 199–201
  in Moscow Oblispolkom 195–9
  in soviets 201–5
bureaucratic group interests 5–6, 209
buro 44–5
  of Moscow Obkom 19–24
  see also party-state relations

cadres 33–42
  training of 42
  turnover of 23–4
  see also nomenklatura, party-state relations
centralisation 3, 210
  in finance 86–7, 91–2, 99, 101–3
  in housing 146
  in Khar'kov city 148
  in planning 111, 136, 141, 142–8
  of norms *see* norms
  see also democratic centralism, dual subordination
cities 1, 124
  general plans of 125
  unplanned development of 124–8
  see also planning, plans
city party committee *see* party-state relations
city soviet *see* departments/administrations, deputies, executive committee
computers 3, 195, 203–5
construction
  illegal enterprise 126–7
  of housing 113, 133, 146
  see also zakazchik, Orel system of planning
control
  control gap 18
  in departments/administrations 201–5
  in ministries 199–201
  in Moscow Oblispolkom 195–9
  party *see* party groups, party-state relations, primary party organisations

decentralisation
  of finance planning 92, 105
  of party work 36
  of planning 147
democratic centralism 4, 12, 90–1, 181

INDEX

departments/administrations
  absence of 143
  finance 103–4
  planning 138–41
  primary party organisations in 30–44 *passim*
  staff shortages in 5, 103–4, 138–9, 166, 211
  transfer of 147, 215
  see also dual subordination, Moscow Oblispolkom
departmentalism 116–17, 130
  in Nizhnevatorsk 129
  in Stary-Oskol 129–30
  in Surgut 128–9
deputies
  new status 10
  participation in budget formulation 102
  participation in sessions of Moscow Soviet 11–12, 217–19
  see also standing commissions
dual subordination 4, 92–3, 181
  in finance departments 92–3
  in planning commissions 139

enterprises
  of different subordination 112–13
  relations with soviets 9, 63–5, 110–13, 213; legislation 114–15; problems of information 117–18; territorial planning 119–20
  see also departmentalism, housing, planning, pooling of funds
executive committee 9–12 *passim*
  rights of 1, 68; finance 20–1; planning 111, 114–15
  see also control, departments/administrations, Moscow Oblispolkom, Presidium, party-state relations

finance department *see* departments/administrations

Gorbachev 54, 148, 181, 193, 199, 211
Gorplan *see* departments/administrations
Gosplan 8, 123, 133

housing 154–77
  enterprise/soviet 155–9
  transfer of 155, 159–68, 211; in Bashkir ASSR 165–6; in Komsomol'sk-on-Amur 161–2; in Moscow 166–7; in RSFSR 160–1; in Saratov 163–5
  see also construction, Orel system of planning, zakazchik

implementation 2, 4, 5, 167, 177, 181–205, 211, 216
  dysfunctions in 183
  in ministries 199–201
  in Moscow Oblispolkom 176, 195–9
  in soviets 201–5
  role of party 3, 18, 51–7
  study of 182–9
  see also bureaucracy, control
incentives 86–7, 104–5, 215
incrementalism 3–4, 216
industrial base 6, 63–5, 78, 110, 112–13, 213
Industrial Production Associations 70, 80–1, 210, 215
information problems 117–18
interest groups 2–6 *passim*, 210
  see also pluralism

Khrushchev 193, 211, 213
Komsomol 31–2

Marxism-Leninism 4, 6, 193

227

INDEX

Ministries
  one-man management in 54–5
  poor control in 199–201
  primary party organisations in 51–6
  types of 8
Moscow Oblast Soviet
  departments of 13
  deputy participation in 11–12, 217–19
  executive committee of 12–13
  Orel system of planning in 175–7
  party membership of 37
  planning commission of 140
  presidium 196
  zakazchik functions 169
Moscow Obkom
  buro 19–24
  crossover of members 38–41
  departments of 20–3, 46–8
  secretariat 19–21, 24, 46–8
  turnover of members 23–4

nomenklatura
  definition of 33–4
  in Leningrad 34
  in Moscow 34
  party 33–4
  state 35
norms 130–2, 144–6

oblast soviet *see* departments/administrations, deputies, executive committee, Moscow Oblast Soviet
one-man management 54–5
Orel planning system 172–7

party groups
  elections and functions of 28–30
  in control 43
  increased activity of 29
  in formulation of policies 28–30

party leadership
  'political broker' role 3, 17–18, 214
  selection of cadres 33–42; *see also* cadres
  theory of 24–8
  over policies 31–3
party-state relations
  and control 43–51; coordination problems 48–51; buro 44–5; departments 46–8; secretariat 45–6
  crossovers 38–42, 213
  dual membership 17, 37–8
  horizontal party leadership 17
  joint decisions of 27
  party and ministries 18, 51–7
  party membership of soviets 31–2, 37
  petty tutelage 18, 214
  podmena 26–7, 214
  theory of 24–8
  unified leadership pool 42, 213
  vertical party control 17, 51–7
  see also cadres, nomenklatura, party groups, party leadership, primary party organisations
planning
  branch and territorial plans 1, 4, 114, 115–20
  commissions *see* departments/administrations
  in Moscow city 142
  legislation 111, 114–15
  process 141–2
  role of party in 136–8
  the infrastructure 128–30
plans 134–8
  branch and territorial *see* planning
  complex 1, 114–16, 135–7
  enterprise 118

general plans 125, 134–5
soviets 119, 135
USSR state 141–2
pluralism 2–3, 111, 194, 216
political culture 155, 211
pooling of funds
rights of soviets 69, 107, 120–4; breaking of contracts 121–2
Presidium 9–10, 196
primary party organisations
and formulation of policies 30–1
in ministries 51–6
in soviets 30–44 *passim*
new rights of control 44
profits 6, 82, 86

sanctions
use by soviets 121, 189–92, 199, 214
scientific and technological revolution 3, 193–4, 210
scientific organisation of labour 3, 193, 210
secretariat 45–6
see also Moscow Obkom
sovnarkhozy 67, 69
standing commissions 9–10, 32–3, 43–4, 102
structural problems 2, 4–5, 183, 185–8 *passim*, 209

taxes 82–5
enterprise and cooperative 85
population 6, 82, 83–5
turnover 6, 82, 83–5, 215

zakazchik 110, 155, 168–72